The End of Modern Literature

On Permanent Revolution

Kojin Karatani

Edited by Hiroki Yoshikuni,
Jonathan E. Abel, and Yoshiki Tajiri

VERSO
London • New York

First published by Verso 2026
The essay 'The End of Modern Literature' appeared in *Shisoteki Jishin* [An Earthquake of Thought] © Chikuma 2016
Fredric Jameson's 'Ancient Society and the New Politics' appeared in *Criticism*, 58:2 (Spring, 2016) © The estate of Fredric Jameson 2016

The manufacturer's authorized representative in the EU for product safety (GPSR) is LOGOS EUROPE, 9 rue Nicolas Poussin, 17000, La Rochelle, France
contact@logoseurope.eu

1 3 5 7 9 10 8 6 4 2

Verso
UK: 6 Meard Street, London W1F 0EG
US: 207 East 32nd Street, New York, NY 10016
versobooks.com

Verso is the imprint of New Left Books

ISBN-13: 978-1-83674-390-3
ISBN-13: 978-1-83674-392-7 (US EBK)
ISBN-13: 978-1-83674-391-0 (UK EBK)

British Library Cataloguing in Publication Data
A catalogue record for this book is available from the British Library

Library of Congress Cataloging-in-Publication Data

Names: Yoshikuni, Hiroki editor | Abel, Jonathan E., 1971– editor | Tajiri, Yoshiki, 1964– editor
Title: The end of modern literature : on permanent revolution / edited by Kojin Karatani, Jonathan E. Abel and Yoshiki Tajiri.
Description: London ; New York : Verso Books, 2026. | Includes bibliographical references and index.
Identifiers: LCCN 2026012589 (print) | LCCN 2026012590 (ebook) | ISBN 9781836743903 paperback | ISBN 9781836743927 ebk
Subjects: LCSH: Literature, Modern – History and criticism – Theory, etc. | LCGFT: Literary criticism
Classification: LCC PN710 .E5655 2026 (print) | LCC PN710 (ebook)
LC record available at https://lccn.loc.gov/2026012589
LC ebook record available at https://lccn.loc.gov/2026012590

Typeset in Minion by Hewer Text UK Ltd, Edinburgh
Printed and bound by CPI Group (UK) Ltd, Croydon, CR0 4YY

Contents

Introduction: Kojin Karatani in the Structure of World History

Hiroki Yoshikuni

1.

Kojin Karatani was born in 1941 in the village of Sonoda, which was later incorporated into the city of Amagasaki, near Osaka, Japan. This was immediately before the war with the US. His uncle was drafted and killed in the Pacific (Karatani has no memory of him). Karatani's single, vague memory of the war is of an air raid and an evacuation to a shelter in the middle of the night. He was a healthy, ordinary boy, except that he did not speak at all at school. He had the ability to speak, and talked with other students during recess, but never in class. One day, however – at the end of his second grade – a substitute teacher came in and casually asked Karatani a question without knowing his condition; he unwittingly responded and started speaking. He never fell silent again.

It was around that time that Karatani saw a picture of a burnt *koban* – a small neighbourhood police substation – in a newspaper. In 1951, under the guidance of the Soviet Union and China, the Japan Communist Party (JCP) had adopted the 1951 platform, which stated that, since national liberation and democratic reform in Japan could not be achieved by peaceful means, it was necessary to use violence and terrorism. Police substations were attacked with Molotov cocktails, and young party members were sent to farming villages to prepare for guerrilla warfare in Maoist fashion. Popular support for the JCP plummeted, and the party lost all of its seats in the Diet in the 1952 election. The militaristic strategy was brought to a halt in 1955. The photograph young Karatani saw was a product of the JCP's 1951 platform. His father, who had a bookshelf in the living room full of works by leftist authors, explained the photo and mysteriously told his son, 'You will do something like this, too', as if making a prediction.[1]

Karatani never became a member of the JCP or threw a Molotov cocktail. When he entered the University of Tokyo in 1960, he instead joined the Communist League, nicknamed the Bund. The Bund was formed in 1958 in the aftermath of the JCP's disastrous 51 platform, the Soviet leadership's retrospective criticism of Stalinism, and the Soviet Union's intervention in the Hungarian Revolution. The Bund was an association of communist workers and students, but it was independent of the official communist parties. 'Before knowing it', Karatani found himself 'immersed' in the Bund's direct actions, rather than its ideology. He always felt 'strange' about his own political engagement because in high school he had 'thoroughly despised' his classmates' activism.[2]

In 1960 the Bund sought to prevent the revision of the US–Japan Security Treaty, known as 'Anpo' in Japanese. Following its defeat in World War II, Japan had recovered its sovereignty through the Treaty of San Francisco in 1951, but by the late '50s tension was already growing in Vietnam and the intensity of the Cold War was palpable in Asia more generally. The revised security treaty established a military alliance that implicated Japan on the side of the US and its capitalist bloc by permitting American military bases on Japanese soil and formalizing Japan's active involvement in the event of war between the US and the Soviet Union or China. Most Japanese preferred a more neutral position.[3] With the JCP's popular support evaporating, the Bund emerged in the void of political alternatives available to the youth of Japan. As Karatani notes,

1 Kojin Karatani, 'Watashi no nazo: Karatani Kojin kaisoroku [My Mystery: The Memoirs of Kojin Karatani]', second installment, 2023, book.asahi.com/jinbun/article/14858084.

2 Kojin Karatani, '60 Nendai to watashi [The '60s and I]', in *Inyu toshite no kenchiku* [Architecture as Metaphor] (Kodansha, 1983), 284.

3 See, for example, Osamu Mikami, *1960 nendai ron* [Thoughts on the 1960s] (Hihyosha, 2000), 41.

the Bund was the first 'New Left' movement in the world, preceding the global protests of 1968.[4]

On 15 June 1960 more than 300,000 workers, teachers, and students assembled in front of the national Diet to protest the treaty. After a bloody clash with police, who killed a student, they were dispersed. The revised treaty was soon ratified. Although the prime minister and other ministers resigned over their role in causing the unrest, and although Eisenhower's scheduled visit to Japan was cancelled, the ratification represented a defeat for the activists.[5] The Bund subsequently split into sects, each aiming to be an organized vanguard party (the existence of a vanguard party being generally believed to be a necessary precondition for revolution and the establishment of communism). Karatani did not join any of these groups. Instead he wrote a public appeal for the reorganization of the Socialist Student League, which had been a student division of the Bund before its absorption into the parent organization amid the excitement of the Security Treaty protests. The Student League was successfully re-assembled in 1961, though Karatani himself did not participate. He discerned in the reconstructed League an inclination to form a vanguard party of its own.[6]

In the lull that followed the frenzy of the protests, Karatani chose to study English literature at graduate school. He was uninterested in established disciplines such as economics, politics, or philosophy. He wanted to reflect on what underlay these disciplines, and it was literary criticism that ended up satisfying this intellectual desire.[7] In Sartre's words, which Karatani cites in 'The End of Modern Literature', literature was 'essentially the subjectivity of a society in permanent revolution'.[8] At that time in Japan, as in France, literary criticism was a totalizing discipline. Critics were not limited to discussion of literary texts. For literary critics, there was no distinction between literature, philosophy, history,

---

4 Kojin Karatani and Fredric Jameson, 'Seiji to hihyo [Politics and Critique]', *Gendai Shiso: Revue de la pensée d'aujourd'hui* [Modern Shiso: A Review of Contemporary Thought], 19:2 (1991): 60.

5 George Packard's *Protest in Tokyo: The Security Treaty Crisis of 1960* (Princeton University Press, 1966) provides detailed accounts of the 1960 crisis.

6 Kojin Karatani, *Nyu asoshieshonisuto sengen* [New Associationist Manifesto] (Sakuhinsha, 2021), 88.

7 Kojin Karatani, *Karatani Kojin chikara to kokan yoshiki wo yomu* [Reading Kojin Karatani's Power and Modes of Exchange] (Bungei shunju, 2023), 11.

8 Karatani, 'The End of Modern Literature' in this volume, 26.

politics, religion, economics, and anthropology. In modern Japan, beginning with Soseki and Ogai and continuing through to Hideo Kobayashi, Jun Eto, and Taka'aki Yoshimoto, many of the leading public intellectuals were literary critics. Karatani belongs to this tradition of Japanese literary criticism; he is, arguably, the last in the line.[9]

Karatani started writing literary criticism after the 1960 Anpo protests; an essay on Soseki won a major award in 1969. It was around this time, as the global protests spread in 1968, that social movements again gained momentum in Japan. Aside from the Bund – which had reorganized itself in the mid-'60s – and some other New Left sects, the main actor in the Japanese '68 was the All-Campus Joint Struggle Committee (*Zenkyoto* in Japanese), a coalition of students who were not only non-JCP but also non-sectarian, 'non-sect radicals'. They fought in various universities over tuition increases, the construction of Narita Airport, the war in Vietnam, and other issues. Their tactics included setting up barricades and shutting down the universities. By the end of 1969, however, most barricades had been dismantled following the intervention of the state, and campus life had returned to 'normal'.

While many non-sectarian students went back to school, graduated, or got jobs, the New Left sects continued their struggles and eventually attacked each other in an increasingly violent manner. Some of them went as far as starting to kill each other. The violence, which was called *uchi-geba* (infighting), claimed more than 100 lives during the '70s, decisively altering the New Left's public image for the worse. The final blow to the New Left was delivered by one of these militant sects, the United Red Army (URA). A group of Maoists, they armed themselves, established a base in the mountains, and trained themselves to prepare for guerrilla warfare in the anticipated revolutionary war. When, in 1972, the police searched the base with the aim of arresting the militants, some URA members escaped and took a hostage in a mountain lodge. When they were arrested following a ten-day confrontation, which caused three deaths, it was revealed that they had tortured to death fourteen of their own members whom they considered unfit for revolution and had buried their bodies in the mountains. This destroyed

9 As for Karatani's position in the history of Japanese criticism (*hihyo*), see Yoshiki Tajiri's chapter in this volume.

Japan's New Left. Up until then there had been widespread sympathy with the student movements, if not substantial support, but since the '70s the New Left in Japan has primarily been associated with the infighting and the URA in popular memory.[10] Beginning with a spontaneous, popular protest in 1960, Japan's postwar social movements thus ended in violence and sectarianism in 1972.[11]

2.

In 1973 Karatani responded obliquely to this conjuncture with an essay on Shakespeare's *Macbeth* published in *Bungei*, a literary magazine. Karatani starts by referring to Banquo's remark that when Macbeth hears the witches' predictions, 'he seems rapt'. Karatani reads this description not as an expression of Macbeth's enjoyment but of his lack of emotional response; 'rapt' here comes close to its etymology, being 'raped', seized, or transported to somewhere else. Macbeth does not enjoy the image of his glory when he is told that he will be king. Nor does he discover a latent ambition. He is simply absent-minded, seeing in himself a man who does not find any meaning in the throne; indeed, he can find nothing to give meaning to his life at all. From this point on, for Macbeth, everything assumes a dream quality. He says: 'If chance will have me king, why, chance may crown me without my stir.' His action or inaction does not matter; everything happens as if dictated by 'chance', which, in fact, operates as necessity. History takes its own course, regardless of Macbeth's volition: the visionary dagger leads him to murder Duncan. Macbeth feels as if someone else is conducting his actions in his place. He lives the meaninglessness of his own life.[12]

But the statement that there is no meaning in life is itself meaningful, presupposing as it does an optimistic view that life *should* have a meaning (even though it unfortunately lacks it at present). As Albert Camus

10 See William Andrews, *Dissenting Japan: A History of Japanese Radicalism and Counterculture from 1945 to Fukushima* (Hurst, 2016), 134–46.

11 See Nick Kapur, *Japan at the Crossroads: Conflict and Compromise After Anpo* (Harvard University Press, 2018), 154.

12 Kojin Karatani, 'Makubesu ron [An Essay on Macbeth]', in *Imi toiu yamai* [Sickness Called Meaning] (Kodansha, 1998), 29–42.

argued in his reading of the myth of Sisyphus, some conception of the absurdity of life is necessary to recover meaning at a higher level. Karatani subtly invokes the sentiment of the student movements: '"your existence is meaningless, you are alienated, inauthentic", these appeals are the drivers of faith and revolution.'[13] Macbeth does not stop at absurdity, however: he goes as far as depriving meaninglessness itself of meaning. Macbeth does not surrender but keeps fighting to the death – a death which is never shown on stage – because if he stops and dies the death of a tragic hero, he will be again involved in the circulation of meaning-production. Macbeth negates any kind of negation. For him, the world is no longer meaningful, meaningless, or absurd; it is simply there. His action is merely physical movement, rather than a meaningful resistance to absurdity or meaninglessness. 'Signifying nothing' literally signifies nothing.

Karatani's *Macbeth* might sound like an extreme version of existentialism in its emphasis on radical alienation, but the essay also carries a hint of structuralism. While Macbeth is reduced to the zero degree of subjectivity that leaves nothing behind, not even its own negative form, the witches' words communicate inhuman necessity, which manifests itself through Macbeth's murderous actions. Karatani writes: 'without any actual cause or ground, the events occurred out of the idea of "necessity" that haunted them. Men do not seize ideas, but ideas seize men. Men do not consume ideas, but ideas consume men.'[14] There is some structural force operating behind this sickness called meaning. The existential internality implodes to reveal the operations of external force.

While reading the galley proof of this essay, Karatani was surprised to learn that the URA leader had committed suicide in prison on New Year's Day 1973. He was surprised not at the suddenness of his death, but at the fact that, for Karatani, his death felt as inevitable and self-evident as Lady Macbeth's death had done for her husband when he said: 'She should have died hereafter. / There would have been a time for such a word.'[15] Karatani had a sense of a force working behind the '60s

13 Ibid., 64.

14 Ibid., 54.

15 Kojin Karatani, 'Daini-han he no atogaki [Afterword to the Second Edition]', in *Imi toiu yamai*, 311.

social movements and the violence to which they subsequently gave rise. Under the influence of this force, history takes on a certain kind of logic, structure, or repetitiveness – in which light the news of the suicide seemed almost natural. In Karatani's description of his own experience of the post-'60s situation, he is no exception to this dynamic:

> I did not feel any of the sense of defeat that was prevalent at that time. I might have been introverted, but it had nothing to do with the result of the political movements. On the other hand, however, even though I wasn't interested in external events at all, I never denied the *external* existence of compulsive, structural force.[16]

This passage was written in the early '80s, but the structural force has haunted Karatani's entire work, as shown in the titles of works such as *The Structure of World History* (2010) and *Power and Modes of Exchange* (2022). In a sense, Karatani himself experienced the force: just as Macbeth hears the witches' predictions, so too does Karatani hear his father's comment on the burnt *koban*, perhaps in a state of being 'rapt'. Karatani never approved of the violent sectarianism of the late '60s and '70s, but he does not explain it away as a mere product of madness or illusion. If it was the product of an illusion then it must have been the kind of illusion that is planted deep inside, that structurally conditions humanity, and that returns periodically and unexpectedly, as if from outside. For Karatani, the force is not a metaphysical idea; it has a concrete structure that has real effects on history.

3.

During the 1960s, members of the Bund debated the 'theoretical foundation' of their movement, believing that such a foundation could be provided by historical materialism. But to Karatani the whole debate looked 'fabricated'.[17] Karatani has never been convinced by the teleological view of history, though he has always maintained an interest in Marx nonetheless. Indeed, he saw the compulsive, structural force primarily

16 Karatani, '60 Nendai to watashi', 285–6.

17 Ibid., 285.

in economic terms, and although the New Left significantly undermined Marxism's credibility as a matter of practical policy, Marx was always at the centre of the intellectual space in Japan. As Gavin Walker notes, 'the most Marxist country on earth was postwar Japan',[18] and Karatani repeatedly stresses his indebtedness to the tradition of Japanese Marxism. Figures such as Taka'aki Yoshimoto and Wataru Hiromatsu were important to Karatani's theoretical development, and Kozo Uno's impact was exceptional. Uno was a Marxian economist who specialized in theory of value, as well as that of financial crises.[19] Spending his undergraduate years in the University of Tokyo's Department of Economics, which was heavily influenced by Uno, Karatani claims that he derived the idea of the structural force from Uno's reading of *Capital*, which was marked by its distinction from historical materialism. According to Karatani, he learned from Uno that, 'while historical materialism is ideology, *Capital* is science, and therefore no practical policy or objective can be deduced from *Capital*, but its logic penetrates us beyond the reach of our volition'.[20] This logic brings about neither the withering away of states nor the establishment of socialist states. It manifests itself in the form of economic force, but it does not derive from the economic base that historical materialism postulates as the determining ground of superstructure. Nevertheless, it 'penetrates us' through and through. The logic has a real force that works at a deeper level than what historical materialists call 'economic'.

The structural force was always on Karatani's mind, but it was not until the end of the Cold War that he became thoroughly engaged in investigating it. Before 1989 Karatani had been 'rebuking Marxist states and communist parties'; if the socialist states represented the negation of capitalism based on historical materialism, Karatani's task was to tirelessly negate such negations without having any teleological goal in sight. When the socialist bloc disappeared, however, he realized that his 'critical stance had been paradoxically relying on their being'. Without the existence of these socialist states, Karatani's negation became its own

18 Gavin Walker, 'Karatani's Marx', in Kojin Karatani, *Marx: Towards the Centre of Possibility* (Verso, 2020), 13.

19 For detailed analysis of Uno's thought, see Gavin Walker's *The Sublime Perversion of Capital: Marxist Theory and the Politics of History in Modern Japan* (Duke University Press, 2016).

20 Karatani, '60 Nendai to watashi', 285.

objective: negation for negation's sake. He then felt that he 'had to state something positive'.[21]

Karatani thus introduced the concept of modes of exchange in *Transcritique*, giving a 'positive' presentation of that structural force which he initially learned about from Uno – positive, that is, in the sense that it can be explicitly articulated, not in the sense of hope or promise. The concept was born out of Karatani's contention with historical materialism, according to which state and nation were parts of an ideological superstructure determined by the economic base (capital). They were expected to wither away when communism abolished capitalism. This did not occur, of course: state and nation only became more powerful in the Soviet Union, China, and ostensibly communist societies. Even when capitalism received a serious challenge, state and nation were only reinforced. After the Great Depression, nationalism developed into fascism in Germany, Italy, and Japan, and while the Soviet Union arguably succeeded in bridling capitalism, it also gave rise at the same time to an extreme form of statism. This shows that state and nation operate independently of capital. Karatani is not the first theorist to take issues with historical materialism; he names as his predecessors Weber, Durkheim, Freud, and Foucault, all of whom insisted on the autonomy of such superstructures as religion, society, the unconscious, or the state. The theoretical limitation of the economic base – as proposed by many Marxists of the New Left generation – allowed historical materialism to become more supple. If the economic base's determining power is limited, however, then historical materialism loses a significant amount of its theoretical potential.[22] Instead of negating the economic base, therefore, Karatani attempted to replace it with 'something positive', reconceiving the idea of the 'economic'. Inspired by Karl Polanyi's triadic concept of economy – reciprocity, redistribution, and market exchange[23] – he replaced modes of production, of which the economic

---

21 Kojin Karatani, *Transcritique: On Kant and Marx*, trans. Sabu Kohso (MIT Press, 2003), ix.

22 Karatani, *Karatani Kojin chikara to kokan yoshiki wo yomu*, 107.

23 Karl Polanyi, 'The Economy as Instituted Process', in *Trade and Market in the Early Empires: Economies in History and Theory*, ed. Karl Polanyi, Conrad M. Arensberg, and Harry W. Pearson (Free Press, 1957), 243–70. Polanyi lists only 'exchange' for the third term, but it is clear in his argument that it specifically means market exchange.

base consisted, with modes of exchange. Karatani thus introduced the triad of nation–state–capital based on modes of exchange. If we want to abolish capitalism or nation–state, all three have to be overcome at once because they are tied together and complement each other in a Borromean knot.

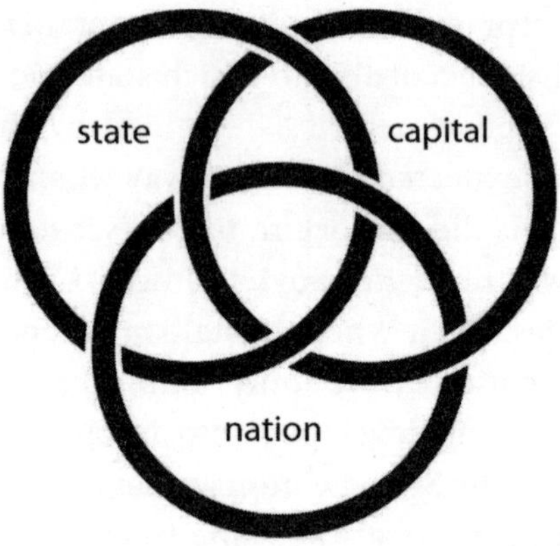

A Borromean knot

Each of the three is 'rooted in its own distinct economic base – its own distinct mode of exchange': nation, state, and capital respectively correspond to modes of exchange A, B, and C.[24] Mode A is reciprocal exchange, as described by Marcel Mauss in his analysis of gift and return in primitive communities. Mode B is the exchange of plundering and redistribution, or dominance and protection. It might appear strange to call this transaction 'exchange', but Karatani argues – along the lines of Hobbes's social contract – that the subject offers their submission to the sovereign in exchange for the sovereign's protection. After all, the plunderer must redistribute what he plunders in order to make his plundering sustainable. Mode C is commodity exchange, as analysed by Marx in *Capital*: exchange between independent individuals who buy and sell commodities, including the commodity of labour power. There is also a fourth mode – mode D – that, unlike the other three, either does not invariably exist or is repressed but occasionally returns in the form of revolutionary or religious movements that disrupt the concatenation of the other three modes. But it is not an

24 Kojin Karatani, *The Structure of World History: From Modes of Production to Modes of Exchange*, trans. Michael K. Bourdaghs (Duke University Press, 2014), 10.

ideal that transcends the other three modes; Karatani always stresses that mode of exchange D is 'the return of mode of exchange A in a higher dimension.'[25]

Modern Social Formations

B	A
State	Nation
C	**D**
Capital	X

Modes of Exchange

B	A
Plunder and Redistribution (Dominance and Protection)	Reciprocity (Gift and Return)
C	**D**
Commodity (Money and Commodity)	X

Karatani puts more emphasis on nation and state than most Marxist theorists do, as he takes them to be economic categories to the same degree as capital is. Nationalism reflects a return of mode of exchange A – reciprocity, with the concomitant allure of the communality of primitive society – primarily in order to counter the dominance of capitalism. Though often culminating in fascism, it also brought about the liberation of colonized nations. For Karatani, the framework of nation persists even as globalization advances; it cannot be abolished as an ideological

25 Ibid., 8.

illusion. Nationalism has always been Marxism's stumbling block: the Second International dissolved at the beginning of World War I amid what Lukács called 'war psychosis'. It is extremely difficult to expand a single nation's resistance to capitalism beyond that nation because each has its own economic base. The same can be said regarding the state. The state is based on the plunder-redistribution exchange; each state has its own bureaucracy and military to maintain the exchange. One state's revolution, therefore, inevitably invites other states' intervention, as in the Russian Revolution. Karatani always emphasizes that a state exists never by itself but always in relation to other states. Thus, state and nation have their own social-economic grounds. As for mode C, according to Karatani's idea of the economy, capitalism is 'a certain force that regulates humanity beyond its intentionality, a force that divides and recombines human beings. It is a religio-generic entity.'[26] Commodity exchange is based on trust and credit – on a blind belief that exchange will always be successful. When this belief is belied, what is known as a 'crisis' ensues. Hence, as Uno pointed out, crisis is not accidental but essential to capitalism.[27] In effect, through his theory of modes of exchange, Karatani spiritualized capitalism, materialized nation and state, and reconceived the concept of the economic.

By introducing modes of exchange, Karatani has provided a new basis for the Marxian concept of historical materialism, which he criticized for its teleology (that is, for its belief in the coming of communism after the abolition of capitalism). The structure of world history being based on modes of exchange is definitely a 'grand narrative', but it is not a story of linear development. This is instead a narrative that takes seemingly random events into account, with a sense of the subtly oxymoronic coupling of 'structure' and 'history'.[28] As Jameson points out, Karatani's structure of world history has the capacity to 'conceptualize transition, or, in other words, a revolution that could lead from one system to another, radically different one'.[29] What these modes of exchange represent is the structural necessity of tension, conflict, or antagonism: both

26 Karatani, *Transcritique*, 5.

27 Kozo Uno, *Keizaigaku* [Economics], vol. 1 (Kadokawa, 2019), 145.

28 Joel Wainwright indeed points out *spatiality* of history in Karatani's thought. See his 'The Spatial Structure of World History', *Journal of Japanese Philosophy* 4 (2016): 33–59.

29 Fredric Jameson, 67 in this volume.

the possibility and the impossibility of the triad of nation–state–capital. When a mode of exchange dominates the other modes, the latter do not disappear but persist in a state of relative repression, ready to return and disturb the current arrangement. Karatani sees emergence of religious movements, which are often indistinguishable from revolution, as the return of the repressed mode of exchange A in a higher dimension. Again, this occurrence is called mode of exchange D.[30]

4.

In 2003, shortly after publication of *Transcritique*, Karatani delivered a talk entitled 'The End of Modern Literature', included in the present volume. The modes of exchange are not mentioned there, but, since the essay was written precisely when Karatani was developing his thought on modes of exchange, it is possible to locate that linguistic entity which we have known as literature within the structure of world history. In so doing, I would like to connect Karatani's theoretical works to the essay on modern literature. For Karatani, literature is neither a pure entity independent of anything external to it nor an ideological or ideal product exclusively determined by capital. Literature has its own economic base, its own modes of exchange.

By 'modern literature' Karatani primarily means the genre of the novel, the most dominant form of literature in modern times. But its 'end' does not mean that it will become the postmodern novel or simply disappear, or that there will no longer be great writers or great novels. The 'end' in question refers instead to the present state of affairs in which novels do not have as much impact on society as they used to. In the past, as Sartre suggested, literature was considered a manifestation of society's revolutionary force, but as of the mid-2020s it is difficult to detect a significant relationship between literary works and social movements. Karatani describes how the novel assumed such a privileged position and then lost it.

Historically speaking, the rise of the novel marked the beginning of a new era in which the idea of individual freedom became a central topic. When Lukács defined the novel as the epic of a world abandoned by

30 Karatani, *The Structure of World History*, 14.

God,[31] this meant that its hero or heroine was liberated from religion and tradition. In the novel, a common, ordinary person could be as important as an epic hero. Karatani points out that, for modern Japanese writers, the task of literature was to establish the 'autonomous subject'. The novel dramatizes a gap or discrepancy between said subject and his or her surrounding realities – whether social order, political system, or cultural institution – and the struggle between them constitutes the novel's plot. In this respect, the novel reflects the possibility of social transformation, and the rise of the novel in Europe was indeed accompanied by revolutions that abolished absolute monarchies and brought civil society into existence.

In terms of social structure, the agents of those civil revolutions were the merchant class, the bourgeoisie.[32] The novel was a manifestation of the force of the rising bourgeois class, a force that made social mobility possible for those individuals who lacked any privilege other than their own talent in the now-godless world. And novels are, of course, commodities. The novel is based on mode of exchange C. Commodity exchange, as it proceeds through money, takes place in principle between equal, independent individuals; when one party has paid money and received a commodity, which the other party has given in exchange for the money, their relationship is over. Commodity exchange is marked by the equality of its participants, their anonymity, and their lack of an actual, social relationship. The novel was the style of the free independent individual in industrialized society. Heroes and heroines of early European novels were very often orphaned or otherwise separated from their families. Japanese literature saw the development of the I-novel, which represented an individual's internality as an inaccessible, inalienable essence. Absolutism was a situation in which mode of exchange B, plunder and redistribution, dominated the other two modes; the bourgeois revolution was mode C's struggle to subordinate mode of exchange B. In the course of this transition of power, the novel also nurtured the shared sense of a nation; as Benedict Anderson suggests, the novel helped its readers to imagine a community to which

31 Georg Lukács, *The Theory of the Novel: A Historico-philosophical Essay on the Forms of Great Epic Literature*, trans. Anna Bostock (MIT Press, 1971), 88.

32 See, for example, J. M. Bernstein, *The Philosophy of the Novel: Lukács, Marxism and the Dialectics of Form* (University of Minnesota Press, 1984), 40.

they all belonged. According to Karatani, nation is a social formation determined by mode of exchange A: it presents an appeal of primitive community based on reciprocity. Modern literature was thus a composite of modes of exchange C and A, through which free individuals reimagined a community.

As Karatani's chart on page 42 indicates, the novel is above all the major art form of the long nineteenth century, from the rise of nation-states to the fall of the British Empire and World War I. In the 1990s we reached the so-called 'end of history'. The Cold War ended, capitalism became the only reality, and, for the likes of Francis Fukuyama, what Hegel called the 'fight for recognition' was over. In developed countries, the emergence of consumer society meant that 'post-historical animals of the species *Homo sapiens*' were meanwhile enjoying 'abundance and complete security'.[33] History stopped. Equality of rights and opportunity (though not of wealth) was seemingly achieved, or at least improved to the degree that the demand for individual freedom ceased to exist. There would be no further revolutions. Literature had lost its social significance, not because what it represented had been repressed, but because it had already completed its task of cementing the bourgeois revolution.

The novel had revolutionary force because it was a style of a rising social class and because its play of subjection challenged authority, long-established hierarchies, and pre-bourgeois values. When such authority is gone, the novel's subversiveness can work only in conservative or cynical ways. In a post-historical society, lacking ideals or ideologies worth fighting for or against, the novel became an expression of atomized individuals, who are sceptical of any kind of political engagement or association with others. It became an empty form of negation of negation, or a commodity for entertainment. In other words, the death of modern literature marks the completion of the nation–state–capital triad, in which the environment is destroyed, natural resources are exploited, and wealth is monopolized by the few, while atomized individuals live according to 'values completely empty of all "human" content in the "historical" sense'.[34]

33 Alexandre Kojève, *Introduction to the Reading of Hegel: Lectures on the 'Phenomenology of Spirit'*, ed. Allan Bloom, trans. James H. Nichols (Cornell University Press, 1980), 159.

34 Ibid., 162.

Around the end of the twentieth century, as in the 1999 Seattle protest, there was a hope that social movements from individual countries would eventually be united, and that resistance to global capitalism might be possible. Karatani himself started the New Associationist Movement (NAM) to counter the nation–state–capital trinity.[35] After the events of 11 September 2001, however, it became clear to Karatani that such resistance could never be transnational. Resistance was doomed to fail because such movements would be torn between nation-states, religious and ethnic groups, and, especially, the North and the South. The NAM dissolved. Contra Michael Hardt and Antonio Negri's prediction, Karatani took the view that globalization would not facilitate the withering away of nation-states but rather reinforce their powers, as well as hostility between them. Karatani agrees with Immanuel Wallerstein's suggestion that there is a parallelism or repetition between the 1848 revolution and the 1968 protest as events that transformed the world,[36] though his reasons for thinking this are different from Wallerstein's. Just as, after the 1848 revolutions, the British Empire began to lose its hegemony, for which nation-states started fighting each other, so what came after the 1968 unrest was not what Hardt and Negri called Empire but the decline and fall of the American Empire with its subsequent imperialistic conflicts, which are still in process as of the mid-2020s.[37] We are atomized individuals living in an age of world war without the kinds of association needed to counter the operation of nation–state–capital. This is the situation from which 'The End of Modern Literature' emerged.

We therefore cannot expect the revival of that once socially important formation known as 'literature'. Literature was an expression of bourgeois individualism and nationalism, both of which are now integral parts of nation–state–capital. And yet literature was once a name for discontent with the contemporary arrangement of the trinity. Individual freedom and nationalism were once motives of social transformation. The structural force that has haunted Karatani and led him to develop these theoretical works is also the agent that both produced literature and brought it to an end. The vicissitudes of the novel attest to

35 Principles of the NAM can be found online at: s3.us-west-1.wasabisys.com/p-library/books/98bc4c46c88f5eb9a97a5339878eba6d.pdf.

36 Giovanni Arrighi, Terence K. Hopkins, and Immanuel Wallerstein, *Anti-systemic Movements* (Verso, 1989), 97.

37 Karatani, *Structure of World History*, 280–1, 293.

the instability, fluidity, or mobility of the structure of world history. There is no one fixed utopian mode of exchange or a perfect balance of the three. There is always a repressed mode or two, and these re-emerge to disrupt the trinity of nation–state–capital. If this return is articulated, the articulation in question should not necessarily be called 'literature' or take the form of prose fiction. It will have a different name and different form, a new means of manifesting itself.

5.

This volume begins with the first English translation of Karatani's 'The End of Modern Literature', along with a short preface by the author. The essay is followed by responses to issues raised by it and by Karatani's other texts; the contributors examine Karatani's thinking in broader contexts and, by so doing, open up its potential to afford new and different ways of conceiving both literature and politics. In 'Ancient Society and the New Politics: From Kant to Modes of Production', Fredric Jameson situates Karatani's theoretical works – *Transcritique* and *The Structure of World History* – in the tradition of Marxism. According to Jameson, Karatani's originality within this tradition lies first in his overcoming of the teleology of historical materialism (which has come to be seen as a more or less failed prophecy) by revamping the concept of modes of production, and, second, in his reconfiguration of Marxism's system of infra- and superstructures by introducing the triad of nation–state–capital, which is a manifestation of the modes of exchange at work in social formation. Jameson also describes the historical background of utopian attention to primitive communism – from Mauss and Claude Lévi-Strauss to Marshall Sahlins – and points out Karatani's unique intervention in this discourse by way of a strange coupling of Kant and Wallerstein, of world republic and world system. This chapter was originally published as a review of Karatani's *The Structure of World History*, and Jameson intended to revise and modify it for this volume. This became impossible for obvious reasons, but since Jameson's essay is the best examination to date of Karatani's significance not only in the tradition of Marxism but also in intellectual history more generally, it is reproduced here as it was first published.

In 'A Single Portobello Mushroom' Bruce Robbins argues against Karatani that modern literature still has a certain degree of socio-political importance, 'though a lesser one' than the strongest claims made for it might suggest. Robbins suggests that, while democracy might not *need* literature, literature can nonetheless work to democracy's benefit by way of its capacity to enable us to share the experience of others. He also points out that literature's ambition to represent the social totality is in fact reflected in the boldness of Karatani's own grand narratives, and that there is in both cases an underlying desire for human emancipation. According to Robbins, a continuation of literature can in this sense be found today – 'under other names and by other means' – in subfields of literary study such as women's studies or ethnic studies.

The novel form's aspiration to represent the social totality is also at issue in Kenneth W. Warren's 'Novel-haunted: Kojin Karatani, Doris Lessing, and Ralph Ellison'. In both the UK and the US, the relevance of the idea of totality is much in evidence in the '50s and '60s, when Lessing and Ellison worked in their novels to give voice to voiceless peoples. Warren points out, however, that after this period – namely, after the decline of Marxism – the idea lost its force for Lessing and became a commonplace, while for Ellison the same idea was transformed into a sociological attempt at 'the truth of Black life', which was indeed a vehicle of racialized cliché. This is precisely the end of modern literature as Karatani describes it. To counter this predicament, Warren suggests, Ellison reasserts the primacy of the art form that disrupts the 'truth' of oppressed peoples.

Gauri Viswanathan's 'Education, Global Culture, and "The End of Modern Literature"' investigates what Karatani sees as the 'importance' of modern literature in the context of Western colonialism, which used literature – in the form of the *Bildungsroman* – as a means of cultivating civil subjectivity. In the age of globalization and multiculturalism, Viswanathan writes, this imperialist literary apparatus has been appropriated by novelists in non-Western societies for their own non-Western contexts, whereas mass culture – social media in particular – continues to employ the *Bildungsroman*'s format of individual development well after its apparent demise. Between identity politics and reactionary regression to traditional humanism, Viswanathan suggests that the useless, irrelevant remnant to which literature has now been reduced might be able to open up a fantasy space of wonder capable of harbouring a new subjectivity beyond the bounds of ideological critique.

Beginning with a brief history of 'the end of literature' discourse, Andrew Gibson's 'Ends Without Ends: Kojin Karatani and the Death and Afterlife of Literature' examines Karatani's idea of literature in relation to those of Jacques Rancière and Maurice Blanchot. Gibson points out that Karatani and Rancière have both considered literature's political impact, but that the former has departed from the latter's position – which still attributes to literature a minimum degree of significance – by declaring an 'end' to literature. It is this idea of an end that Gibson attempts to deconstruct, and, in so doing, he suggests an opening in which the end overrides itself, a zone of ongoing ending, which is compared to Blanchot's idea of the space of literature.

Young-il Cho's 'The End of Modern Literature and Korea's World Literature' describes the impact of Karatani's essay in South Korea. Even though Karatani declared the *global* ending of literature, his statement somehow ended up fuelling Korean exceptionalism and literary nationalism: 'Japanese literature is dead, but Korean literature is still alive.' Eventually this nationalism gained government support, which facilitated the translation of Korean literature and thereby made it 'world literature' – culminating in Han Kang's winning the Nobel Prize in 2024. In reaction to Karatani's essay, a strange afterlife of literature emerged in the form of a nation-state's project on the stage of global capitalism, a project which indeed attests to the end of literature.

In 'Questions of Modernism and "The End of Modern Literature"' Yoshiki Tajiri considers Karatani's essay from the perspective of modernist literature. After situating Karatani's career in the history of the unique genre of Japanese 'criticism' (*hihyo*) – as inaugurated by Hideo Kobayashi – Tajiri argues that Karatani's lack of interest in the experimental modernist literature represented by Riichi Yokomitsu and Yasunari Kawabata is due to the fact that Japanese modernism was historically insignificant compared with its English counterpart. Tajiri nonetheless tries to find ways of meaningfully connecting Karatani's essay and modernism, while also reconsidering the fundamental question of what Japanese modernism was.

Michael K. Bourdaghs's 'Mode of Exchange D, (F+f), and the Ends of Literature' examines Karatani's argument concerning the end of literature in relation to his idea of 'mode of exchange D' and Soseki Natsume's theorization of literature as (F+f). Pointing out that, for both Karatani and Soseki, literature is an imagined synthesis of understanding and sensibility, Bourdaghs explicates its ambiguous status: literature is an expression of people's resistance to capital–nation–state, but it also serves to reinforce that very trinity. The chapter concludes with an analysis of 'the end of literature' within this conceptual constellation.

This volume ends with Jonathan E. Abel's 'AI Novels and the New Real: How Literature Ends with New Modes of Exchange', which shows how Karatani's concept of the end of literature might help to explain the recent advent of AI novels in Japan. Is the rise of AI novels the harbinger of a new moment in literary history or the final death knell of literature? In the context of Karatani's more recent work on modes of exchange, Abel argues that AI novels may both demonstrate a new literary mode of exchange and instantiate the end of literature as such. Regardless of whether literature survives or not, paying attention to who is writing and who is reading continues to matter for elucidating the literary.

Juxtaposing Karatani's provocative essay with these responses, I hope that this book suggests a link between the utopian politics found in Karatani's recent works and the literature that is to come – or whatever comes after literature. Thinking about the end of literature doesn't simply mean historicizing it; it also means thinking about something new that is different from literature, something that emerges from what once made literature possible and meaningful.

Preface to the English Edition of 'The End of Modern Literature'
Kojin Karatani

The essay 'The End of Modern Literature' was born by accident. It stems from an interview published in a magazine at the end of the last century. At that time I had been saying to my friends that I no longer felt like talking about literature while there were still many people who expected me to be a leading figure in the literary world. Then a young editor at the magazine asked me for an interview about my loss of interest in literature. I was reluctant to do this interview, but I accepted the request because the editor was a former student of mine and I wanted to help him. Consequently, my words in the interview were mentioned frequently in literary magazines and elsewhere. At that point, I felt it necessary to express my fully developed view on this topic and wrote 'The End of Modern Literature'.

As this episode suggests, I was not eager to claim that modern literature had ended. I just wanted to look at the history of society from the perspective of 'modes of exchange'. The idea of modes of exchange occurred to me in 1998, leading me in a new direction. As that process unfolded, I gradually distanced myself from literature, even though that had not been my original intention. It happened naturally.

Several people have recently pointed out that my début work 'Consciousness and Nature', an essay on Soseki Natsume, already implies the idea of modes of exchange. If so, that means the concept of modes of exchange developed not from Marx's *Capital* but rather from literary criticism. Maybe this is true. Also, a few years ago, I received an email from a Swedish person who had taken part in the selection process for the Nobel Prize in Literature. In the course of our exchange, he said to me: 'I know you stopped writing about literature in the narrow sense, but what you are doing is fundamentally literature.' His words somehow made me very glad.

In retrospect, I became a 'philosopher' also by accident. It happened as follows. In 2005 I became a book reviewer for *The Asahi*. A couple of years before that, I had declined the same offer to be the reviewer because I felt that I was expected to read only novels. They persisted and allowed me to review any kind of book, so I finally accepted. There was a problem, however: my job title was required. Reluctantly, I chose to introduce myself as a 'philosopher'. I had an aversion to the title of 'philosopher', and that is why I had previously identified myself as a 'critic'. I had chosen literary criticism as my field because I thought it was free and creative, unlike specialized disciplines such as economics, philosophy, and politics.

In this sense, I neither abandoned literature nor abruptly became a philosopher; I have simply been working on the problem that lies at the very basis of literature *and* philosophy. Today we are facing the possibility of the end of the human world rather than the end of literature. That is the end I am now writing about.

By the time I heard about the project of this book, I had forgotten all about 'The End of Modern Literature'. Rereading the essay, I found it difficult to understand. That always happens to me when I reread my past works. Seeing the table of contents, however, I am deeply grateful for the contributions made by so many prominent authors. I am also grateful to Yoshiki Tajiri, Hiroki Yoshikuni, and Jonathan E. Abel for organizing and editing this volume.

The End of Modern Literature

1.

Today I will talk about *the end of modern literature*. This does not mean, for example, that something like postmodern literature will come after modern literature; nor does it mean that literature will disappear entirely. What I would like to argue today is that, in the modern period, a particular meaning was attached to literature, as well as a particular importance and a particular value. And yet, today, those things have disappeared. This is not really something that needs saying, but a simple fact. There are few people nowadays who believe literature is important, and it is therefore unnecessary for me to demonstrate that literature has come to an end. What does need pointing out, however, is that there was once a time when literature bore an incredible weight of meaning.

I myself have been deeply committed to literature, but I wouldn't say that you should follow me in this; there is no necessity for it whatsoever. We should instead seriously consider, first, the reasons why there was once a time when literature was thought to be eternal, and, secondly, the implications of literature's having lost this high status. By so doing, I would like to consider certain questions about the age we live in today.

When I say modern literature, I am thinking of the novel. Modern literature is not exclusively limited to the modern novel, of course, but a distinctive feature of modern literature lies in the fact that the novel assumed a new significance. Valued by the ruling class and by intellectuals, literature predated the modern period, but the novel did not feature in the canon of classical literature. Europe had been cultivating the tradition of poetics since Aristotle, but the novel (unlike drama) had not been included within that tradition. Similarly, in Japan, *literature* (*bungaku*) used solely to mean Chinese literature (*kanbungaku*) and the Japanese classics, and intellectuals were not interested in the novel (*shosetsu*) or common people's history (*haishi*).[1] It was only in the Meiji 20s (1887–96) that the novel came to be regarded as something deserving of intellectual attention. The regard for modern literature means, in short, that *novels* were held in high regard.

Accordingly, the 'end of modern literature' suggests the end of the period during which the novel and novelists were important. To demonstrate this point, I would like to start with a single novelist: Jean-Paul Sartre. This might seem an inapt choice, since Sartre was seen as a philosopher, dramatist, novelist, critic of art in general, journalist, and social activist. In my view, however, he was essentially a novelist.

I was recently reading a collection of Gilles Deleuze's essays, interviews, and conversations, in which he says that Sartre was his only 'teacher'.[2] Distinguishing 'private thinkers' from 'public professors', Deleuze says that Sartre was the only private 'teacher' for him. This is precisely what I mean by asserting that Sartre was a *novelist*. He was not a philosopher lecturing at a university. His philosophy was essentially akin to literature, or, rather, to the novel. Deleuze quotes Sartre's words: 'In a word, literature is essentially the subjectivity of a society in permanent revolution.'[3] That is to say, when revolutionary politics grows more conservative, it is literature that should continue the permanent revolution. Notice that Sartre says 'literature' rather than 'philosophy'. His activity was not limited to writing novels, but it was the perspective of the novel or a novelist that made his versatility possible.

1 [Trans.] *Shosetsu*, the Japanese word for the novel (which was adopted as the translation of the English word 'novel' by Shoyo Tsubouchi in *The Essence of the Novel* (1885–6)), originally meant 'small tales' in the Chinese classics – in contrast to *daisetsu* (big tales), which referred to the official history of monarchs and states. *Haishi* (trivial/vulgar history) also refers to a Chinese classical genre composed of stories of the daily life of ordinary people.

2 Gilles Deleuze, 'He Was My Teacher', in *Desert Islands and Other Texts, 1953–1974*, ed. David Lapoujade and trans. Michael Taormina (Semiotexte, 2004), 77–80.

3 Ibid., 78.

In France, Sartre's enormous influence overwhelmed those who came after him. A plethora of authors criticized or ridiculed Sartre in order to shake off his influence, but, as Deleuze admits, every apparent detractor actually admired him. Indeed, Sartre had anticipated all of what was subsequently attempted by way of criticism of him. For example, Derrida's critique of the 'metaphysics of presence' was exactly what Sartre was talking about in his writings on 'imagination'. Sartre was also one of the earliest proponents of the anti-novel (*nouveau roman*); his *Nausea* was virtually the first anti-novel.

To give you another example: the concept of *writing* (*écriture*) has been widespread since the 1960s. It designates a kind of work that is neither novelistic nor philosophical. To speak frankly, it seems to me that writers working in Sartre's wake, finding that they could not write novels like Sartre's, opted instead to denounce him and replace what he said about 'literature' with their own new concept – *writing*. The prevalence of the concept of *writing* therefore points to the fact that the novel as modern literature (including the anti-novel) has already come to an end. Hence it is nothing but an illusion if you expect any possibilities of new literature in *writing*.

Based on my own experience of working in the field of literary criticism in Japan, it seems to me that modern literature came to an end in the 1980s. It was the time of the so-called bubble economy, of consumer society, and of postmodernity. At that time the majority of young people were reading 'contemporary thought' (*gendai shiso*) rather than novels. In other words, literature lost the radical status it had once held. In this sense, what Sartre called 'literature' had been replaced by critical *writing*. This situation did not last for long, however. When I say 'the end of modern literature', I mean that all *writing* – including the deconstructive criticism, theory, and philosophy that emerged as a critique of modern literature – has ended. It was in the 1990s that this fact became obvious. In Japan it happened right after the death of Kenji Nakagami.[4]

4 [Trans.] Kenji Nakagami (1946–92) was a novelist who identified himself as a member of *Burakumin* (a group of people that has been discriminated against as the outcast in Japan) and intensely described the life of the *Burakumin* community.

2.

What does it mean to say that the status of literature – or the influence of literature – has declined? I will come back to this problem later. For the time being I would like to contend that this phenomenon has not only occurred in Japan. I have just mentioned the case of France, and in the United States the fall of modern literature happened even earlier. This is because popular culture, centred around television, developed earlier there (that is, in the 1950s) than it did anywhere else. The US, with its large minority population, has of course seen the literature of minority writers develop since that time. After the 1970s, Black women and Asian women writers have appeared on the scene with amazing literary vitality. And yet none of them had influence on the entire society. The significant role played in Japanese literature by minority writers such as Kenji Nakagami, Yangji Lee, and Yuko Tsushima during the 1980s was similarly constrained.[5] The change happened much earlier in the US. This is attested to by the fact that creative writing programmes have only recently been established in Japanese universities (with many novelists being hired as professors). In the US this same phenomenon began back in the 1950s. Faulkner once said that to be a writer one had to be the owner of a brothel,[6] but this advice makes little sense today; nowadays writers come from creative writing courses in universities. Departments of literature in the US are now quite unpopular, however – to the extent that they cannot survive without incorporating the study of film. In Japan, too, literature departments are disappearing.

But what really made me aware of the end of modern literature was the sudden decline of literature's influence in South Korea. It was shocking. In the 1990s I participated in the Japan-Korea Writers Association and had many opportunities to speak with Korean authors. At that time, my guess was that even if modern literature had ended in Japan, it would continue in South Korea. In 2000 I went to Seoul and declared at a press conference that literature had died in Japan. In saying this I meant that, even though Japan was still producing literary works that, as

5 [Trans.] Yangji Lee (1955–92) was a second-generation Korean-Japanese novelist. Yuko Tsushima (1947–2016) was a novelist known for works depicting the lives of marginalized women.

6 James B. Meriwether and Michael Millgate (eds), *Lion in the Garden: Interviews with William Faulkner, 1926–1962* (Random House, 1968), 239.

commodities, sold well globally – the works of Haruki Murakami, for example – the erstwhile role or meaning of literature in Japanese society had already disappeared. I heard afterwards that my speech had been taken seriously by the Korean audience, who considered it very pertinent to their own situation (by that point young people had started reading Murakami in South Korea too). When I was asked what I thought about the future of Korean literature, I replied that literature would continue to play a significant role in South Korea; since political movements were set to last, literature would likewise persist.

This turned out not to be the case, however. Although the student movement has declined, the South Korean labour movement is still very active in South Korea. Molotov cocktails were thrown during a workers' rally held in the autumn of 2003. The student movement was once an active force in South Korea because it served as a substitutive expression during a period when state suppression made the labour movement – or indeed any political movement – impossible. It is therefore unsurprising that when the political movement and the labour movement did become possible, the student movement declined. Literature underwent a similar process. Indeed, in South Korea, literature was in the same position as the student movement; since political movements were impossible in reality, literature undertook all of the substitutive roles.

Nonetheless, the decline of literature in South Korea since the 1990s has been remarkably rapid. Jong-chul Kim, a famous literary critic there, has quit working on literature and now engages in the ecology movement, publishing a journal entitled *Green Review*. In the autumn of 2002 he invited me to give a talk. He knew very well that I had already ceased attending to literature and was working on more directly political activities such as the New Associationist Movement (NAM).[7] Let me clarify, however, that he was the kind of person who, as he told me, had just finished reading Jun'ichiro Tanizaki's *The Makioka Sisters* for the fourth time. I asked him why he had stopped writing about literature. He replied that he had originally been interested in literature because he had thought that it would engage with all kinds of matters, from politics to personal problems – including some contradictions that could not be resolved in reality – and yet, he continued, literature now seemed limited

7 [Trans.] The New Associationist Movement (NAM) was a movement against the state, nation, and capital organized by Karatani from 2000 to 2002.

to a very narrow range. It was therefore no longer necessary to him, and so he abandoned it. I agreed with him.

What I learned later was that all the Korean literary critics I knew in the '90s had abandoned literature. In South Korea, it was typical among critics not only to write criticism but also to edit journals and manage publishing companies. But all of them quit working for literature at once. I do not think that this was because they got old and could no longer keep up with the sensibility of the younger generations. It rather suggests that what they used to consider 'literature' had come to an end. I had never imagined that the situation would change that rapidly in South Korea. It was then that I truly realized that the end of literature was an indisputable fact.

3.

Let me now consider why modern literature or the novel used to have a particular significance. Classical literature existed before the modern period, as did theories of literature – called poetics. As I have noted, however, poetics did not take an interest in the novel. And yet novels (prose fiction) did exist before the emergence of the modern novel, and they were popular among the common people. But they were not seriously considered.

In this context, it is remarkable that the notion of 'aesthetics' appeared in the eighteenth century. Aesthetics originally meant the science of sensibility – this is essentially how Kant uses the term in his *Critique of Pure Reason*, for instance. Aesthetics was, in short, the science of – a radically new intellectual concern with – sensibility or emotion. Before aesthetics, philosophy had disregarded sensibility and emotion as inferior human faculties. The best thing was to be rational, by distancing oneself from emotions. But then a new idea that sensibility and emotion were actually connected with intellectual and moral capacities (with understanding and reason) – and that imagination mediated those capacities – emerged. Until then, imagination had been understood in negative terms, as something causing illusions, but since the era in question it has been taken instead as a creative faculty. This development is intimately connected to the fact that literature came to be regarded as important.

Aesthetics had its origins in Britain, but it would soon be developed by the German Romantics. Interestingly, something similar happened in

Japan during the same period. In the late eighteenth century, Norinaga Motoori, in opposition to the cerebral and moralistic Cheng-Zhu school of Confucianism, emphasized the superiority of sympathy and imagination, which he termed *mono no aware* (the pathos of things).[8] He also argued that it was in the Japanese classic *The Tale of Genji* – a quite immoral narrative by Confucian standards – that the true morality could be found. This apparently Romantic idea emerged independently of any European influence. Yet Motoori and the German Romantics certainly had something in common, and this is because their attitude prioritizing sensibility and emotion originated in the same historical conditions: the ascendancy of the bourgeois class working for commerce and industry.

To put it differently, this was the moment when the novel, which had formerly been read solely for sensationalistic entertainment, was rediscovered as something that could be epistemologically and morally *truer* than philosophy or religion. The novel became the foundation of a community of sympathy – that is, in line with Benedict Anderson's formula, the foundation of a nation as an imagined community. The novel, unifying intellectuals and the common people, or all the social classes, was able to establish the nation.

As a result, the novel began to rise from its hitherto lowly status. But it was as a consequence of this rise that the novel now took on a heavy burden. If the novel is to be regarded as an aesthetic object, it cannot be a mere instrument for *sensible* pleasure. If literature was to supersede the intellectual and ethical traditions, it would also have to shoulder the burden of being both intellectual and ethical. The 'defence of poetry' used to be made with recourse to religion and moralism. In later periods, political or Marxist aspects of literature represented its intellectual and ethical task. Debates on such topics as 'religion and literature' or 'politics and literature' took place when literature rose above the rank of mere entertainment.

In the old problematic of 'religion and literature', literature's defenders argued that, even when it *looked* anti-religious, literature actually had more of a religious and ethical tendency than (institutionalized) religions themselves. Or, even though literature was fictional (they argued), its representations could be more true than what was thought to be the

8 [Trans.] Norinaga Motoori (1730–1801) was a scholar who led *Kokugaku*, the Japanese academic movement that re-evaluated early Japanese classics instead of concentrating on the then-dominant Chinese Confucian texts.

truth. By the same token, in the 'politics and literature' debate, the defenders of literature mainly argued that even though literature seemed impotent, meaningless, and even anti-political, what it described could actually be more revolutionary than (institutionalized) revolutionary politics – or that, even if it was fictional, it represented a vision that surpassed conventional perspectives. This is exactly what Sartre meant when he said that 'literature is essentially the subjectivity of a society in permanent revolution'. Sartre's words, that is to say, are indicative of the status of literature (or art in general) since the post-Kantian era.

Nowadays, however, no one attempts this kind of definition or defence of literature. This is in turn because no one criticizes literature. Today's society praises literature to a certain extent, but it also considers it to be nothing more than child's play. Until thirty years ago, people were always discussing issues like 'politics and literature' or literature's independence from politics. More concretely, they talked about the question of what novelists should do in relation to politics or the Communist Party. Therefore, when the authority of the Communist Party disappeared, so too did the problematic of 'politics and literature'. No one discusses these matters today. Writers can write whatever they like so long as they don't talk about obsolete nonsense like politics – this is how everyone seems to think.

But it is not that simple. Literature's increase in status meant that it bore a heavy ethical burden. When it was released from this burden, literature had the option of becoming mere entertainment again. If no one sees any problem here, then that's fine. Literature should pursue this direction. As it happens, I do not think we should painstakingly seek ethical and political qualities in literature alone. To be candid, I believe that there are many things that are far more important than literature. I also think that the novel, the literary form that constituted modern literature, was a historical product, and that it has already fulfilled its historical role.

4.

Up until the modern period, the world was covered by several empires. Each of the empires had a common written language – Chinese in East Asia, Latin in Western Europe, and Arabic in the Islamic world. These are the world languages, which the common people in each area could not read and write. Those empires were divided into modern nation-states, which, importantly, abandoned their world languages and created national languages based on their nations' vernaculars.

Over the course of this process, the nation-state created its national language not by simply writing down its vernacular language but rather by translating a world language (such as Latin) into a vernacular language. Luther translated the Bible into a vernacular language, which became the basis of modern German. The same is true for Dante's works. He wrote *La vita nuòva* in the vernacular of an Italian region, and this became the standard Italian language. Intellectuals at that time lamented that Dante did not write in Latin, since he was well known for his Latin writing, and yet his Italian writing later became the standard. And this is because he actually wrote it as a translation of Latin.

According to Dante, emotions such as love could not be expressed in Latin. Similarly, in Japan, Lady Murasaki, who was well versed in Chinese writing, did not use Chinese vocabulary in *The Tale of Genji*. For her, Chinese writing was too intellectual to capture subtle emotions. However, the Japanese language (*yamato-kotoba*) that she used was not derived from a vernacular language actually spoken in Kyoto, but was instead written as a translation of Chinese writing. That is why it could later become the classical standard of Japanese language.

In this way, every modern nation-state created a new written language by translating a universal intellectual language such as Chinese or Latin into a vernacular language. In Japan it was necessary, once again in the Meiji era, to create a new written language based on a vernacular (spoken) language.[9] This was called *genbun itchi*, literally meaning the unification of the spoken and written language. Again, this movement was carried out by novelists. In aesthetics, as I have noted, imagination came to be appreciated as the ability to mediate between sensibility and reason. The same is true for vernacular language. *Genbun itchi* was intended to connect sensational, emotional, and concrete experiences with intellectual and abstract ideas.

A similar process invariably occurred whenever a modern nation-state was established. In China, for instance, the *genbun itchi* style

9 [Trans.] The Meiji era (1868–1912) was the age of Westernization and modernization following the long-lasting Edo period (1603–1868), which was presided over by the Tokugawa shogunate.

became the standard way of writing. It is said that many young Chinese students, who studied in Japan after the First Sino-Japanese War, learned from *genbun itchi* in Japan and started the New Culture Movement in China. In this case, again, the novel played a significant role.

Today, however, with the nation-state nexus already established all over the world, national identity has completely taken root. Literature was once indispensable to nation-building, but we no longer have to *imaginatively* construct a sense of identity. Instead, people now think about nations in terms of pragmatic and economic interests.

At present, nation-states all over the world are being culturally eroded by capitalist globalization. This is giving rise to a small amount of push-back, but we are not seeing naked nationalism erupting as it did in the past – though economic disadvantages may end up prompting vehement resistance. The strongest current basis of opposition to globalization is neither nationalism nor literature, but rather movements such as Islamic or Christian fundamentalism, which are in fact hostile to modern literature.

5.

To repeat: 'the end of modern literature' could be paraphrased as 'the end of the modern novel'. What characterized modern literature was the fact that the novel dominated other literary forms. I have remarked that the novel shouldered an intellectual and moral task that it had not shouldered before modern times. But why was it the novel that did this, rather than other literary forms? This problem should be considered from another point of view. In the first place, the novel as an art form was related to the development of technologies such as printing.

Novels in Edo Japan (from the seventeenth to the nineteenth centuries) were published with illustrations. For example, Bakin Kyokutei's *Eight Dogs* was illustrated by *ukiyo-e* artists because there were not many literate people. Those novels were also read aloud. Well into the middle of the Meiji era, novels, including those printed in the newspaper, used to be read aloud by a reader and listened to by others. The pseudo-traditional rhythmical style was more enjoyable to listen to than the *genbun itchi* style. In this sense, it can be argued that the modern novel was established only when illustrations and voices were eliminated. The modern novel is supposed to be read silently. It is natural that one becomes introverted when reading the modern novel silently and alone. Conversely, it is difficult to read an introversive novel out loud.

Related to this point, however, a strange phenomenon arose in the middle of the Meiji era. Shimei Futabatei wrote *Ukigumo* (*The Drifting Cloud*) in the *genbun itchi* style, but he gave it up halfway, and the unfinished work had little influence at that time, even though it is highly regarded today as the first modern Japanese novel. By contrast, his 'Aibiki' – a translation of Turgenev's short story 'The Tryst' – had a significant impact on the early stages of modern Japanese literature. Why was it that *Ukigumo* was comparatively neglected?

I used to think that it was because Futabatei was so strongly influenced by Edo literature such as the *kokkeibon* that he was unable to break away from that tradition.[10] I actually wrote as much in my *Origins of Modern Japanese Literature*. Even if that is true, however, it should be added that the Western literature that inspired him was quite similar to *kokkeibon*. It wasn't modern realists such as Turgenev that inspired him, but rather the genealogy of Gogol and Dostoevsky. For example, Dostoevsky's novels, which were composed by means of dictation, are more suitable to listen to than to read silently.

Futabatei was moved by Dostoevsky's novels when his Russian teacher read them aloud. When he later read them silently, however, he found them less impressive. This makes it clear that his *Ukigumo* was aligned with the genealogy of Gogol and Dostoevsky, which was different from the realism of modern literature. It was, as it were, a *Renaissance* novel in the Bakhtinian sense. The same is true for Soseki Natsume.[11] Laurence Sterne, Soseki's favourite author, is likewise a Renaissance novelist. These authors will assume a different kind of significance depending on whether one takes them as preceding realism or surpassing it. However, at that time, they were seen as *premodern* in both Britain and Japan.

For instance, Soseki published *I Am a Cat* for the first time by reading it aloud to his friends. Other of his works, including *Botchan* and *The*

---

10 [Trans.] *Kokkeibon* (literally 'comical book') was a literary genre of the Edo period. It was full of word play, parody, and comical depictions of ordinary people.

11 [Trans.] Soseki Natsume (1867–1916) was a novelist and a scholar of British literature. He introduced Laurence Sterne into Japan for the first time, and his first novel *I Am a Cat* (1905–6) is particularly well known for being influenced by Sterne's *Tristram Shandy*.

Three-Cornered World, are similarly more enjoyable if you hear them read aloud. The same can be said of Futabatei's *Ukigumo*, which is why it deviated from the mainstream of modern literature. Modern literature, after all, is realistic, Romantic, and based on silent reading. In this sense, that episode which Deleuze recounts about Kafka reading *The Trial* aloud and the audience convulsing with laughter is important.[12]

6.

The modern novel was independent of voices and illustrations, and this meant that it demanded a powerful imagination on the part of both writer and reader. Once visual media appeared, however, such a faculty became unnecessary. For example, until the appearance of the cinema, novelists tried to write what one might call film-like novels, and they developed various methods for doing so. Once the technology of cinema had actually emerged, however, such strategies lost their meaning.

This is in a sense comparable to what happened to painting when photography emerged. When photography appeared in mid-nineteenth-century France, the painters who had previously made their living by painting portraits could not survive – for up until then painting had been based on the same principle as photography (the camera obscura). Linear perspective was based on that principle. With photography, however, such technical facility became meaningless, and so impressionist painters tried to do what photography could not. It might be said that this was the moment when contemporary painting began. It was also the moment when Western painters encountered Japanese *ukiyo-e*. Ironically, however, it was right after that that Japanese artists in the Meiji era adopted the pre-impressionist principle of Western painting as their new standard.

The same happened to the novel. The distinctive feature of the novel is, after all, its realism. How to make it real, even though it is only a story (fiction) – this was the problem with which the modern novel engaged. Erwin Panofsky considers what made painting realistic from two points of view: the object and the form that captures it. As far as the object was concerned, there was a shift from religious and historical themes to

12 Gilles Deleuze and Félix Guattari, *Kafka: Toward a Minor Literature*, trans. Dana Polan (University of Minnesota Press, 1986), 95.

ordinary people and landscapes. As for the form (or 'symbolic form', in Panofsky's words), the crucial development was the adoption of linear perspective – a method by which it is possible to give depth to a two-dimensional image by showing the object from one fictional fixed point.[13] The same is true for the realism of the novel.

As far as the object is concerned, little is needed by way of explanation. To put it succinctly: ordinary landscapes and people were brought into focus. This required a great inversion, as I have shown elsewhere, taking Doppo Kunikida's 'Unforgettable People' as an example.[14] What is 'unforgettable' in Kunikida's work actually refers to an insignificant, ordinary landscape. As for the form, what makes realism possible is the form of third-person objective description. This is a method by which it is possible to make the narrator transparent without completely removing them from the novel. When the narrator is visible and lacks a single fixed viewpoint, the novel lacks reality and a certain sort of depth. As I have said in relation to Futabatei, however, just as Western literature started to doubt the realism of third-person objective description, Japanese writers painstakingly adopted it. In this regard we can again see a parallel between literature and painting.

Japanese writers probably stuck to the I-novel because they could not get accustomed to the 'symbolic form' of third-person objective description.[15] In quite a few I-novels a limited third-person point of view is employed, such that the narrative voice is undifferentiated from the perspective of the protagonist: what the protagonist cannot see is also invisible to the reader. In contrast, the position of a third-person objective narrator is, like linear perspective, fictional. For the I-novelists, whose realism aimed at uncovering an individual's inner life, there was therefore something vulgar about the third-person objective novel. They certainly were not wrong in saying that third-person omniscient description (like linear perspective) is based on a kind of falsity.

---

13 See Erwin Panofsky, *Perspective as Symbolic Form* (Zone Books, 1991).

14 See Karatani, *Origins of Modern Japanese Literature*, chap. 1. [Trans.] Doppo Kunikida (1871–1908) was a novelist who, in Karatani's reading, accomplished the *genbun itchi* style in works such as 'Unforgettable People' (1898).

15 [Trans.] The I-novel (*shishosetsu*) was a subgenre that predominated on the Japanese literary scene throughout the early twentieth century. It was a sort of confessional literature, in which the events in the story were expected to correspond to the real experience of the author.

Since those days, some people have criticized the I-novel for being a backward and deformed subgenre that deviated from authentic modern literature. The I-novel has its own raison d'être, however. I-novelists tried to be thoroughly *realist*. In so doing, they found the fiction of the third-person objective to be unacceptable. Ryunosuke Akutagawa appreciated the I-novel, recognizing in it a novelty corresponding to that of post-impressionism. Akutagawa, in his 'In a Grove', likewise shows – by skilfully juxtaposing three perspectives – that the third-person objective is nothing but a fiction.[16] Later, in France, Sartre was among the first to doubt the perspective of the third-person objective point of view, and he was succeeded by the *nouveau roman*. It could henceforth be said that the third-person objective had been abandoned. When one renounces the value of the realism enabled by the third-person objective, however, the radical significance of modern literature also disappears.

When photography appeared, painters attempted to do what photography could not – to do what only painting could do. The modern novel did the same when the cinema appeared. It could be said that the early-twentieth-century modernist novel was the embodiment of the novelty of the novel as defined against the cinema. In other words, modernist writers sought to do what only the novel could do. James Joyce is a typical example, along with the *nouveau roman* in France. These writers were extremely conscious of the cinema. Moreover, they deeply engaged with the cinema. Marguerite Duras directed ten or more films, and she wrote the screenplay of *Hiroshima mon amour*, which Alain Resnais directed. (By the way, Duras chose Vietnamese when she took her *baccalauréat*; French was a foreign language for her. Whereas other writers of *nouveaux romans* were merely intellectually sophisticated, she was a true 'novelist' – one somehow reminiscent of Kenji Nakagami. She passed away four years after Nakagami's death.)

But the cinema is not the novel's only rival. New media have emerged to challenge the cinema, including television, video, and the digitalization of audiovisual information by the computer. It is unsurprising that

16 [Trans.] Ryunosuke Akutagawa (1892–1927) did not himself write I-novels, but he argued for a 'novel without plot' in his essay 'Literary, All-Too-Literary'. His short story 'In a Grove' achieved international fame thanks to *Rashomon*, the film version directed by Akira Kurosawa.

the superiority of print culture and the novel, which was originally introduced by way of the novelty of letterpress technology, has come to an end during this era. For instance, in the case of Japan, the popularity of manga could mean a return to the novel of the Edo period: the majority of the Edo novels were illustrated and composed almost entirely of conversations.

As I have said before, it is an undeniable fact that the modern novel was foundational to the formation of modern nations. Since the late twentieth century, however, there have been few cases in which literature has served as a foundation for nationalism, and there will be even fewer cases in the future. At the present time, in developing countries, we cannot expect that many more novels will be written, or that they will find a growing audience. Even if there are some readers out there, will they not in all likelihood be reading *Harry Potter*?

To give you an example, I heard this story about Icelanders. Perhaps because theirs is an isolated island country, they have historically been proud of being authentic Icelanders. In fact, their language has not changed significantly since the *Sagas of Icelanders*, and their traditional culture has been strikingly visible in their dances, songs, and youth culture. But once the restriction on television was lifted, everyone became Americanized in a single night.[17]

This kind of phenomenon does not entail the disappearance of nationalism. It simply means that it is now difficult for literature to be the foundation of nationalism. For political purposes, making films would be more efficient than writing novels. And manga might be even better. In short, it would be more effective to create a work with audio-visual culture than with print culture. For such media are easier for the public to approach. Passing through the process of modern literature or the novel is, therefore, not an indispensable and inevitable condition for all nations. Of course, there may be a huge problem in 'leaping over' this stage. I think that in the future some will have to pay for what they have skipped over.

17 See Pico Iyer, 'Iceland: Rock 'n' Roll Ghost Town', in *Falling Off the Map: Some Lonely Places of the World* (Vintage, 1993).

7.

Let me talk at this point about an Indian writer, Arundhati Roy. She won the Booker Prize in 1997 for her novel *The God of Small Things*, which became a bestseller and made her very famous. Yet, after getting the prize for her first novel, she quit writing novels while also becoming closely involved with movements such as anti-dam and anti-war activism in India.[18] In her capacity as a writer, she has exclusively published non-fiction essays on these socio-political issues. It is common among Indian writers who become popular in the West to migrate to the US or the UK, living in style in the literary world there. When asked why she gave up writing novels, however, she replied that she would not write a novel just because she was a novelist, that she would write only when she has something to write, and that she could not write a novel in a carefree manner in this critical time.

Doesn't Roy's behaviour suggest that the social role of literature has come to an end? If the age during which literature seemed able to change society has ended, that would mean that it is no longer possible to write a novel or to be a novelist in the original sense, and that being a novelist is merely one profession among others. It is not that Roy abandoned literature and chose social movements instead, but she has actually inherited what was authentically 'literature'.

By the way, the recent winners of the Booker Prize have mostly been from minority populations or foreign nations, including Salman Rushdie and Kazuo Ishiguro. This is the same phenomenon that I have mentioned in the cases of the US and Japan. This tendency will not prolong the life of literature, however. The anglophone world is far more multi-ethnic and multicultural than Japan, and its literature therefore has the potential to last a bit longer; nonetheless, the period during which literature exerted a strong influence due to its ethical and intellectual tasks has basically ended. What we see now is nothing more than its afterimage.

Some say that literature still exists. If a few writers who are resolved to be voices in the wilderness dare to defend literature, I have no problem with that. In fact, I have written many pieces to encourage

18 See Arundhati Roy, 'The End of Imagination', in *The End of Imagination* (Haymarket, 2016).

those writers, and I may even continue to do so. But in recent times it has not been these committed writers who have been asserting that literature is still active. On the contrary, it is those people whose very existence attests to the death of literature who have been asserting this sort of nonsense. Literary magazines continue to be published in Japan even today; their ads appear in the newspapers every month. They do not sell at all well, however; the circulation figures are pretty dismal. If a novel sells well, it is thanks to some sensational topic unrelated to literature, but this creates the false notion that literature is still flourishing.

I am not trying to encourage writers to restore 'literature' now that it has been lost. Nor do I criticize novelists who write books that are intended to be entertaining. In the historical context of Japan it is only natural, now that the modern novel is over, that literature will come to resemble premodern entertainment such as *yomihon* or *ninjobon*.[19] That's OK. In the best-case scenario people will write well and produce global commodities; manga has in fact accomplished this. Indeed, there are actually quite a few writers who can pull this off in genres such as mystery fiction. But there is something absurd about the arrogant claims made by writers who pretend to write *pure* literature (*jun-bungaku*) but who actually write commonplace works that are only read within a small Japanese literary circle.

8.

Thus, I have briefly illustrated the end of modern literature. The problem will be neither intelligible nor meaningful if we consider literature or the novel in isolation, however. In the first place, the notion of 'modern' is very unclear. Discussing fashionable topics such as the critique of modernity or postmodernism would merely obscure our understanding. In my view, the problem should be examined in relation to the development of world capitalism. I would like to trace the end of literature by way of a simple periodization chart.

19 [Trans.] *Yomihon* and *ninjobon* were popular literary genres in the Edo period. *Yomihon* is typically a collection of strange/supernatural tales (such as Bakin's *Eight Dogs*), while *ninjobon* is typically composed of sentimental/erotic stories.

Stages of World Capitalism

	1750–1810	1810–70	1870–1930	1930–90	1990–
World capitalism	Mercantilism	Liberalism	Imperialism	Late capitalism	Neoliberalism
Hegemonic state	(Imperialist)	Britain (liberal)	(Imperialist)	The US (liberal)	(Imperialist)
Capital	Merchant capital	Industrial capital	Financial capital	State monopoly capital	Multinational capital
World commodity (staple)	Woollen textiles	Fibre textiles	Heavy industry	Durable consumer goods	Information
State	Absolutism	Nation-state	Socialism/ fascism	Welfare state	Regionalism
Ideology (ethos)	Consumerist	Ascetic		Consumer society	
Social types	Tradition-directed	Inner-directed		Other-directed	
Major art form	Narrative	Novel	Cinema	Television	Multimedia

At first glance, this chart illustrates the transition coinciding with the development of productive force. This is obvious, for example, in the 'World commodity' and 'Major art form' (media) items, which show the development of technology. On the other hand, however, the chart also testifies to circular (repetitive) changes. This much is obvious from the 'World capitalism' row.

It should be noted that when the chart shows that the stages of world capitalism are mercantilism, liberalism, or imperialism, it does not mean that the entire world assumed the same economic system. For instance, when the chart says 'liberalism', that was the economic policy adopted by Britain, which established overpowering superiority at that time; other nations were far from being economically liberal, but instead contended with Britain by way of protectionism. Japan was still in its Edo period at that point. And 'imperialism' means the economic policy adopted by a few great European powers – with which a rapidly developing Meiji Japan caught up – while the large majority of nations were colonized by those powers.

It is still possible, for instance, to call the period from 1810 to 1870 the *liberal* stage, because whatever economic policies each state employed, they belonged synchronically to world capitalism, in which the British economy obtained hegemony. Under world capitalism, nations in various stages coexist, forming an international division of labour. This global synchronic structure, in which each national economy is situated, is crucial to bear in mind when looking at this chart.

Meanwhile, the stages of mercantilism (1750–1810) and imperialism (1870–1930) mean the periods when formerly hegemonic states declined and competed with newly rising states. The imperialist stage and the liberal stage come in turn on a roughly sixty-year cycle.

In this regard, the stage from 1930 to 1990 is usually called late capitalism or the Cold War era, but from another point of view it was the stage of *liberalism* based on American hegemony. During this stage, the developed capitalist nations cooperated with each other on account of seeing the Soviet Bloc as the common enemy, and, domestically, they employed policies for the protection of workers and the social welfare. Even though this period looked like an age of hostility and crisis, the communist nations (internationally) and socialist parties (domestically) were far from threatening world capitalism but, rather, stabilized it. In turn, the era after the 1990s should be seen as the *neo-imperialist* stage, in the sense that the US declined economically and the real hegemonic state disappeared.

We can thus see the transition taking place in tandem with the development of capitalism on the one hand and repetitive circulation on the other. This is obvious when we look at the items in the 'Capital' row. Merchant capitalism, which makes a profit from the price differences caused by circulation, was replaced by industrial capitalism, which makes a profit from production. Financial capitalism or speculative capital, which became dominant after industrial capitalism, is in a certain sense a revived version of merchant capitalism. Max Weber emphasized that what caused industrial capitalism was not the desire for consumption, as was the case in merchant capitalism, but, rather, the ascetic attitude restraining desire. In late capitalism, or so-called consumer society, which was based on mass production and mass consumption, this ascetic attitude was marginalized. We can see this kind of transition in the successive 'Ideology' items.

9.

Consider the row on 'Social types'. I have briefly mentioned the US in the 1950s; actually, what took place in the US at that time anticipates almost all of what would later be theorized as postmodernism. Accordingly, the works of the North American sociologists and critics who engaged with the relevant social issues during that period were predictive. For example, Daniel Boorstin pointed out that events were being replaced by pseudo-events. This is what Jean Baudrillard would later call simulacra. The Canadian literary critic Marshall McLuhan meanwhile undertook a prescient investigation of the radical changes to which television was giving rise.

Take David Riesman's *The Lonely Crowd*, for example. Riesman paid attention to the fact that these changes had happened as the problem of 'subjectivity'. Classifying societies as the 'tradition-directed', 'inner-directed', or 'other-directed', Riesman argued that American society had shifted from being inner-directed to being other-directed.[20] Inner-type people possess an autonomous self, which is not easily influenced by tradition or by other people. In terms of social class, they had been represented by yeoman farmers in the Midwest. But, according to Riesman, they quickly became other-directed.

Unlike tradition-directed people, other-directed people have no fixed objective standards. As in Hegel's theory of recognition, being other-directed means behaving in accordance with the desires of the other – that is, with the desire to be recognized by the other. The 'other' towards which other-directed people orient themselves is what they imaginatively construct out of their preoccupation with other people. What the sociological theories of the 1950s – those theories of pseudo-events and new media – grasped was precisely this kind of floating individual (in other words, the masses).

This was not a phenomenon peculiar to the US. It could be observed wherever industrial capitalism was shifting from the primary and secondary sectors to the tertiary sector of industry, or from the manufacture of goods to the production of information. Still, it happened in the US first, and this was because of a lack of tradition-directedness

20 David Riesman, *The Lonely Crowd: A Study of the Changing American Character* (Yale University Press, 1950).

there, and because inner-directedness was in fact quite fragile as well. The farmers in the Midwest, whom Riesman regards as being archetypally inner-directed, were in many cases immigrants who had rejected the tradition-directedness of their home countries. And yet the communities that they formed tended to be extremely other-directed, on account of their having no traditional standards.

Inner-direction is internal autonomy rising up against tradition-direction, in a situation where tradition is predominant. In the US, however, where tradition had never been predominant, an individual's behaviour was not based on his or her own principles. There was instead a standard shared among people who were all watching each other, and this standard served in the place of tradition. For this reason it was often pointed out that even though the US had no state control of the kind seen in the Soviet Union, there existed there another variety of intense conformism. This is why mass society and consumer society were first realized without resistance in the US.

It is worth bearing in mind here the distinction that Hegel made between desire and need. Desire is the desire of the other – that is, the desire to be recognized by the other. According to Hegel, this desire and the struggle to fulfil it drive world history. But what happens if it is actually fulfilled? Then history will end. It was in this theoretical context that the Hegelian philosopher Alexandre Kojève reflected on humans after 'the end of history', which he associated with future communism. But, in addition to arguing that it would be realized in the future, Kojève also saw this 'end of history' as being present in the here and now. He took the 'American way of life' – that is, the mass consumer society based on mass production and mass consumption that first appeared in the US in the 1950s – as being exemplary in this regard.

According to Kojève, this was a society without struggles and without classes, and therefore a society of 'animals' who did not have to speculatively understand the world or the self. Kojève's 'American way of life' is, in Riesman's terms, the other-directed world, in that it is neither tradition-directed nor inner-directed. It should also be noted that what Kojève calls 'animals' are the opposite of real animals, since the term refers to individuals who desire only what the other desires.

Kojève thought that the world would be 'Americanized' in the future. However, after visiting Japan in 1959, he experienced 'a radical change of opinion'. He found in Japan another post-historical world, one which had had no experience of internal war since the Battle of Sekigahara.[21] For instance, the Japanese could commit 'gratuitous' suicide (*seppuku*) without any 'human' reason but for the sake of pure formality, which Kojève calls 'snobbery'. Kojève's conclusion was as follows: 'the recently begun interaction between Japan and the Western World will finally lead not to a rebarbarization of the Japanese but to a "Japanization" of the Westerners (including the Russians)'.[22]

What Kojève calls 'America' and 'Japan' are not of course real objects out there in the world, but only exist as philosophically theorized categories – very much as in Hegel's writings. As such, the Japanese snobbery Kojève described really means the set of conventions that stake one's life on an empty formal game that is devoid of any historical ideas, or indeed any intellectual or moral content. It is neither tradition-directed nor inner-directed, but an extreme form of other-directedness. There exists only the desire to be recognized by the other. Indeed, in today's society, we can find innumerable examples of those who, in spite of only ever thinking about what the other would think, have never really cared about the other as such, and who also lack any kind of interiority.

Kojève found the end of history in *the Japanese way of life* of the Edo period, and this turned out to be a prescient insight. For, twenty years after Kojève had made this claim, the era of Japanese economic prosperity (the bubble economy) – which was also known as postmodern – saw the re-emergence of the peculiar snobbery that had taken a particularly elaborate form during the 300-year peace of the Edo period.

Originally, the inner-directed type did not exist in Japan. It appeared in modern Japanese literature and philosophy after the Meiji Restoration. The intellectuals of the Meiji era tried hard to establish the autonomous

21 [Trans.] The Battle of Sekigahara (1600) was a decisive battle whose winner, Ieyasu Tokugawa, inaugurated the long-lasting Edo period (1603–1868), also known as Pax Tokugawana.

22 Alexandre Kojève, *Introduction to the Reading of Hegel: Lectures on the Phenomenology of Spirit*, ed. Allan Bloom and trans. James H. Nichols (Basic Books, 1969), 162. [Trans.] By 'snobbery', Kojève refers to the conditions of life after the end of history, which adhere to 'totally formalized values – that is, values completely empty of all "human" content in the "historical" sense', rather than to an exaggerated regard for wealth or social position or a sense of superiority in cultural taste. Kojève includes 'the Noh Theater, the ceremony of tea, and the art of bouquets of flowers' in such snobbery and refers to the kamikaze attack as one of 'gratuitous' suicides (162).

'subject'. What became remarkable during the 1980s, however, was the opposite attitude – an attitude that ridiculed the 'subject' and 'meaning' and indulged in formal linguistic play. In place of the modern novel, manga, anime, computer game design – or literature and art related to these new media – became predominant. It was an even emptier, yet more aesthetically sophisticated, version of the popular culture that had first appeared in the United States.

The Japanese bubble economy quickly collapsed and, from that time onwards, the kind of mass culture described above has proliferated globally. In this sense, it does seem as though the world started being 'Japanized'. All this means, however, is that the global capitalist economy has been uprooting tradition-directed and inner-directed cultures and introducing other-directed cultures in their place. Modernity and modern literature have thus come to an end.

10.

As I have already mentioned, Weber emphasized that it was neither interests nor desire but 'worldly asceticism' that advanced industrial capitalism; it was asceticism that laid the groundwork for the industrious work ethic that resulted in modern (industrial) capitalism. Weber also pointed out that such asceticism had developed from Protestantism (Christianity). But what about in Japan, in that case? The answer is that it did not have to be Protestantism in particular that drove Japanese capitalism; what really matters is that worldly asceticism entailed the delay of the fulfilment of desire.

Of course, Christianity (specifically Protestantism) had no small impact in Meiji Japan. In fact, many authors, including Tokoku Kitamura and Doppo Kunikida, were heavily influenced by Christianity. Even before that, however, there was an ideology that introduced the industrious and ascetic life into Japan on a large scale: the ideology of the self-made man – *risshin shusse shugi*.[23] This was the idea underlying the early Meiji policies, educational reform, and conscription. It was

23 [Trans.] This literally means 'ideology of upward mobility and success', but it is sometimes translated as 'careerism', 'meritocracy', or 'ideology of the self-made man'.

already expressed in the Charter Oath.[24] And, in concert with the Oath, Yukichi Fukuzawa's *An Encouragement of Learning* and Samuel Smiles's *Self-help* (translated by Masanao Nakamura) were published in Japan and became bestsellers.

The ideal of the self-made man was a great source of intellectual energy for modern Japanese people. And besides the self-made man, there were myriad discourses arguing against the feudal status system in Meiji Japan. But the mere claim that everyone was equal was little more than hollow words. What *did* change during the Meiji era, which was far from being an egalitarian society in reality, was that Japan adopted a new system that determined one's status in accordance with one's educational background. The Edo period had actually had more social mobility than we imagine today, but it was really after the Meiji era that such mobility increased in a significant way. As a result, the majority of the Japanese, both children and parents, worked hard to achieve success. This has continued until recent years in the form of fierce examination competition. Without taking all this into consideration, we cannot understand Japanese modernity.

That being said, the self-made man did not immediately manifest himself in modern literature. On the contrary, modern literature expressed a disillusioned sense that one *cannot* be the self-made man. This phenomenon appeared in roughly the year Meiji 20 (1887). Both Ogai Mori's *The Dancing Girl* and Futabatei's *Ukigumo* treat this kind of depressed character.

It is often pointed out that the modern self or interiority in Meiji Japan originated from the failure of the Freedom and People's Rights Movement.[25] Tokoku Kitamura is a representative example.[26] But the Freedom and People's Rights Movement had a great deal of internal variation, and as such it contained within itself significant early opposition to the idea of the self-made man. For example, D. T. Suzuki and

---

24 [Trans.] The Charter Oath (*Gokajo no Goseimon*) outlined in 1868 the main aims and priorities of the Meiji government, setting the direction of Japanese modernization.

25 [Trans.] The Freedom and People's Rights Movement (*Jiyu Minken Undo*) was a Japanese political movement for democracy in the Meiji era, especially in the 1870s and '80s.

26 [Trans.] Tokoku Kitamura (1868–94) was a poet and literary critic who initially engaged in the political movement but soon shifted to Christianity and the Romantic literary movement.

Kitaro Nishida, who were sympathetic to the Movement, quit school in order to resist the centralization of the education system and, after the failure of the Movement, devoted themselves to religion.[27] Futabatei also quit school as part of the trend represented by the Freedom and People's Rights Movement in its broadest sense. This is part of the background to *Ukigumo*. Soseki Natsume, apparently doing well on the elite track, was always driven by the impulse to deny and destroy the world of the self-made men. Although he did not start writing literary works until much later, Soseki was a contemporary of Kitamura, Futabatei, and Nishida's. Indeed, he quit his post as a professor at Tokyo Imperial University to become a novelist. This is why I am inclined to associate Kitamura and Nishida (in the years of the Meiji 10s) with K and Sensei, the characters of Soseki's *Kokoro*.

It would furthermore be true to say that it was Christianity that brought modern interiority – and, at the same time, romantic love and modern literature – into Meiji Japan. However, it is difficult to understand why it was Christianity in particular that caused such radical transformations at that time. As I wrote in *Origins of Modern Japanese Literature*, many of those who converted to Christianity were former subjects of the Tokugawa government. Because their prospects of career advancement had become uncertain in the new society, and because they had lost the 'lord' who had once been the object of their loyalty, they chose another lord (Christ). If this analysis is correct, it is, again, impossible to understand the significance of Christianity without the historical background of *risshin shusse shugi* – the ideology of the self-made man. It is obvious that the interiority of these subjects appeared under the pressure of this ideology. They sought to stand on their own two feet against the social pressure of *risshin shusse shugi*, and it was then that they encountered Christianity (Protestantism).

It was the ideology of the self-made man that introduced the industrious and ascetic ethos into Japan after the Meiji Restoration. In Riesman's terms, this ideology is not tradition-directed; it challenges the system under which one inherits one's status from that of one's parents. Nor is it inner-directed. It is, instead, other-directed; it is driven by the

27 [Trans.] D. T. Suzuki (1870–1966) was a Buddhist author and philosopher famous for his English works on Zen. Kitaro Nishida (1870–1945) was a philosopher who founded the so-called Kyoto School.

desire to be recognized by the other. The modern self desired autonomy beyond tradition and the other, but this is difficult to achieve in reality. People therefore found it in Christianity, or, ultimately, in 'literature' imported from Europe.

But what about today? In Japan, for example, a kind of educational credentialism has developed, or a system that determines one's 'status' in accordance with the hierarchy of universities (at the top of which resides the University of Tokyo). However hard you try to challenge it, the hierarchy has endured. And yet, under globalization since the 1990s, it seems that the system is rapidly being dismantled. Many people are happily quitting their jobs in spite of having been hired by good companies after a lengthy competitive process. They become part-time workers. They might write novels. Still, there is no interiority or ressentiment – of the kind that originated in dropping out of or being excluded from the track of the self-made men – that is in any way akin to what one associates with modern literature. This is not a negative development, in my view; I have no inclination to say that these people ought to be involving themselves in literature. I would really prefer them to create alternative forms of life in the real world.

11.

In Japan, what Weber theorized as worldly asceticism becomes most remarkable in the context of love and sex, rather than in that of labour. In the Edo period, too, merchants were ascetic. But once they had diligently hoarded up their money, what did they do? It was always sexual debauchery. Koyo Ozaki wrote about these kinds of sexually debauched affairs in his novels.[28] It was Tokoku Kitamura who severely criticized Ozaki's novel (*Kyaramakura*). He criticized the world described by Ozaki, naming it *iki*, which according to Kitamura was nothing but plebian nihilism born in the red-light districts (*yukaku*) of a feudal society. He proposed romantic love (*ren'ai*) over against *iki*. In his 'The Pessimistic Poet and Women', Kitamura argues that 'romantic love serves not for the battle between the imagined world and the real world,

28 [Trans.] Koyo Ozaki (1868–1903) was a popular novelist and poet known for old-fashioned and entertainment-oriented works.

but as a bastion where the loser of the imagined world barricades himself', and that 'romantic love is a clear mirror, which, once you have sacrificed yourself, mirrors the "self" of yourself'.[29] The notion of romantic love that had been imported from Europe was, in this manner, thought to have an epoch-making significance.

Kitamura argued for Platonic love. Unlike younger writers such as Toson Shimazaki or Katai Tayama, who had been making this case since the beginning of their careers, he had experienced in his youth the dissipated world described by Ozaki. For he was precocious to the extent that he participated in the Freedom and People's Rights Movement when he was an elementary school student. And he understood the actual difficulties of romantic love. For example, he says: 'it is deplorable that, as romantic love easily bewitches a pessimist, marriage easily disappoints him. Getting married with too much expectation will cause despair in comparison to the first expectation, ending up with miserable opposition between husband and wife.'[30] Indeed, Kitamura himself divorced Mina Ishizaka – and committed suicide at the age of twenty-five.

Now what about Ozaki, who was criticized by Kitamura as a dissolute figure? Ozaki admired and imitated Saikaku Ihara to the extent that he edited Saikaku's complete works.[31] I do not think Kitamura's criticism of plebian nihilism is applicable to Saikaku. Rather, writers in Osaka in the Genroku period (1688–1704), such as Saikaku and Monzaemon Chikamatsu, captured the rising power of the merchant class. Kitamura's notion of *iki* is applicable only after the Bunka-Bunsei period (1804–30). (The philosopher Shuzo Kuki theorized the plebian nihilism of red-light districts as the 'structure of *iki*', but it only became a phenomenon after the Bunka-Bunsei period.)

But Ozaki, allegedly a successor to Edo literature, did not understand Saikaku in spite of having edited his collected works. Even worse, Ozaki did not understand the age that he himself was living in. What Ozaki learned from Saikaku was the insight that everything is governed by the commodity economy. This insight suggests totally different meanings depending on which period of time one is talking about, however; Saikaku

29 Tokoku Kitamura, 'Ensei Shika to Josei', in *Kitamura Tokoku Shu*, ed. Odagiri Hideo, *Meiji Bungaku Zenshu*, vol. 29 (Chikuma Shobo, 1976), 65, 66.

30 Ibid., 67.

31 [Trans.] Saikaku Ihara (1642–93) was a novelist, playwright, and poet in the Edo period.

revealed this insight at the beginning of the eighteenth century – in a feudal society governed by samurai – whereas Ozaki offered the same insight during the Meiji 20s (1887–96). In the Meiji 20s, the merchant capitalism described by Saikaku had already been replaced by industrial capitalism. What had thrived under merchant capitalism had simply become commercial capital (*shosha*, general trading companies) or usury, which was, when industrial capitalism developed further, replaced by banks, giving rise to a system that was very different from traditional usury.

Ozaki himself thought that he had later changed his mind about romantic love. And yet his views did not change fundamentally, as we can see in his last work: *The Golden Demon*. This work was written in Meiji 36 (1903), right before the Russo-Japanese War – that is, when Japan's economic trajectory was towards heavy industry and its political trajectory towards the imperialist stage. But what Ozaki wrote in this novel is the story of a man (Kan'ichi) whose lover (Omiya) has left him for a wealthier man (Tomiyama) and who plans to take his revenge on her by becoming a usurer. The entire setting is anachronistic – wholly removed from the contemporary reality. In contrast to Ozaki's anachronism, it could be argued that Kitamura's romantic-love ideology dovetailed perfectly (even if this was not his intention) with the ethos that is indispensable to industrial capitalism: worldly asceticism. Delaying desires rather than satisfying them instantly, or storing up the right to satisfy one's desires. This is the 'spirit' of industrial capitalism.

In retrospect, however, the fact that in Meiji 36 (1903) and thereafter *The Golden Demon* became a phenomenal bestseller would seem to suggest that people's way of thinking had not changed substantially since the Edo period. For instance, in a well-known scene, Kan'ichi kicks Omiya with his sandals on the seashore of Atami, accusing her of betrayal. Kan'ichi then says that next year, the year after next, and for many years hence, 'this moon shining above tonight will be clouded with my tears'.[32] He condemns her betrayal because, in his account, they 'used to be like husband and wife'. I thought this was exaggeration, but, rereading the text closely, I found that they had actually lived together for five years – a situation tolerated by her parents. Yet Tomiyama, in spite of being aware of their relationship, boldly asks Omiya to marry him. She then calculates that she can be got 'at a higher price'. These are the actual words that appear in the novel.

32 Koyo Ozaki, *Konjiki yasha* [The Golden Demon] (Iwanami Shoten, 2003), i, 81.

Omiya's candour might be shocking to today's readers, but Ozaki's original readers would have taken it in their stride; indeed, the novel was very popular. Beginning with the shinpa drama version in the Showa era (1926–89), however, *The Golden Demon* was greatly altered from the original. I first got to know *The Golden Demon* – I think this might have been just before I started at middle school – via the 1954 film version featuring Fujiko Yamamoto. In the film, Omiya is a pretty maiden who innocently loves Kan'ichi but who tearfully consents to Tomiyama's sudden proposal after considering Kan'ichi's likely future.

The situation was different when Ozaki wrote the novel in the Meiji 30s (1897–1906). It was only in the Meiji 20s (1887–96) that values such as virginity or Platonic love had become live issues, and it was Kitamura who had argued for the new ideas. But it took longer for these ideas to take root among the common people, let alone in rural areas, where such customs as *yobai* continued well into World War II and even beyond.[33] Similarly, no one in the cities cared about virginity. But one thing that differentiated cities from rural areas was that in the former there was a tendency to view sex in terms of money – that is, to view oneself as a sort of commodity. The idea, to speak plainly, was that it was wasteful to have sex with someone for no reward. Unsurprisingly, there was little hesitation about carrying out this sort of work in the red-light districts. Families of samurai were exceptional, since they were imbued with the Confucian morals that, with an admixture of Western morality, gradually permeated all the other classes after the Meiji era.

When reading *The Golden Demon*, however, we can see that, even in the Meiji 30s, sexual norms had not drastically changed among the common people from those of the previous era. Even though Omiya graduated from a girls' school, she is, essentially, not very different from a geisha. Well into the middle of Meiji, there were many politicians and scholars who married geishas. Indeed, parties at the Rokumeikan were managed by ex-geisha women.[34] Common women did not know how to behave in fashionable society. That is why girls' schools were established

33 [Trans.] *Yobai*, literally meaning 'night-crawling', is an ancient Japanese custom in which unmarried men silently enter the beds of unmarried women at night to have sex, with or without the latter's consent.

34 [Trans.] The Rokumeikan was a gaudy building in Tokyo, constructed in 1883 for the housing and parties of foreign guests. It became the symbol of Meiji Japan's Westernization.

in the Meiji era. When Ozaki describes Omiya as a girls-school graduate, it therefore means that she is little different from a geisha. Which is why Omiya, calculating the value of her beauty, thinks that she deserves better than Kan'ichi. This does not, however, imply that Japan was backward or un-Western. In psychological novels set in the French court, for instance, many duchesses and countesses are former high-class prostitutes. It was not a particularly scandalous fact. It is said that during the era of Napoleon III, one in three women in Paris was a prostitute. Of course, in Protestant culture sexual debauchery was strictly forbidden. Kitamura was a Quaker, so the culture of red-light districts was intolerable to him. Nevertheless, this culture cannot be said to be un-Western. For example, Shuzo Kuki compares *iki* (the plebian nihilism) to *chic* in French. (By the way, Heidegger greatly appreciated Kuki's work on *iki*, though I personally doubt that a German farmer-type philosopher like Heidegger could really have understood the meaning of *iki*, which had its origins in the red-light districts.)

On the other hand, although Tomiyama in *The Golden Demon* has studied in Europe, his behaviours are not very different from those of a master of the merchant or artisan class having fun in red-light districts during the Edo period. Accordingly, he can propose to Omiya even while knowing that she has been living with Kan'ichi, just as one can buy the freedom of a geisha from her employer. And, as so often happens, once the man redeems the woman, he loses interest in her. And then Omiya is filled with regret as she remembers her life with Kan'ichi – this is the story of *The Golden Demon*.

I said earlier that today's readers would be shocked by the story of *The Golden Demon*. But I actually think that they wouldn't be shocked at all; instead they would be disgusted at Tokoku Kitamura. For there is nothing rare nowadays about Omiya-like women who calculate their commodity value and try to sell it at a higher price, and neither men nor women care about virginity. A few years ago there was a sociologist in Japan who tried to find revolutionary significance in a new form of prostitution among teenage girls known as *enjo kosai* (compensated dating). But all that that phenomenon means is that capitalism is permeating ever deeper. If that kind of prostitution is revolutionary, then Saikaku's *The Life of an Amorous Woman* was revolutionary in a far more powerful sense.

There are also many young people who – like Kan'ichi in a sense – are gambling in speculation in order to earn money quickly. What does this mean? In terms of the stages of capitalism, it means that a new stage following on from industrial capitalism – the stage of a sort of merchant capitalism – has arrived. These young people are seeking to acquire surplus value not by way of production but from the difference caused in the process of circulation. It is this kind of merchant capitalism that is being foregrounded today, and we can call this the stage of neoliberalism. We can hence discern clear parallels between the present time and an earlier epoch. This is the evidential ground for the 'repetition of history' hypothesis.

To conclude, let me repeat once again that, considering the situation today, I do not believe that literature (novels) can possibly play the same role in today's situation as it did before. However, even if modern literature has come to an end, the movements of capitalism and the state that determine us are not over. They will survive even after they have destroyed all human and natural environments. Within this situation, we have to keep resisting. In this regard, however, I no longer expect anything from literature.

Based on a recording of a series of lectures I gave in October 2003 at the Osaka College of the International Institute for Research in the Humanities, Kinki University.

Ancient Society and the New Politics: From Kant to Modes of Production

Fredric R. Jameson

At a time when the so-called 'death of theory' has alternately been celebrated or lamented (and compensated by the revival of academic philosophy and its barren subfields such as ethics and aesthetics), we may well be grateful that the most original and exciting Japanese theorist of our time, Kojin Karatani, is finally becoming more widely known in what we used to call the West.[1] With the ambitiously named *The Structure of World History: From Modes of Production to Modes of Exchange*, indeed, Karatani's new work arrives in English at virtually the same time as its publication in Japanese. Not only is it a new turn in his own work and preoccupations, it opens some welcome new paths for our own theoretical and political discussions, reviving a number of crucial but virtually abandoned debates and (hopefully) starting some new ones. *The Structure of World History* critically rereads a number of classic texts in new perspectives, combines new uses of current theory, and reopens the traditional debates on modes of production in new and more productive directions, taking controversial political positions, as well as

1 [Editors] When the editors first asked Fredric Jameson to respond to the Karatani essay, he replied that he could revise and expand the following essay, which was initially delivered as the opening lecture of the 2014 conference at Duke University organized by Jameson to discuss the issues raised by *The Structure of World History*, and subsequently published in *Criticism* in 2016. We regret that, because of his untimely death, the revision was not possible, but we reproduce the essay here with the permission of his estate as a way of giving a sense of his first thoughts about the end-of-literature essay.

philosophical ones, particularly on the relationship of Immanuel Kant to Marxism; in short, not only does it revive a much-maligned approach to history (world history, the philosophy of history, and so on), it also intervenes in economics, Marxology, theory, and philosophy itself.

Karatani's preceding book *Transcritique: On Kant and Marx* (1995) had already proposed a new approach to Kant, one unusual and unexpected even in the midst of what looks like a generalized Kant revival. We are far from the days in which Jean-Paul Sartre remarked that any return to Kant always marked a regression to pre-Marxist and anti-Marxist positions (a proposition that surely retains much of its relevance). It is at least not true of Karatani, whose strategic move lies not in using Kant against Hegel and the dialectic, but, rather (at least on my reading), in treating Kant as one who invents the dialectic in the first place by way of the antinomies. Karatani thereby confirms the more traditional dialectic's impatience with the pettiness of the law of non-contradiction and abandons the attribution to Kant of the 1763 refutation of the existence of negativity in nature as such.

Two more interesting features of Kant emerge in the earlier book: the ideal of the world republic, which becomes central in *The Structure of World History*; and the overcoming of the impasse of the *Ding-an-sich* (thing-in-itself) and the unknowability of the real by way of the figure of the parallax, an attractive astronomical conception that seems to be making its way in contemporary philosophy (for example, in Slavoj Žižek's work) as a result of Karatani's speculation.

For the more standard 'enlightenment' view, Kant subscribed to a view of so-called transcendental realities as being fundamentally unknowable (however much we may still require them ethically). The figure of the parallax, however, suggests that we can nonetheless deduce the position and the volume of such realities, as it were, blindly and by indirect computation, even where we can never confront them directly or in some unmediated way. The shift at issue here is one from metaphysics to representationality, and it has, indeed, seemed to me a useful index to the difference between modernity and postmodernity: for modernity, this failure of knowledge or representation was an agonizing experience, which, in literature and philosophy alike, led to grandiose schemes and forms for its evasion – forms that constituted a kind of triumph over it. For postmodernity, this particular 'death of god' is no longer so fraught with anguish, and the anti-representationality of the parallax has seemed to offer a new form of representation as such at the very moment of its impossibility.

But the other (non-Kantian) originality of *Transcritique* – and the one that led most directly to the present work – was a revision of Karl Marx that seemed to offer a new kind of political praxis – namely, the cooperative movement at the base, or dare I say in the interstices, of actually existing capitalism. Some will remember that Lenin's very last writings were devoted to cooperatives and to the praise of Robert Owen. Others will object that the central polemic of *Capital* – at least on the left and against Proudhon – was the slashing and omnipresent attack on the idea that circulation could be the central framework for understanding capital as such let alone for changing it: production, for Marx, always comes first, and new value cannot be created in circulation. The very subtitle of *The Structure of World History* would seem to suggest that Karatani thinks otherwise, and to that effect I quote a crucial sentence from *Transcritique*: 'While capital organizes social relations globally, the moment to overturn capital – inexorably at the same time as following it – is folded within, namely, in the process of circulation.'[2] This would seem to be a serious practical issue, particularly inasmuch as the dominant ideology of our time – free-market dogma – is clearly a fundamentally circulationist one.

But I am not personally scandalized by this heterodoxy, this heretical – and, indeed, traditionally heretical – displacement of Marxist orthodoxy. What interests me more is the way in which Karatani has arrived at this point (which in his formulation I hasten to say is not anti-Marxist, post-Marxist, or indeed pre-Marxist) – namely, by way of the whole matter of modes of production, which does interest me greatly and to which I devote the rest of this discussion.

Let me briefly summarize the history of the problem, which Marx himself alludes to as follows (in the 1859 preface to *A Contribution to the Critique of Political Economy*): 'In broad outline the Asiatic, ancient, feudal, and modern bourgeois modes of production [*Produktionsweisen*] may be designated as epochs marking progress in the economic development of society.'[3] The syntax thereby implies that these four modes of

2 Kojin Karatani, *Transcritique: On Kant and Marx*, trans. Sabu Kohso (MIT Press, 2003), 293.

3 Karl Marx, *A Contribution to the Critique of Political Economy*, ed. Maurice Dobb (International, 1999), 20–2.

production would be completed by a fifth – namely, that from which progress has been made or, in other words, primitive communism. Meanwhile, the very thrust of Marxism as a theory and a praxis alike suggests the need to specify a sixth mode of production, the one that closes off the series of 'antagonistic forms', as he calls them, and brings 'the prehistory of human society' to an end – namely, socialism or communism. This is, however, clearly a list and not even a description, let alone a theory (or 'philosophy of history' as it is contemptuously called nowadays). But what people did not know for eighty years was that Marx had indeed written a substantial account of these modes of production in his 1857 manuscript, that trial run of *Capital*, which we call the *Grundrisse* (floorplans) and which was not published until 1939.

Nonetheless, and in whatever form, it is surely this list of the fundamental structures of human society that has earned Marxism (and Hegelianism before it) the most virulent contemporary attacks on its alleged teleology and its imputed idealistic reading of the meaning of history as such. To be sure, real historical developments account for the widespread appeal of such attacks, not least the omnipresence of late capitalism (which Francis Fukuyama thought could justify the relevance of a slogan such as 'the end of history'), as well as the collapse of state socialism, which seemed to invalidate Marxian teleological notions of the ways in which socialism was coming into being within capitalism itself. Scarcely irrelevant either is the contemporary emphasis on state power and its emergence (or omnipresence) insofar as that casts a different kind of light on the other end of the sequence of 'modes of production' – namely, on the notion of so-called primitive communism.

But perhaps two deeper theoretical trends need to be mentioned in any discussion of this much-maligned form or genre called 'universal history', to which Karatani makes so interesting a new contribution here. On the one hand, we have to remember the fundamental tension or antagonism between the historical and the sociological or structural, and the consequent unwillingness to reduce unique historical facts or events to philosophical or theoretical frameworks or abstractions – universal history then becoming one more example of that bad thing called totalization. On the other hand, it is precisely fear of Eurocentrism and its universalism, the sense that other cultures and their histories, their specificities, are being reduced to a single matrix, that is a fantasy of Western provenance. I believe that we can locate the scandal here in geography itself, in the contingencies of our own unique globe and its spatial configurations. (They are contingent only from the historical perspective and not from the geological or astrophysical one.) Thus, universal history turns out to be an attempt to philosophize geography, to make philosophical sense out of its unique spatial folds and configurations. Thus, Hegel felt obliged, in the greatest and most scandalous of all universal histories, to find dialectical meaning in the landscapes in which his various world spirits originated, thereby giving rise to often grotesque kinds of landscape symbolism or allegory. My favourite is the moment in which he explains that, in contrast to the Nile or the Rhine, the immense rivers of the Americas – the Amazon, the Orinoco, the Mississippi – somehow express in their very overwhelming formlessness the youth and newness of the New World, as such. But surely the philosophizing of geography is still as illicit and as scandalous as it was in Hegel's day?

I want to take as an emblem of the transformation of this situation in our own time the figure of Immanuel Wallerstein, whose own universal history is very precisely based on a philosophizing or theorization of landscape in his notions of core, semi-periphery, and periphery.[4] To be sure, he is the inheritor or synthesizer of many contemporary trends – Fernand Braudel's historical vision of the Mediterranean, dependency theory in Latin America, radical geography, and ecology; in this sense, he epitomizes the spatial turn in modern thought. But he also benefits from globalization or, in other words, the subsumption by capitalism of all those far reaches of the globe that once were outside the boundaries of the capitalist market system: this is to turn the reproach of Eurocentrism inside out and to grasp Europe as simply a marker for the uniquely dynamic and self-perpetuating autopoietic virus of capitalism, as such; it is also to make new research into Europe's others possible as spaces whose ability to resist the emergence of capitalism becomes an important object of inquiry in its own right.

At any rate, I will argue that Karatani's assimilation of Wallerstein endows his new version of universal history with a relevance and a plausibility that the older, more purely cultural syntheses could never have. In particular, this new global framework lends his treatment of culture

4 Immanuel Wallerstein, *The Modern World-System I: Capitalist Agriculture and the Origins of the European World-Economy in the Sixteenth Century* (Academic Press, 1974).

– here concentrated in the emphasis on religion (and on world religions) – a unique opportunity to rethink much of our cultural past, as well.

Karatani's place in all this, however, will no doubt be exacerbated not merely by his revival of the modes of production debate in general, but also by his seemingly idealistic revival of Kant's appeal to a world republic that could alone secure universal peace.

Late capitalism, which already has of course its own not at all utopian world market, has not encouraged 'one-world' fantasies of the type so current after World War II. But it might all have been otherwise: in a forgotten yet unforgettable exercise in counterfactual history, Arnold J. Toynbee sketched out what might have happened had Megalexandros not died so young and been able to pursue his restless Homeric vision to the pillars of Hercules and perhaps, in a second attempt, persuaded his soldiers to venture down the Silk Road. Then, a new multi-cultural world empire might have ensued, with its two official languages – Greek and Persian – its offerings to the Olympians (in the welcome absence of the bloodthirsty monotheisms), and its peaceful rule by the Alexander XXXVII of the present day.[5] He does not say whether that empire would have known capitalism: whether, to use Wallenstein's language, it would eventually have undergone a mutation from world empire to world system; but it is a question scarcely addressed by Kant either, and one that once again demonstrates the vanity of purely political speculations when devoid of economic considerations, such as the swelling reserve army of the unemployed, the closing of the frontier (otherwise called 'the falling rate of profit'), and the incessant emergence of new forms of 'primitive accumulation' within the apparently mature, completed system whose new features some have already begun to theorize. At any rate, pre-Alexandrian Greece is there to remind us that multiple states always mean warfare, something that does not necessarily guarantee its absence from the universal empire as such.

As for the other end of the historical spectrum, in Marx's own lifetime, the omitted mode – namely, primitive communism – was suddenly brought to unexpected life by an American, Lewis Henry Morgan, in his 1877 book *Ancient Society*, which Claude Lévi-Strauss hailed as the foundational act of anthropology, as such, with its extensive account of that

5 Arnold Toynbee, 'If Alexander the Great Had Lived On', in *Some Problems of Greek History* (Oxford University Press, 1969), 441–86.

complex, yet at that time altogether unsuspected, form of social organization called the kinship system. Marx devoted the final years of his life to exploring this newly discovered continent of human social organization in his so-called *Ethnological Notebooks*, which Engels wrote up in his 1888 classic *Origins of the Family, Private Property and the State*, the latter then, for another fifty years or more, standing as the fundamental statement of Marxist orthodoxy on history and the modes of production, as such. The problem is that this work does not square with the description Marx made in the *Grundrisse*, and Morgan's extraordinary celebration of the Iroquois *gens* as the most perfect human society so far in history does not quite fit into Marx's list, save as a kind of second state of so-called primitive communism (the first one being the Palaeolithic life of hunters and gatherers). In effect, Morgan's and Engels's encomia to this 'military democracy' of the Iroquois sets our problem off in a new direction – namely, that of the problem of the emergence of the state and of state power – which will now deflect the economic problematic of the original Marxian 'modes of production', as we shall see in a moment.

Yet, before 1939 (or perhaps we should say, before 1953, when the *Grundrisse* became more widely available), the principal object of debate and contestation was the concept of an Asiatic mode of production, which Marx does indeed briefly touch on in *Capital* and which specifies a stagnant, virtually unchanging world of isolated villages capped by the rule of the despot to whom all land belongs and who is supported by an imperial bureaucracy without a traditional nobility or aristocracy.[6] Perry Anderson, in a destructive and fairly definitive historical review, has demonstrated the origin, via Hegel, of this stereotype in Montesquieu, who based it on the Ottoman Empire, buttressed by imperfect travel narratives on Moghul India.[7] We may ignore the East/West prejudice of the term Asiatic; and indeed more recent scholarship – most notably that of Maurice Godelier – has revived this concept for other parts of the world, most notably the Inca Empire. The problem with removing this particular mode of production from the active list is that in that case you are left with nothing but feudalism as far as the eye can see. Feudalism,

6 Karl Marx, *Grundrisse: Foundation of the Critique of Political Economy*, trans. Martin Nicolaus (Penguin Books, 1993), 472–3.

7 Perry Anderson, 'The "Asiatic Mode of Production"', in *Lineages of the Absolute State* (New Left Books, 1974), 462–549.

then, like the petty bourgeoisie, becomes one of the most tiresome of orthodox Marxian stereotypes. It should be noted that one of the most interesting problems involved in Marx's original excursus lies in the multiple ways in which he links the various 'modes' to one another, suggesting alternate thematic links that turn this seemingly chronological (or diachronic) list into a multidimensional constellation of forms. Thus, the unity of primitive communism is in Marx paired with the Asiatic mode in a Hegelian fashion: each one incarnates the One of the society without individualism; only the *one* or unity of the primitive village is now projected outward and upward into the *one* of the despot who is in that Hegelian sense the only individual, the only concrete subject in that social formation. On the other hand, the self-sufficiency of the isolated village can also be seen to migrate alternately into the form of the Greek city-state or the more rural isolation of the Germanic village – from which then feudalism seemingly arises. Both of these outcomes remain Hegelian in their opposition of universality and particularity; but where in the earlier version the identification of village and despot fails to produce the individuality of its multiple subjects, the distance between universal and particularity in the German, and later the feudal, form leads to an individuality that will reach its fullest realization only in the social atomization of capitalism. Still, its multiple centres must take the path of an antagonism towards each other, and paradoxically Karatani sees the structural and well-nigh eternal warfare between them as yet another kind of Hegelian reciprocity. Marx thereby already grasps war as an integral and structural creature of primitive communism and not merely some external accident, which is a discovery that Pierre Clastres and, in his different way, René Girard both thought supplied ammunition against Marx.

Yet, the despot himself returns, as we shall see, and becomes a figure for state power, a function retained in Karatani's work, who views the state as essentially a matter of the looting and plundering of the foreign or nomadic conqueror from whom the state evolves (modern taxes being a civilized form of such plunder or tribute).

In the postwar period, and after the publication of the *Grundrisse* and its exposition of the very concept of the mode of production, a new set of debates emerges. In the immediate postwar, which can be said to extend up to the failure of the 1960s, let us say around 1975, we have a utopian celebration of primitive communism, as Lévi-Strauss derives it from Jean-Jacques Rousseau: I am extremely happy to find a discussion here, in Karatani's work, of that great utopian classic that is Marshall Sahlins's *Stone Age Economics* (1972), supplemented by the inevitable structuralist adopted classic, Marcel Mauss's book on the gift. But this utopian moment is itself a reflex of the obsession with the state and with the emergence of state power, which can easily take a negative turn after 1968, as it ultimately does in Michel Foucault's work and in the various anarchist fixations with power as such, which both politically and theoretically serve to distract us from the fundamentally economic problem of capitalism as Marx diagnosed it. The utopian upward slope of the period before the state is then matched with the triumph of the state by a decidedly dystopian downward path into the innumerable apocalyptic scenarios with which mass culture today is peopled, or unpeopled, as you prefer.

Meanwhile, at least until recently, the matter of socialism or communism as a mode of production has vanished from theoretical view, as seemingly has the utopian nature of primitive societies, just as both social formations seem to have vanished from real life and from the actually existing (dare I say, dystopian) world of globalized capitalism.

But it is here that Karatani's book takes an interesting turn, and that Kant returns in unexpected form, precisely as the theorist of a new form of globalization in his famous essay on universal peace and the world republic. Here he meets the Marx of the world market – that outer limit of capitalism which is its most fundamental and destructive contradiction – and Wallerstein, whose replacement of the Asiatic mode as the *world empire* with capitalism as the *world system* has, as I have already said, done so much to invent a radical geography for a Marxism in which it was only implicit, and only anticipated in a fragmentary way in Lenin's theory of imperialism.

Now let me summarize what I take to be the originalities of Karatani's synthesis – first of all, a modification in the object of our study, which was once called a 'mode of production'. The standard Marxian, and also structural Marxian, schema of this object was a system of levels: first the level of the base or infrastructure and then the level of the superstructures. The latter were multiple and could be identified as the ideological, religious or philosophical superstructure, the juridical superstructure, the political superstructure (assuming that you position politics as a superstructure), and so forth. The former – the base – is essentially made up of two levels: that of the relations of production (classes, for example, or property relations) and that of the forces of production (technology and productivity). The most rigorous and consequent Althusserians – Barry Hindess and Paul Hirst – then defined a mode of production as a specific articulation of these two levels upon each other. There are as many different modes of production, according to them, as there are distinct forms of such articulation – the crucial question thereby emerging as to what exactly an articulation is and what you mean by 'to articulate'.[8]

Karatani has, at any rate, replaced this system with another, more striking, but perhaps equally structural one – namely, Jacques Lacan's Borromean knots, in which three circles are inseparably intertwined. For capitalism, he insists that these three circles are to be identified as the state, the nation, and capitalism as the law of value or commodity exchange. Now the question addressed to the older paradigm was always what the ultimately determining level is, and the short answer, as far as Marxism was concerned, was always the economic: production, or, in other words, the base. But remember that, given the dual nature of the base, this ultimately determining instance could always be ambiguously inflected, either towards the forces of production, in which case you come up with technological determinism (the industrial revolution and so forth), or towards one of the relations of production (which might most often be the social classes, but which could slip off into this or that idealist or culturalist deviation).

In Karatani's work, it is not possible to evade the economic circles: attention to the state then also secures the political questions, the questions of power, but, here, a problem arises: for the mode of production that precedes state power – primitive communism – what fills this role, what constitutes this particular circle? Or does the Borromean scheme not yet exist at that point? As for the third circle, the nation, its equivalent in the older modes is clear enough; beginning with the kinship system, it is what secures the existence of the community, whether imagined or not. In certain systems, two of these three dimensions get identified with each other, and we have the nation-state. Is it possible to imagine a system in which the place of community is conceived as being vaster than the

8 Barry Hindess and Paul Q. Hirst, *Pre-capitalist Modes of Production* (Routledge and Kegan Paul, 1975), 9–12.

nation, as such? Is this then the role of Kant's world republic, of an association of nations or a supranational entity of some sort (one that is neither a Wallersteinian world empire nor that capitalist world system we call globalization)? It is with this question that the book ends.

However, we must now observe that Karatani's tripartite scheme is shadowed by a fourth term, sometimes here identified as *religion*. Clearly, in the present state of things, where militant or fundamentalist religion has replaced the secular parties as the only active, violent force for revolutionary change, it is altogether fitting for religion to take its place in the analysis, functioning as what I would more generally term *ideology* – that is, the driving superstructural force for legitimation of the various modes of production. But, clearly enough, religion is something a little more concrete and existential, a little more collective and social, than some mere philosophical value. To see where this fits, we need to retrace our steps and review again the sequence of the modes of production as Karatani outlines them, and also to grasp why he should wish to substitute the term 'exchange' for 'production' in the formula while always insisting that exchange here means not only capitalist circulation but a larger, more all-encompassing economic category – an emphasis Marx argues tirelessly against in his polemics against Proudhon and the latter's version of associationist anarchism. And, in that respect, of course, Karatani does reveal himself to be fully as much a follower of Proudhon as of Marx himself.

As I have said, Karatani's history follows a traditional sequence: societies before power (clan or tribal societies, primitive communism); power societies, in which the state exists; and, finally, capitalism as a society organized not so much around power relations as around economic and monetary categories. But over each of these forms presides what we may call a mode of extraction (if you do not like the word 'exchange'). Primitive communism is the world of Marcel Mauss's gift, of what Karatani calls reciprocity or pooling (it has several forms, but we omit those); in power societies, often constructed on the basis of conquest, distribution takes the form of plunder and looting (Republicans would, I think, welcome this notion of the state and its taxation as a form of plunder and theft); capitalism is then organized *grosso modo* as what we can call commodity exchange. Now, it is clear that just as the structuralists liked to specify the individual social formations as combinations of several modes of production all at once, so also Karatani conceives of the persistence of earlier kinds of social relations or modes of exchange in this sense of social interaction within later stages. Thus, the mode of reciprocity persists at some deeper, more repressed level within power society and then the capitalist one, whereas power itself clearly persists within capitalism's more purely economic arrangements. Here, Karatani develops a new concept of historical repetition in order to conceptualize such returns of the repressed, very often detectable in the emergence, or shall we say eruption, of the great universal religions (among which I take it he includes Marxism or communism itself).

So, now, we can better understand where religion fits in Karatani's scheme and how a fourth term might emerge from his scheme without any accompanying specific mode of production to ground it. The universal religion in general marks the return, the repetition, the eruption, or repressed force of reciprocity into systems organized to replace it (with power and domination or with unequal distribution and exploitation). It is generally transmitted by great prophecy and takes on an ethical or moralizing form (even though its metaphysical or superstitious figuration in reality carries a radically different and more concrete type of social relationship within it).

The premise here is, on the one hand, the proposition that each social system includes a mechanism to ward off and pre-empt its own dissolution, a kind of self-preservation or immune response that neutralizes the effects of potential revolutionary change. Thus, the later modes of social organization have had somehow to disable such mechanisms in order to supersede their predecessors: repetition and the return of the repressed then mark moments in which – for good or ill, it should be noted – one of those older layers then, for whatever structural reason or on whatever uniquely propitious conjuncture, comes back to life.

The cooperative scheme, reciprocity, pooling, and their various equivalents in contemporary times seem to Karatani to represent such a return of the repressed. At any rate, this antagonistic layering of the social archaeology can usefully be compared to Bloch's nonsynchronous synchronicity in a new and fruitful way; and, indeed, it seems to me that the political uses of the new utopian movement are both drawn on here and enhanced by this conception of the deep social, which, far from being anthropomorphic, in fact suggests that our representations of the individual and the subjective or psychic are, in fact, enabled by a social objectivity from which they draw their figuration (as with Sigmund

Freud's archaeological accounts of the unconscious). Social being comes first, and existential experience draws on its possibilities for its own self-understanding (in much the same way, I would argue, as the discoveries of science are enabled in their very structure by new forms of the organization of social life).

Thus, Karatani's work concludes with immediate, and surely immensely controversial, proposals for a new and concrete politics for the present day and our current situation. Those will no doubt receive further attention of a critical or exegetical nature. But I should like to close with a more general remark on the value for us of such speculations on modes of production long extinct and surely belonging to a history that no longer concerns us. Indeed, Hindess and Hirst, in that most rigorous of all monuments to Althusserian scientific thinking (*Precapitalist Modes of Production*, 1975), conclude, in their painstaking interrogation of the various concepts of modes of production, that not only is this concept not historical, but even that 'the study of history is not only scientifically but also politically valueless'. As over against their Master, who called for a new 'science of history', they observe that 'it is the notion of a Marxist history, of a Marxism confined within the conditions of the historian's practice, which is the contradictory enterprise . . . The object of history, the past, no matter how it is conceived, cannot affect present conditions. Historical events do not exist and can have no material effectivity in the present.'[9] This astonishing conclusion, which, in fact, spells the end of the entire Althusserian enterprise (and, appropriately, results in the authors' renunciation of Marxism, as such), is admirably predicated on the insistence that Marxism, if it is to be anything, must be part of a political and not merely epistemological praxis. And their stumbling block was, to be sure, the failure of the theory of modes of production to conceptualize transition, or, in other words, a revolution that could lead from one system to another, radically different one. They are right, and we should continue to work on that.

But, before Hindess and Hirst reached that sorry point in their rigorous argumentation – either unfinished business or outright renunciation – earlier in their book, they had achieved a rather remarkable description of primitive communism as a mode of production (a determinate articulation, you will remember, of the forces and the relations of

9 Ibid., 312.

production), thus integrating Marx and Morgan. They thereby demonstrate the way in which, in what they call complex redistribution, the relations of production (the kinship system) articulate the forces of production (or a certain stage of productive metabolism with the earth). The political level, the level of power, the level of the state, as such, is omitted from this interaction between the two essential levels, and the possibility of a comparable 'withering away of the state' is projected into the concept of socialism or communism, as well.

But I prefer to end on another note, which might well tempt us to juxtapose Karatani's practical conclusions with rather different but related ones. I therefore conclude with the peroration of Lewis Henry Morgan's *Ancient Society*, in which that blood brother of the Iroquois and enthusiastic admirer of the Paris Commune, evoking 'the next higher plane of society to which experience, intelligence and knowledge are already tending', cries, 'It will be a revival, in higher form, of the liberty, equality and fraternity of the ancient gentes.'[10]

10 Lewis Henry Morgan, *Ancient Society* (Henry Holt, 1877), 552.

A Single Portobello Mushroom

Bruce Robbins

In a recent seminar on contemporary American fiction, I assigned Patricia Lockwood's internet novel *No One Is Talking About This*. Having come to the internet much later in life than my students and acutely aware that I do not possess their skills in interpreting its rapidly changing vocabulary and protocols, I felt I needed extra preparation, so I spent some time immersing myself in that somewhat alien world. In the course of poking around I came upon the following specimen of Lockwood's social media prose, with which those more familiar than I am with her or with social media may already be familiar: '"I'm pregnant!" shouts Jonathan Franzen's wife. He places a finger on her lips. "No, it is I who am pregnant," he says. "Pregnant with the next great American novel." He walks into the backyard and places a single portobello mushroom upon the grill.'[1] By my standards, this tweet is pretty amusing. (I am not sure my students agreed.) It is a joke on men taking themselves too seriously, on male writers taking themselves too seriously, and on the putatively male ambition to write something that can be called *the* Great American Novel. Let me murder the wit here by laying out its components: first, Franzen's Great American Novel as (in his mind) the real baby, more real than the biological baby that Franzen's wife has just announced she is pregnant with. Second, the Great American Novel figured as a single portobello mushroom placed on a

1 Posted by Lockwood (@TriciaLockwood) on X on 9 July 2014.

grill. Third, the repetition of the verb 'place', so that the mushroom or Great American Novel on the grill is likened to the silencing finger placed on the wife's lips. Celebrating the masculine ambition to produce the great national novel is as ridiculous as it would be to celebrate the grilling of a single portobello mushroom, the singleness of the item to be grilled reflecting back on the silly singularity of the literary ambition: *one* novel to capture an entire nation's history and identity?! But the ambition to singularity performs the additional function of silencing women, which is not a joke. Lockwood's wit is also amplified by the fact that it comes in the form of a tweet, with the modesty and concision of Twitter, or X, presumably offered as a post-literary contrast to the overblown, pretentious grandiosity of the Great American Novel, or of literature itself, which Kojin Karatani in his essay 'The End of Modern Literature' identifies with the fate of the novel.

Like Karatani's essay, in other words, this tweet could be taken as a barbed announcement of the end of modern literature, or at least a call for efforts to be directed elsewhere.

If that hypothesis is worth following up, the next step would be to ask whether for Lockwood it is the internet that is killing off literature, or perhaps the internet conceived of as more female-friendly, in which case so much the better. (Given the notorious harassment of women and minorities on social media, however, is that a serious proposition?) We would also have to ask whether, for Lockwood, literature is properly imagined as a single (masculine) meta-narrative, a mega-portobello subordinating and even erasing all smaller narratives and fungal growths. Is Lockwood even as hostile as she sounds to the Franzen-style social novel? The first half of *No One Is Talking About This* deals with social life on social media, which has, inexplicably, made the protagonist famous (famous for a single tweet). There she conjures up social life as represented once upon a time by Jane Austen: '"what someone said at breakfast over cold mutton, a fatal quadrille error, the rising of fine hackles in the drawing room." Pale violent shadings of tone, a hair being split down to the DNA. A *social* novel.'[2] Again funny, again hostile. In the age of the internet, it seems, the social novel à la Austen or Franzen is dead, and justifiably so. But, here, the presumed cause of death seems to be different. Not too much ambition, but too little: a fatal preoccupation with hair-splitting

2 Patricia Lockwood, *No One Is Talking About This* (Riverhead, 2021), 26–7.

among the privileged, a fatal neglect of the social reality behind or below what is murmured over cold mutton or in the drawing room. It is an old complaint about Austen, but a complaint that makes sense only if it is pronounced *on behalf* of the social novel, not to rebuke its ambition.

And, as it turns out, a social novel is, arguably, what Lockwood herself has written. In the first half of *No One Is Talking About This*, Austen's violent shadings of tone and rising of fine hackles faithfully reappear, this time as the tones and hackles of people who conduct most of their social lives on the internet. As with the novels of Austen and Franzen, the manners of the characters reflect the realities of her country and her time, which include an upward-mobility story (the tweeter's success) as well as (perhaps not unrelated) the social havoc made possible by the internet and aggressively exploited by the followers of Donald Trump. One might say that Lockwood has placed her own portobello mushroom on the grill. If so, the question is not to grill or not to grill, but what is on your plate in the end. How does Lockwood's novel end? It does not end in marriage, like Austen's, but it courts comparison with the most traditional of social novels by allowing its second half to flee virtuality and centre itself firmly, as if to make a point, on a biological family. And not just a family, but a family gathering its dispersed members around, of all things, the birth of a baby. Her lips unsealed, Jonathan Franzen's wife thus gets to reply that the real pregnancy is hers, that bearing a child matters more to the world than firing up a literary barbecue. But the reply takes a known generic form. After all, Lockwood and Franzen share the same ambition, which is that of the social novel: a representation of social totality showing that, for better or worse, private life and public life are decisively enmeshed in each other.

What Lockwood puts on the table will not satisfy anyone who shares Sartre's hope, cited by Karatani, that in a non-revolutionary period the novel can substitute for revolutionary politics. The most radical case that might be made for *No One Is Talking About This* is that the baby is not destined to survive, and the quasi-religious cult that arises around its final hours displays a certain desperation, perhaps the desperation of a society which no longer believes, even in the face of internet chaos, that its identity can be re-established (that is what the splitting of Lockwood's novel in half suggests) by the successful reproduction of family values. I cannot say I find that argument, or the novel itself, especially persuasive. Like the tweet, the novel seems committed to the higher reality of female reproductive biology, this time aligned, a bit confusingly, against the disembodiment of the internet rather than against embodied patriarchy.

Karatani notes that women writers, especially women who also belong to minorities, have retained some of the success with readers that the novel otherwise seemed to be losing to visual media. Lockwood's mockery of 'the Great American Novel' is one answer to the question that Karatani addresses to these women and minority writers: are they still animated by the ambition to speak of and to the imagined community of the nation? A number of the most vibrant and vigorous subfields in literary study today present their subject-matter, as Patricia Lockwood presents hers, as unrecognized, unprecedented, its value wrapped up in its identity. To the extent that this is true, the knowledge that the subfields produce will tend to be self-contained, defined in opposition to the culture at large, even in opposition to the idea that there exists such a thing as a culture at large. The subfields, often incubated by literary study until they could stand on their own, are then counted (in terms of majors and enrolments) as separate disciplines when it is claimed that the numbers in literary studies itself are declining, and they may well count themselves as distinct enterprises, beyond the horizon of literature, at least as literature is presently known and practised: women's studies, ethnic studies, and so on. What can look like the end of literature, then, might be better thought of as a continuation of the literary project under other names and by other means, the goal held steady as the shared project of making American democracy more genuinely democratic.

If the national ambition is still justifiable, given the irreducible differences of perspective that women and minority identities bring to literature and the fact that capitalism itself is transnational, the obvious reason would lie in political action. Political action largely remains national in its sites and its organization. And if political action is the option the novel is set against – a very different question than its competition with the internet or visual culture – Karatani seems clear that this is a contest that literature cannot win, and no doubt should not, the world being in such dire need of radical change. But this is an existential question – a question of what to do with one's life – that cannot be properly dealt with in a volume like this one, dedicated as it is to literature. All one can say, on the one hand, is that the binary choice (literature or politics?) may turn out to be a false one and, on the other, that a wise choice of what to do with one's life would have to include a serious assessment of the particular moment in national and global history to which one's lifetime has been confined. No reader of Karatani will have missed his globalizing tendency, his impulse to lay out an inclusive scheme of world history into which different modes of cultural production take their place. It is his version of the portobello mushroom on the grill: the seemingly impossible, hugely ambitious crystallization of a profusion of historical realities. As I read him, however, there is an internal tension here: his aspiration to build a global frame does something to undermine the existential urgency of the literature-versus-political-action dilemma. For why throw one's life away on a political project that, according to the structure of history as Karatani lays it out, is not fated to succeed? Piety towards activism will not resolve that question, which depends on the contingencies (and the structures) of history.

Karatani mentions the Indian novelist Arundhati Roy, famous both for her 1997 novel *The God of Small Things* and, in the wake of that novel's immense global success, for her decision to forsake literature and put her fame in the service of activism. Karatani's essay came out before the news that Roy had returned to fiction writing after twenty years with another powerfully political novel, *The Ministry of Utmost Happiness* in 2017. Roy is a useful reference point here because her fiction is not merely political in a marginal sense. There is an argument to be made that by focusing on atrocity, as she does in both novels, she revives the political *function* of the novel at the national level. And she does so for a period of globalized moral consciousness, that is, with a kind of unarticulated recognition that in our time every nation is also part of a world system. Atrocity committed by one's own nation is not a common subject in fiction, and the reason is obvious: it is a matter of national shame, not of national pride. And, yet, when acknowledged, it is also the kind of trauma that invites a new national self-description or self-definition. After the climactic murder of a *dalit* in *The God of Small Things*, the mass killing of Kashmiri Muslims by the Indian army in *The Ministry of Utmost Happiness* establishes Roy as, in a strong sense, a national novelist – one who represents her nation to itself precisely because, speaking as she does to a global readership, she brings to bear on this violence a more-than-national sensibility. Much the same might be said of Haruki Murakami, another novelist who is suspiciously successful outside his own nation. I cannot speak to his value as a writer of Japanese, or as seen within the long tradition of Japanese literature that Karatani has so eloquently laid out. But Murakami's *The Wind-Up Bird Chronicle* presents the murder of Chinese prisoners of war by the invading Japanese army in the 1930s and '40s – an atrocity – as a defining shame for Japan, one which has hidden but determining consequences for Japanese society in the present and on whose long-delayed acknowledgement the plot of the novel will turn.

No one is likely to describe *No One Is Talking About This* as a political novel. But political novels – novels that are about political activists and seem intended in part to inspire political activism – are still being written and sometimes have notable success. One example is Richard Powers's novel *The Overstory*, which shared with Lockwood a place on my contemporary American fiction syllabus. *The Overstory* is a novel about, and in favour of, environmental activism. It is, arguably, a candidate for the Great American Nature Novel. But it pays a price for its advocacy. Part of its call for activism is the claim that no one has ever really seen trees before, or recognized them for the sentient, wise, communicative creatures they are. If the recognition is unprecedented, there is an obvious limit to how much literature it can be hooked up with except as a bleak chronicle of *non*-recognition. Literature, as a product of humans, is not the hero of the story. Its protagonists are the redwoods, charismatic megaflora. If they represent Nature, then Nature is an innocent victim. Fungi, bark beetles, and Dutch elm disease, all of which kill trees, are left out of Nature, which is all about uncanny subterranean communication and saintly mutual aid. Humanity, other than its activists, is left with the role of evil perpetrator. Powers looks forward with some eagerness, therefore, to humanity's extinction. Not the end of modern literature, but the end of humanity. Arguments of the form 'the end of X' tend to be quite compelling, but where does the compulsion lead, politically speaking? Taking the side of nature against humanity could also be seen as rejecting politics.

One of the virtues of Karatani's audacious anthropological perspective is that it welcomes both gender and nature, categories which have been taken as challenging Marxism's claim to totality, its singular grilled portobello, and insist that they are necessary components of Marxist materialism. As I read Karatani, he is trying both to retain the commitment to a singular structure of world history and to stretch his vision of that structure so as to make it include the full plurality of particular voices and agents. To put this another way: his primal commitment is less to political activism, urgent as that activism is, than to a vision of history oriented around and mobilized by the ongoing project of human emancipation. It is this project that organizes a range of knowledges in Karatani's work that seems almost superhuman.

Consider books like *Isonomia and the Origins of Philosophy* and *The Structure of World History*. *The Structure of World History* argues that in order to see history from a materialist perspective, you cannot look exclusively at modes of production, as Marxists have traditionally done. You have to examine circulation, or modes of exchange. Modes of exchange are more universal, both historically and geographically; they make modernity, the break in mode of production that occurred with the Industrial Revolution, less dramatic a break. They give more importance to shifts that occurred both before the Industrial Revolution and outside Europe. This gesture would be consistent with various modes of anti-Eurocentrism, some of them explicitly anti-Marxist. For Karatani, it is simply incumbent on any Marxism that would claim to be genuinely materialist. In order to be materialist, Marxism must also be anthropological; the time has come for Marxism to embrace the pre-capitalist, the non-capitalist, the other. Karatani is not unique in drawing this conclusion; for example, the word 'anthropological' is everywhere in the theoretical career of Étienne Balibar. As in Balibar and in other left-wing thinkers over the past decades, this shift in emphasis to exchange, which decentres the Industrial Revolution and the birth of the industrial working class in the West, could be seen as an adaptation to cultural or 'identity' politics, politics not centred on the traditional industrial working class, politics that registers identities and issues located closer to the sphere of consumption, politics that has a great deal more to say about matters of gender and sexuality, as Karatani does in the latter part of his essay. I am not well versed enough in Karatani's thinking to evaluate this line of thought in him or to pursue it as far as it seems to go. I only acknowledge that the project of sustaining Marxism clearly entails doing something like what Karatani has been doing: keeping it tightly bound to political emancipation as well as to the analysis of the changing material conditions in which actors are spurred to resist the system.

In *Isonomia*, Karatani places himself within a left-wing tradition that is perhaps better described not as humanism, but as historical humility. For this tradition, tradition itself is enlivening and emboldening.

Progressives are not unprecedented; they can believe in progress without denying that others in the distant past have recognized many of the same problems and, if they have not resolved them, have at least made efforts that continue to inspire. Think of Marx's doctoral thesis on Democritus and Epicurus. Like 'The End of Modern Literature', *Isonomia* presents us with a perhaps idealized 'before': in this case, the politically radical philosophy of the Greek city-states of Ionia, on the coast of Asia Minor, in the sixth century BCE, the century before democracy was supposedly discovered in Athens. For Karatani, 'isonomia' ranks higher than democracy. The term refers to the equal distribution of resources, an equality achieved without rule, without state-like social organization. The word 'democracy' comes from the word for 'rule' (*krateia*) as well, of course, as the word for 'people' (*demos*); isonomia meant a sort of democracy *without* rule. (*Akratia* would, arguably, have been the preferable term.) It also meant, for some, that events could be explained without reference to the rule of the gods. Unsurprisingly – Karatani makes no attempt to conceal this – the Ionian cities were not militarily oriented, and they did not do well when threatened by hostile imperializing powers in the region, Lydia and then Persia. They decided not to join together in a mutual defence league; they were conquered one by one, and the experiment was swiftly brought to a very decisive, verifiably historical end. Still, the experiment persists at the level of thought – Karatani's book takes us through it, lovingly, thinker by thinker, chapter by chapter.

I would argue that Karatani idealizes somewhat the reciprocity urged by this constellation of thinkers. He links it to nomadism and makes it dependent on the fact that, as colonists who had come from Greek-speaking areas to the west, the Ionians continued to afford decisive significance to mobility and the universal right to exit. (Here, the resonance today is with the work of Michael Hardt and Toni Negri.) When Karatani compares the Ionian cities to New England townships in the early US, alarm bells will go off for American readers: What about the indigenous people who already lived in those supposedly empty spaces? And, even if some land was uninhabited, are we obliged to assume that true equality demands endless supplies of it? Are we assuming, in fifth-century Ionia, something like the infamous Frontier thesis by which Frederick Jackson Turner linked American democracy to the pioneer push westward? This seems a dangerous idealization. But, if Karatani does indeed idealize this lost moment in human history, the idealizing seems less important than the gesture of registering that something like this did once exist. As a vestigial Hegelian and dialectician, Karatani leans on criteria of socio-political judgment that are not merely utopian wishes or imaginings, but a part of lived human history in all its imperfection. That seems to me exactly right – and right about the very imperfect politics that came out of the 1960s as well, even for those of us who are rightly impatient with the neoliberal versions of multiculturalism (today, Diversity, Equity, and Inclusion) that have been complacently institutionalized, leaving economic inequality untouched.

Rightly or wrongly, those who have tried to find an existing social location for political dissent have often turned to the category of the intellectual. And, perhaps for that reason, the category of the intellectual has attracted narratives that make use of formulas like Karatani's: 'the end of X', 'the decline of X', 'the disappearance of X'. Among the titles that immediately come to mind are Russell Jacoby's *The Last Intellectuals* (1987), Richard Posner's *Public Intellectuals: A Study of Decline* (2002), Eric Lott's *The Disappearing Liberal Intellectual* (2006), and Shlomo Sand's *The End of the French Intellectual* (2018). In New York, anyone aspiring to be recognized by others *as* an intellectual has surely faced the temptation to throw their hat in the ring by means of just this sort of apocalyptic announcement: the species, alas, is extinct. It used to exist, and maybe it still does exist elsewhere (perhaps in France or Japan), but not here, not now, and that is very sad. It is our society's immeasurable loss. The idea that the end of the intellectual is a loss to society, and not just to would-be intellectuals who would like to be so categorized, is key. Titles that follow the end-of-X formula make a greater than normal claim to the public's interest, thus also to sales. If what we mean by intellectuals now is *public* intellectuals, intellectuals recognized as such outside the academy, in mainstream public media, even those on whom is bestowed the status of celebrity, like Jean-Paul Sartre, Susan Sontag, or Bernard-Henri Lévy, the publicity is of the essence. And if self-promoting publicity is what the eulogist-of-the-intellectual is seeking, who can blame them?

Otherwise, what this narrative accomplishes is the idealization of an absence. In the case of the so-called 'New York intellectuals', for example, what is idealized is an earlier moment, the 1930s and '40s, and the journal *Partisan Review* around which those intellectuals clustered.

Today no review has equal resonance. Heroic figures like these have disappeared, and since their disappearance, the story goes, no one has been able to fill their shoes; no other intellectuals have been as radical or as independent or as public-spirited. In effect, the intellectual has died. Under closer historical inspection, however, it usually turns out that these before-and-after narratives cheat a bit on both ends. On the one hand, it turns out that the 'before' moment of the recent past was idealized; it was a good deal less ideal than it is claimed to be. Were the New York intellectuals, many of them men who married women with money, really so independent? If they sold their intellectual wares on the open market, do we want to call this independence? On the other hand, the 'after', the depleted present with which it is being contrasted, turns out to be less empty. In the case of the 'end of the intellectuals' narrative, the present is in fact inhabited by figures who are performing many of the same valued functions, like intellectuals who are feminists and people of colour and who have stretched both ideas of radicalism and ideas of what the relevant 'public' is. As a cliché about the actual or impending non-existence of the intellectual, the 'end of' proposition has been strongly challenged in Stefan Collini's *Absent Minds: Intellectuals in Britain*. Despite its title, Collini's book deals with other national traditions as well as the British, and it reveals that these other nations, too, tend to locate their intellectuals in some other time and some other place. Anywhere, but not here, not now. It is hard not to conclude that none of these narratives can be correct. If they apply everywhere, they apply nowhere. The ubiquity of the cliché is also its refutation.

In the case of modern literature, the critique would go that modern literature never possessed the special political significance that Karatani attributes to it, and therefore cannot be said to have lost it. I stress that what we are talking about is *political* significance – significance in informing and directing action concerning the fate of society as a whole. Given the limited proportion of the citizenry whose lives ever allowed or encouraged them to read much literature, even in the (quite recent) period of near-universal literacy, could literature ever have been as broadly significant to cultural self-definition or the politics flowing from it as, say, popular music? It seems unlikely that the novel ever played the unique and decisive political role with which it is credited. And if not, then, satisfying as 'the end of X' story can be, the novel cannot really be said to have lost a role it never had. But it would seem to follow that once the idealization of the past is abandoned, it becomes possible to see that even today, in the era of Taylor Swift and TikTok and so on, modern literature still *has* a certain socio-political significance, though a lesser one.

As an academic with some historical training, I am always inclined to hesitate in the presence of 'end of X' narratives. But I also recognize a problem with this critique of them. The problem is being satisfied with what amounts to scholarly quibbling – that is, the implication that what our society needs is infinite repetitions of the predictable scholarly move: 'isn't it really more complicated?' Complications: they are valuable, and Lord knows the institutions that produce and reproduce a sense of complexity are endangered. But man cannot live on complexity alone, let alone thrive or make social progress. What we, arguably, need is the boldness of narratives that, even if they can never be firmly or adequately grounded in historical fact, inform and sustain our desire to *change* the facts. From what I know of it, which is far from enough, that seems to me one fundamental impulse behind Karatani's critical and philosophical writing, as in *Isonomia* and *The Structure of World History*.

It may also be worth underlining an assumption that is visible in the latter book's title. *The Structure of World History* posits that world history even on the largest, archaeological scale *has* a structure. A structure, singular – a structure that includes and synthesizes the seemingly infinite number of collective actors and trajectories and meaningless massacres that world history recognizes and struggles to contain. Among scholars of the humanities today, it seems likely that a majority would be sceptical of the proposition that a structure, any structure, is something world history can possibly possess. Hence the easy mockery of the portobello mushroom. This scepticism is arguably an ideological accompaniment to the assumption that our goal as academics is the production of complications. It is not necessarily aimed, in particular, at Marxism, of which Karatani is a distinguished advocate; it reflects a more general sense that while structures or meta-narratives have of course been *imposed* on world history, the truth that underlies all such constructs or imaginative impositions is contingency, randomness, chaos.

My own position, for what it is worth, is that the vision of history as contingency, randomness, chaos is itself a construct or act of imagination – as Wallace Stevens put it, 'the absence of imagination / had itself to be imagined'. And this holds even in the case of atrocity, about which I have written a book, also on a global scale. I assume that it is better to look at the record with an open mind. If structure is what you see, maybe structure is what there is. Karatani has done the job of looking, looking as a materialist, and looking freshly. He makes me want to do the same.

I will end with a minor provocation that follows loosely from this line of argument. Let us assume that only an educated minority is or has been much concerned with modern literature. This is consistent with Helen Small's argument that it is demographically absurd for faculty in the humanities to argue that 'democracy needs us'. It will never be more than a small portion of the population that will ever get higher degrees in the humanities. If higher degrees in the humanities are what democracy needs, then this is an additional reason to say that democracy is in trouble. People who spend significant time reading and thinking critically about literature are doomed to remain a small minority. And if so, then to propose that modern literature retains a certain socio-political significance is to say the same about what J. D. Vance and the American right call, or call out as, the cultural elite. It is to say that the cultural elite retains a certain socio-political significance *as a minority*, and is right to do so. It means, while denouncing the hypocrisy of the right's cultural politics and refocusing attention on the material consequences that the right's cultural politics are trying to disguise, also pausing to mount a *defence* of the minority they are calling a cultural elite. A progressive defence, of course. But a defence that must concede not just that it is a minority, but also that the minority possesses a certain degree of material privilege. There is already a well-established place in the rhetoric of the right for the argument that it is the material privilege of the educated that makes *us* hypocrites, and all the more so when and because we claim to be progressive. When the Trump/Vance ticket won in November 2024, that argument was surely one reason why.

The more limited or nuanced case for the public significance of reading and teaching modern literature – and not just *modern* literature, we should probably add – is not that democracy absolutely needs it, but that democracy benefits from it. It is a case I tried to make in my 2022 book *Criticism and Politics*. An old-fashioned case. Not, as will be obvious, a revolutionary case. I agree with Immanuel Wallerstein, in his 1969 book about the student protests of 1968, that under no circumstances can the metropolitan university, at the very centre of the global capitalist system, be expected to turn into a revolutionary institution. This is not a case against revolution, only a case about the university – and, one might add, about literature, outside as well as inside the university. I put my non-revolutionary case with deliberate crudeness. Literature is a vehicle for the preservation, transmission, and interpretation of the experience of others, often others whose historical experience differs significantly from our own. When we make that experience available to students, or enrich a conversation about it in book clubs and reviews and conversations about reviews, when we add to those conversations some sense of the perhaps inevitable limits on people's understanding of other people's experience, we who teach the teachers, whether in class or in other cultural activities, are doing our bit to make democracy more genuinely democratic. Training in conducting such conversations and conducting them well, acquiring expertise in the subject, involves a certain amount of privilege, even if these days those who have spent time in the acquisition of expertise often find themselves near the bottom of the ladder in terms of salary, benefits, and job security. The way the experts are treated in our society is indefensible, but the expertise itself is not.

Novel-Haunted: Kojin Karatani, Doris Lessing, and Ralph Ellison

Kenneth W. Warren

In the 1971 introduction to her landmark novel, *The Golden Notebook* (1962), Doris Lessing recalls that one of her goals in writing the book was to produce a critique and commentary on the form or genre of the novel as such. She writes

> that if the book were shaped in the right way it would make its own comment about the conventional novel: the debate about the novel has been going on since the novel was born, and is not, as one would imagine from reading contemporary academics, something recent. To put the short novel *Free Women* as a summary and condensation of all that mass material, was to say something about the conventional novel, another way of describing the dissatisfaction of a writer when something is finished.[1]

Accordingly, what become a leitmotiv within Lessing's lengthy novel are periodic engagements with the failings of the conventional novel. For example, in the novel's first section, the Black Notebook, Anna Wulf, the novel's author protagonist, decries the abandonment of philosophical ambition and the capitulation to fragmentation and reportage that she

1 Doris Lessing, *The Golden Notebook* (Harper Perennial, 2008), xviii–xix. All quotations from this book are from this edition and the page numbers are indicated in the text.

sees predominating in the novels of the 1950s. There are now, in her view, lamentably few novelists like Thomas Mann 'who used the novel for philosophical statements about life'. Instead, she laments,

> the function of the novel seems to be changing; it has become an outpost of journalism; we read novels for information about areas of life we don't know – Nigeria, South Africa, the American army, a coal-mining village, coteries in Chelsea, etc. *We read to find out what is going on.* One novel in five hundred or a thousand has the quality a novel should have to make it a novel – the quality of philosophy. I find that I read with the *same kind of curiosity* most novels and a book of reportage. (58–9)

And, as Lessing notes in her 1971 introduction, *The Golden Notebook* aligns the decay of the philosophical novel – which, for her, is also the decay of the realist novel – with the political decline of Marxism. For, notwithstanding the shortcomings of her experiences with the Communist Party, Anna recalls her time in the environs of the party as fellow traveller and party member as having been productive because it had placed at the centre of intellectual and political practice the presumption of the interconnectedness of human experience. Agreeing with Anna, Lessing writes,

> Marxism looks at things as a whole and in relation to each other – or tries to, but its limitations are not the point for the moment. A person who has been influenced by Marxism takes it for granted that an event in Siberia will affect one in Botswana. I think it possible that Marxism was the first attempt, for our time, outside the formal religions, at a world-mind, a world ethic. It went wrong, could not prevent itself from dividing and subdividing, like all the other religions, into smaller and smaller chapels, sects and creeds. But it was an attempt. (xix)

Setting aside 'for the moment' Lessing's insistence that the principle of subdivision is endemic to Marxism, her assertion that what looked like the strength of the novel was really fascination with mere reportage about events from the peripheries and hinterlands of the European bourgeois world tracks reasonably well with Kojin Karatani's contention that the efflorescence of novels by 'minority writers' in the US and Japan,

problematic of "politics and literature"' (32). In lieu of that problematic, the imperative to allow the formerly excluded to 'find their voice', which identifies literary expression with political expression, and holds that authors and critics can perform a political action solely through expression, becomes axiomatic rather than problematic. As a consequence, authenticity rather than narrative form moves to centre stage and the generic necessity for the novel threatens to disappear.

Even for Lessing, the necessity of the novel as form dissolves. Writing somewhat against the grain of her novelist avatar in *The Golden Notebook*, Lessing in her 1971 introduction enjoins her reader,

> Remember that for all the books we have in print, are as many that have never reached print, have never been written down – even now, in this age of compulsive reverence for the written word, history, even social ethic, are taught by means of stories, and the people have been conditioned into thinking only in terms of what is written – and unfortunately nearly all the products of our educational system can do no more than this – are missing what is before their eyes. For instance, the real history of Africa is still in the custody of black story-tellers, and wise men, black historians, medicine men; it is a verbal history, still kept safe from the white man and his predations. Everywhere, if you keep your mind open, you will find the truth in words *not* written down. So, never let the printed page be your master. (xxiv)

No longer do writers and readers face the central challenge of determining what happens when these 'real histories' confront the history of the novel. Rather the literary and political goal becomes that of protecting these expressions from the formal challenges of novelization.

The sensibility that Lessing embraced in writing *The Golden Notebook*, but seemed to repudiate in her 1971 reflections on it, was shared by her American near-contemporary Ralph Ellison (Lessing was born in 1919 and Ellison in 1913). Although scholars have been quite ready to remark on Ellison's sharp criticism of left political praxis in his depiction of 'the Party' in *Invisible Man* (1952) and in his chiding of Richard Wright for having 'found the facile answers of Marxism before he learned to use literature as a means for discovering the forms of American Negro humanity', Barbara Foley has argued provocatively that it was only by working through 'his reliance on Marxist categories of historical and political analysis' – categories he effaced and exiled over the course of the novel's lengthy composition – that Ellison was able to make *Invisible Man* the novel it was, while leaving its achievement short of the kind of fiction it might have been had he not 'abandoned' Marxism as 'both a passion and a paradigm'. Even so, *Invisible Man* appeals to Foley as 'a conflicted and contradictory text bearing multiple traces of [Ellison's] struggle to repress and then abolish the ghost of his leftist consciousness and conscience'.[3]

Where Ellison would have no disagreement with Foley is in acknowledging that the road to realizing the artistic completeness of the novel had to traverse the terrain of political commitment. But for Ellison, as Foley notes, it was only through an assertion of the non-identity of politics and art that the novel could come into its own. In 1964, Ellison observed in his essay 'Hidden Name and Complex Fate: A Writer's Experience in the United States' that however much a novelist may have been moved by some social or political cause or by some personal grievance to produce a literary work, the success of the work produced would not be found in its fidelity or commitment to the conditions that provoked it. Conceding the 'outrageous irony' of his postulate, Ellison nonetheless averred that 'in literature the great social clashes of history, no less than the painful experience of the individual, are secondary to the meaning which they take on through the skill, talent, imagination and personal vision of the writer who transforms them into art'. Accordingly, 'for a writer to insist that his personal suffering is of special interest in itself, or simply because he belongs to a particular racial or religious group, is to advance a claim for special privileges which members of this group who are not writers would be ashamed to demand'. Sentiments such as these constitute one of several reasons why not only Marxist scholars but also many scholars of African American literature have long found Ellison to be a problematic quantity – his arguments threaten to dissolve the basis on which any claim for a distinctive Black art could stand. And at the current moment, when Black literary and artistic production has come to be identified with the

3 Ralph Ellison, 'The World and the Jug', in *The Collected Essays of Ralph Ellison*, ed. John F. Callahan (Modern Library, 1995), 145; Barbara Foley, *Wrestling with the Left: The Making of Ralph Ellison's Invisible Man* (Duke University Press, 2010), 6–7.

travails of the 'Black Body', Ellison's views, at the very least, mark him as a figure of another moment. It was not that Ellison denied the reality and the persistence of racial inequality ('I have shared and still share many of their detailed injustices') but, rather, that he felt that such injustices were, 'at least in a discussion of a writer's experience, as *writer*, as artist, somewhat beside the point'. What made Black writers Black was not what would make them writers.[4]

In insisting that for a Black writer to be a true writer, that person must be, in the first instance, an artist, Ellison did not exactly pit the novel against the project of social justice. For example, he believed in firm but complicated ways that good novels and good democracies shared an essence. He did, however, insist on the non-identity of political and artistic ends, and his attention to this problematic does indeed locate him within a specific moment in literary history that gave us such novels as Lessing's *Golden Notebook*, a moment stretching from the 1930s through the late '60s, punctuated by the late 1930s debates about modernism and realism among Theodor Adorno, Walter Benjamin, Ernst Bloch, Bertolt Brecht, and Georg Lukács; the emergence of now-canonical studies of the history of the novel and realistic representation, including Ian Watt's *The Rise of the Novel*, Erich Auerbach's *Mimesis*, and Wayne Booth's *The Rhetoric of Fiction*; the rise of creative writing programmes as described by Mark McGurl in *The Program Era*; and the third wave of African American literary authorship (preceded by the early Jim Crow efflorescence at the turn of the twentieth century and the Harlem Renaissance of the 1920s). This was a time when the problem of representation in literature and art had not yet splintered on the reefs of deconstruction, and when it was possible to raise the question of totality without some measure of embarrassment. And, finally, this was a time when, as exemplified in Lessing's Anna Wulf, serious practitioners of the novel felt continually called upon to produce an account of whether or not it should matter to the world if not one more novel were ever written.[5] Granville Hicks begins *The Living Novel*, his 1957 edited volume of testimonials from major novelists, with the declaration that

4 Ralph Ellison, 'Hidden Name and Complex Fate: A Writer's Experience in the United States', in *The Collected Essays of Ralph Ellison*, 189–91.

5 As Wulf recalls the genesis of her first novel, *Frontiers of War*, she remembers asking herself, 'Why a story at all – not that it was a bad story or untrue, or that it debased anything. Why not, simply, the truth?' (Lessing, 61).

'This book is dedicated to the proposition that the novel is important, and is addressed to a skeptical world.'[6]

Hicks's summoning of writers rather than literary scholars to make the case for the importance of the novel reflected a belief shared among his contributors (a list that included Saul Bellow, Ralph Ellison, Herbert Gold, Wright Morris, Flannery O'Connor, and Jessamyn West) that, in Ellison's words, 'the best way for a novelist to discuss the problem of the Novel is in the form of *a specific novel*'. Echoing the ambition that Lessing expressed in writing *The Golden Notebook*, Ellison's essay for Hicks's volume stated, 'Every serious novel is, beyond its immediate thematic preoccupations, a discussion of the craft.'[7] In other words, novels themselves are theorizations and criticisms of the novel.

In making this point about the distinctiveness of the novel as a form, Ellison and Lessing assert informally the insight that Mikhail Bakhtin, in such essays as 'Epic and Novel', has made more systematically. Agreeing with the title of Hicks's volume, *The Living Novel* Bakhtin observes that the 'novel is the only developing genre and therefore it reflects more deeply, more essentially, more sensitively and rapidly, reality itself in the process of its unfolding'. Paralleling Ellison's remark that individual novels are inherently 'discussions of craft', Bakhtin celebrates the 'ability of the novel to criticize itself [as] a remarkable feature of this ever-developing genre'.[8] There is then, on Bakhtin's account, no history and theory of the novel outside of the relations that individual novels establish with other novels, other genres, modes, forms, media, and discourses in relation to whatever it is that an individual novel is, or purports to be, about. As a consequence, critical writing on that 'history and theory' is always superseded by the writing of another novel.

I do not take any of what I have just offered about Bakhtin to be at all new; rather, I assume its familiarity to most scholars of the novel. What I hope to bring to light, however, are three subsequent points. The first is the aptness of Bakhtin's insights to the historical moment that gave us such figures as Lessing and Ellison. My second point may count as an emendation or modification of Bakhtin's account of the relation of the

6 Granville Hicks, *The Living Novel: A Symposium* (Macmillan, 1957), vii.

7 Ralph Ellison, 'Society, Morality and the Novel', in *The Living Novel*, 59–60.

8 Mikhail Bakhtin, 'Epic and Novel', in *The Dialogic Imagination: Four Essays*, ed. Michael Holquist and trans. Caryl Emerson and Michael Holquist (University of Texas Press, 1981), 7, 6.

novel to other genres. For Bakhtin, the primary mode of the novel's relation to other genres is that of parody. He writes, 'Parodic stylizations of canonized genres and styles occupy an essential place in the novel . . . Throughout its entire history there is a consistent parodying or travestying of dominant or fashionable novels that attempt to become models for the genre.' To be sure, parody, as disrespect, does not, for Bakhtin, describe fully the posture of the novel to other genres – the form also renovates other genres by opening them up. But, even in this case, the relation does turn out to be a matter of hierarchy, for to the degree that a novel refrains from undercutting the authority of other novels or genres it does so, on Bakhtin's account, by way of annexation – renewing other genres by making them more like novels. Thus, 'in the process of becoming the dominant genre, the novel sparks the renovation of all other genres, it infects them with its spirit of process and inconclusiveness. It draws them ineluctably into its orbit.'[9] What I want to suggest, instead, here, is that, for many novelists of this period, the relation of the novel to its others might better be described in terms of a practice of neutral delineation of or even an attitude of measured respect towards those others, deriving from the idea that for a novel to be a novel it must preserve or even produce the lines of demarcation between it and other forms or arts. A society in which everything was novelized would be society that needed no novels. Wulf, for example, objects not to reportage as such, but to reports that purport to be novels.

My next point is one that I have already made, namely the observation that what exerted some of the most intense pressure on the act of novel writing during this period was the demand that novelists produce works of social engagement. Again, I do not offer this observation as anything new: the relation of modernist fiction to works of social realism or proletarian fiction has been a long-standing interest of literary scholars. What I merely note is what scholars like Foley and Ellison's non-Marxist biographer, Lawrence Jackson, also remark, that the contours of the novel as a form emerge only in the struggle for differentiation from politics. Jackson observes that the problem of the artist's 'social responsibility' which bedevilled 'everyone who picked up a pen in the 1950s' was particularly acute for Black writers, who according to Jackson had to wrestle with 'the difficult decision to join the active

9 Ibid., 6, 7.

struggle to win black rights in face of the real challenges to their craft' – a problem that 'became the chief condition for the black talent that had got on the scene in the 1940s'.[10] In Jackson's view, none of the Black writers of that moment was able to produce a resolution of that problem. What I want to argue, however, is that, through their novels, some writers from this period give us a picture of what resolution might look like.

For Ellison, as we have seen, the problematic of distinguishing between art on the one hand and the social condition and social responsibility of writers on the other remained a central preoccupation. Arguably, the concluding pronouncement of the protagonist of *Invisible Man*, that even an invisible man might have a socially responsible role to play, allegorizes this problematic. Having finished his story, the novel's loquacious narrator now has to figure out what he ought to do – and it is with this dilemma that the novel leaves him, facing the problem of acting politically rather than creating artistically. For Ellison himself, however, the next move was clear: write another novel. Ironically, however, the predicament of his protagonist, having completed his story without yet having laid out a plan of action, became Ellison's as well, who having finished one novel never completed another in his lifetime.

Ellison did, however, complete many essays, and it is in some of these that we can see further unfolding of the problem of art and politics. And, by way of understanding better what Ellison was often up to, I want to take a brief, but I hope illuminating, detour through Michael Fried's landmark 1967 essay, 'Art and Objecthood'. Although it would be stretching the truth to say that, since its publication in 1967, 'Art and Objecthood' has figured centrally in discussions of African American art and literature, it does not require too much effort to see how the claim that – to quote Fried – 'the imperative that modern art defeat or suspend its objecthood is at bottom the imperative that it *defeat or suspend theater*' might be cognate with much of what has preoccupied at least one strain of thinking about Black art and literature since the late nineteenth century.[11] One need only mention the way that the spectre of minstrelsy loomed over the career of Paul

10 Lawrence P. Jackson, *The Indignant Generation: A Narrative History of African American Writers and Critics, 1934–1960* (Princeton University Press, 2011), 403–4.

11 Michael Fried, 'Art and Objecthood', in *Art and Objecthood: Essays and Reviews* (University of Chicago Press, 1998), 160.

Laurence Dunbar as a poet to see the broad outlines that make comparison apt. Although, in Dunbar's case, the problem would not be appropriately described as a problem of modernism, the matter that concerned him was, nonetheless, the more fundamental one that Fried described in 'Art and Objecthood', namely the threat theatricality posed to the very idea of art. When Dunbar bemoaned the world's praise for 'a jingle in a broken tongue' over the lyric poems he aspired to write, he was not only objecting to the strictures on the mode within which the Black writer was expected to work – inevitably the comic – but also inveighing against the belief that no line could be drawn between the dialect poem on the page and the banter of the Black labourer in the cotton field.[12] To indulge a slight anachronism, what Dunbar was objecting to was the type of sentiment that the sociologist Robert Park offered up a few decades later in an article that would later infuriate Ralph Ellison, namely that the Negro 'is primarily an artist, loving life for its own sake. His métier is expression rather than action. The Negro is, so to speak, the lady among races.'[13] On Park's description of Black poetry and art, the line between art and life simply disappears such that all utterance and representation become nothing other than expression. Paradoxically, this could appear to make the figure of the Negro a figure of a peculiar site of absorption, someone capable of producing expression without rhetoric, an expression that would always be the same with or without an audience. Indeed, for Park, whose interest, from the stance of sociology, was in getting at something like the truth of Black life, the lack of self-consciousness in Black

---

12 The poem is Dunbar's 'The Poet' from *The Complete Poems of Paul Laurence Dunbar* (Dodd, Mead, and Co., 1922), 191.

> He sang of life, serenely sweet,
> With, now and then, a deeper note.
> From some high peak, nigh yet remote,
> He voiced the world's absorbing beat.
>
> He sang of love when earth was young,
> And Love, itself, was in his lays.
> But ah, the world, it turned to praise
> A jingle in a broken tongue.

13 Robert E. Park, 'The Conflict and Confusion of Cultures with Special Reference to the Negro', *Journal of Negro History*, 4:2 (April 1919): 130.

folk poetry – in contradistinction to the kind of poetry that was emerging during the Harlem Renaissance – was valuable because it revealed exactly who the Negro was. For Park, the folk Negro, in his milieu, expresses himself unintentionally and unselfconsciously, without the interference of the white reader. And, in this view of Black expression, we are back on the ground of Lessing's account of the real of African history and storytelling. Getting at what art presumably gives us without going through art becomes a feature of what it means to think about Black art forms – for which the commitment to form is at best minimal, giving way instead to a certain stylization, to the way one almost reflexively does things, to that which one cannot help.

In many ways it is against the 'that which one can't help' version of Black art that many of Ralph Ellison's essays on Black art and the novel are pitched, of which perhaps the best known is the aforementioned 'The World and the Jug', where he asserts,

> While one can do nothing about choosing one's relatives, one can, as an artist, choose one's 'ancestors'. [Richard] Wright was, in this sense, a 'relative', Hemingway an 'ancestor'. Langston Hughes, whose work I knew in grade school and whom I knew before I knew Wright, was a 'relative'; Eliot, whom I was to meet only many years later, and Malraux and Dostoevsky and Faulkner, were 'ancestors' – if you please or don't please![14]

That which he can do nothing about is that which makes one's work, so to speak, Black – a set of lived or imputed social relations (hence, relatives) adduced to demarcate one social group from another. It is here that the Parkian, sociological, interest lies. And in Ellison's estimation, it is this set of relations that paradoxically would matter the least for the Black artist. Crucially important would be that which Fried calls '*conviction* – specifically, the conviction that a particular painting or sculpture or poem or piece of music can or cannot support comparison with past work within that art whose quality is not in doubt'. For modernist art – for Fried and for Ellison – 'nothing short of *conviction* . . . matters at all'.[15]

14 Ellison, 'The World and the Jug', 185.

15 Fried, 'Art and Objecthood', 165.

To put the case more strongly would be to say that while what might initially compel interest in a work is everything one might want to collocate with Blackness, i.e. the condition of being Black, the task for the Black artist would, by contrast, be to overcome this interest so that what would ultimately stand forth is the conviction that this is a work of art. This conviction would not be to deny the force asserted on one's social being by those ascriptive practices by which races are constituted. But it would be to deny their precedence and to attenuate their consequence except as a matter of how they matter within art.

Now, I suspect that to some readers this may appear to be little more than an updating of what Langston Hughes alleged against the poet Countee Cullen in his landmark 1926 article, 'The Negro Artist and the Racial Mountain', when Hughes wrote,

> One of the most promising of the young Negro poets said to me once, 'I want to be a poet – not a Negro poet', meaning, I believe, 'I want to write like a white poet'; meaning subconsciously, 'I would like to be a white poet'; meaning behind that, 'I would like to be white.' And I was sorry the young man said that, for no great poet has ever been afraid of being himself. And I doubted then that, with his desire to run away spiritually from his race, this boy would ever be a great poet. But this is the mountain standing in the way of any true Negro art in America – this urge within the race toward whiteness, the desire to pour racial individuality into the mold of American standardization, and to be as little Negro and as much American as possible.[16]

But what should become evident upon re-perusing Hughes's slippery slope is that he has stipulated what needs instead to be argued, namely the apparently inescapable identity of race and poetry – the idea that to be a true poet, one must, from the standpoint of identity, be a particular kind of poet or else be at risk of producing only that which could come from 'the mold of American standardization', which one presumes would be some sort of non-poetry. And to expand Hughes's point slightly differently, the problem he has identified is one that could not be wholly identified with the 'Negro' poet, given that, as it is formulated

16 Langston Hughes, 'The Negro Artist and the Racial Mountain', in *Keeping Time: Readings in Jazz History*, ed. Robert Walser (Oxford University Press, 1999), 55.

here, the path to true poetry for any American artist would have to traverse the terrain of identity. What, according to Hughes, Cullen has missed is that, as Walter Benn Michaels has demonstrated in *Our America*, the great American modernist literature of the 1920s and early 1930s succeeded precisely because, instead of evading the matter of race, it made *identity* its central project.

So the crucial point that makes Ellison's remarks something other than a more artful restating of Cullen's insistence that the putative race of the artist should never matter for aesthetic judgment is a historical one. Ellison is writing after the great achievements of the nativist modernism of the 1920s. For him it is not enough to assert the irrelevance of race as well as the irrelevance of Marxist politics. Rather, he must demonstrate their overcoming. In his own fiction and in his broader discussions of American literature, this overcoming sometimes involves what Ellison saw as William Faulkner's method, which entailed beginning with the necessary theatricalization that race entails, namely the stereotype, which one must 'accept . . . as true, and then seek out the human truth which it hides'. To be sure, much of Faulkner belongs with the corpus of nativist modernism, but for Ellison in that essay Faulkner provides a contrast to the other modernists, who embrace 'technical experimentation' but forget that the novel is also 'an ethical instrument' in which moral truth matters.[17] That is, Ellison invokes Faulkner in an argument that seems intent on pointing out the inadequacy of mere form, only to assert that it is through the form of the novel that one exposes the calcified false forms that masquerade as truth. While it is true that Ellison castigates mere technical brilliance, his criticism remains primarily artistic: by failing to realize that the society in which they exist routinely ignores or stereotypes 'the Negro', these artists merely parrot prevailing beliefs and images. The moral point is an artistic one: although the humanity of Black Americans is given, its realization demands the proper use of artifice.

But, for our purposes here, more pertinent may be the brief reflections Ellison makes about the work of Romare Bearden, who was one of his most important artistic friends. Asked to provide the introduction to the 1967 catalogue *Romare Bearden: Paintings and Projections*, Ellison

17 Ralph Ellison, 'Twentieth-Century Fiction and the Mask of Humanity', in *The Collected Essays of Ralph Ellison*, 98, 99.

took the occasion not to single out for description a few exemplary works (which is one of the essay's limitations) but to limn the overall challenge and achievement of Bearden's work after he turned to collage in the early 1960s when he discovered those 'methods' that 'would allow him to express the tragic predicament of his people without violating his passionate dedication to art as a fundamental and transcendent agency for confronting and revealing the world'. Ellison's essay proffers Bearden's achievement to the would-be Black artist 'who cannot avoid, nor should he wish to avoid, his group identity, but . . . flounders before the question of how his group's experience might be given statement through the categories of a nonverbal form of art which has been consciously exploring its own unique possibilities for many decades before he appeared on the scene'. Lacking any 'specifically Negro American tradition of plastic design to offer him support', the Black artist 'feels, in brief, a near-unresolvable conflict between his urge to leave his mark upon the world through art and his ties to his group and its claims upon him'. I have no doubt that some might quibble with, or outright reject, the contention that Black art before Bearden lacked any viable 'tradition of plastic design', but I want to pass over that now in order to focus on what Ellison insists is the crucial line of battle, namely Bearden's claiming for art all that had been dominated by non-art. Ellison asserts that by working with 'a highly conscious awareness of the resources and limitations of the form to which he has dedicated his creative energies', Bearden reveals a 'world long hidden by the clichés of sociology and rendered cloudy by the distortions of newsprint and the false continuity imposed upon our conception of Negro life by television and much documentary photography'.[18] Standing opposed to art then are, along with Ellison's bête noire, sociology, the newspaper and documentary photography, which, in bits and pieces, figure onto the surface of Bearden's collages. In Bearden's words, 'I feel that when some photographic detail, such as a hand or an eye, is taken out of its original context and is fractured and integrated into a different space and form configuration, it acquires a plastic quality it did not have in the original photograph.' By working with genres of reportage, ripping them out of their context, and making them subject to the composition on the flat surface of his canvas,

18 Ralph Ellison, 'The Art of Romare Bearden', in *The Collected Essays of Ralph Ellison*, 684, 687, 690.

Bearden asserts the primacy of form over the transmission of mere information. Although Bearden began his career as a serious artist under the spell of the idea that 'art . . . [was] an instrument of social change',[19] his mature injunctions insist that 'a quality of artificiality must be retained in a work of art, since, after all, the reality of art is not to be confused with that of the outer world'. But to this he adds, with a self-deprecatory ruefulness,

> I am afraid, despite my intentions, that in some instances commentators have tended to overemphasize what they believe to be the social elements in my work. But while my response to certain human elements is as obvious as it is inevitable, I am also pleased to note that upon reflection many persons have found that they were as much concerned with the aesthetic implications of my paintings as with, what may possibly be, my human compassion.[20]

Although it is not quite right to say that the social elements in Bearden's work stand against its aesthetic implications, it does seem clear that what Bearden – and Ellison through him – want is work that commands attention as an aesthetic object rather than a political statement. Indeed, for Ellison, the political statement that he was chiefly interested in making, which was to affirm 'the irrelevance of the notion of race as a limiting force in the arts', could be made only via a work that commands conviction as a work of art.

But Ellison's *Invisible Man* also concluded with the tentative and apprehensive conjecture that it might speak for its collective readership: 'And it is this which frightens me: *Who knows but that, on the lower frequencies, I speak for you?*' One can argue that the novel's reception, despite ongoing and often effusive praise for its achievement, has tended to deny and deprecate the narrator's proposition in favour of demonstrations of how much and how many lie outside of his bid for representativeness and completeness. And while this pointing-up of all those for whom the novel does not speak is meant to indicate the failure of the novel, the fear expressed in Ellison's final line also suggests something

19 Romare Bearden, 'Rectangular Structure in My Montage Paintings', *Leonardo*, 2:1 (January 1969): 17, 11.

20 Ibid., 18.

other than hubris, something that goes in a different direction, namely a fear of being presumed to be speaking the last word on the human situation. As I have argued elsewhere, Ellison's only completed novel was a statement haunted by its imminent obsolescence,[21] and it may be that what *Invisible Man* shares with its generic counterparts is the sense of dread that Karatani's reflections on the end of modern literature have expressed so starkly. The utopian dream of the novel was that the conditions that had brought it forth would have run their course before the form itself had realized its own limits. The genre's nightmare is not the imminence of its death but rather its ghostly persistence at a moment when, to quote Karatani, 'the movements of capitalism and the state that determine us are not over' (55). And against these movements, we remain novel-haunted, searching for forms that will flesh out our desire for the realization of our humanity.

21 See Kenneth W. Warren, *So Black and Blue: Ralph Ellison and the Occasion of Criticism* (University of Chicago Press, 2003).

Education, Global Culture, and 'The End of Modern Literature'

Gauri Viswanathan

When Kojin Karatani contemplates 'leaving literature', as he puts it, his declaration comes as nothing short of a gut punch. When he ponders the question of what literature can do that other branches of study such as religion and politics cannot do, he finds that he cannot arrive at a positive answer. This is effectively the moment when literature has ended for him. His sobering reflections lament that literature no longer offers him the tools to analyse political positions or ideological contradictions, or even to confront personal issues for that matter. Karatani's insistence on literature's political, or public, role forcefully demands that literature not be tethered exclusively to aesthetics. When literature no longer serves politics or revolution (at times, he problematically applies the terms interchangeably), literature has effectively ended for him. This simple proposition anchors his determination to seek more radical aims outside literature. Crucially, at the same time, he leaves enough of a conceptual space to consider whether literature can be rebooted to serve twenty-first-century needs. His essay's analytic lies within that laser-focused aim.

One is prompted to ask: is Karatani's decision to leave literature a frustrated response to the apolitical consequences of twentieth- and twenty-first-century literary theory, as delineated by Edward W. Said in his seminal essay 'Criticism Between System and Theory'?[1] After all,

1 Edward W. Said, 'Criticism Between System and Theory', in *The World, the Text, and the Critic* (Harvard University Press, 1983).

Said had weighed Foucault's archaeological methods of reading discourse against Derrida's text-based models and found both lacking. While it was unarguable that Foucault attended to the densities of history and historical process in the rise of institutions like the prison and the clinic, Said rejected his deterministic approach, which, in Said's view, deprived human beings of agency and reduced them to mere objectifications of impersonal historical forces. Said was equally alienated by Derrida's attempts to turn the historical and social world into a language game in which notions like undecidability and illegibility had more cachet than historical knowledge. It is hard not to read Karatani as echoing elements of Said's thought when he despairs of the endless self-referentiality of literature. Does literature, then, end for Karatani when it is no longer an expression of what Said called worldliness?

In addressing this question, Karatani's response takes an interesting philosophical turn. Rather than choosing to leave literature because it has become too wrapped in an aesthetics jettisoned from political engagement, Karatani reorients his thought towards seeking out the motive-force that keeps political engagement alive in aesthetics. He regards post-Romantic aesthetics as noteworthy for having newly promoted sensibility and intellect, observing that imagination's new respectability heightened literature's status, not as fanciful or effete, but as purposeful and relevant. An interesting line of thought develops in Karatani's analysis at this point: sensibility and imagination summon moral ideas, which, paradoxically, are present even in so-called immoral tales, such as in *The Tale of the Genji*, which he cites as an example of a lauded text that has endured over time. Morality goes beyond the stark facts presented in narratives or what narratives reveal about their characters and situations. Rather, morality is broadly conceived as meaning itself, untethered from a scale of predetermined values. Viewed thus, morality is disentangled from judgment, eschewing appraisals of characters as good or bad in favour of the implications of their behaviour on plot and action. Herein lies the meaning of morality – and the enduring value of literature – for Karatani, who looks anew at narrative form as a site of meaning-making that scrambles fixed notions of morality. In piercing through morality's conventions, narrative form helps to uncover core truths about the role of social, economic, and political forces in world-building.

Karatani's subtle argument tackles a subject that perturbed me when I wrote *Masks of Conquest*.[2] If British colonizers sought to introduce Indians to English literature in order to inculcate a moral sensibility, what is moral about, say, *Macbeth* or *Titus Andronicus*, leave alone novels like *Joseph Andrews* or *Tom Jones*? How would reading a play about regicide and rapacious greed elevate the minds of colonial subjects, who were derided as benighted by their colonial overlords? Even more puzzling was the fact that Christian missionary schools favoured such literary works over direct instruction in the Bible, citing the power of imaginative works in affecting young minds more directly than scriptural texts. Reading Karatani, I realized that the unravelling of Macbeth's rank ambitions – the fate that befalls the purveyors of power – alone does not represent the play's morality. Rather, *the ability to read for meaning* keeps literature relevant for modern society and provides its moral underpinning. Once literature ceases to be available for reading in this sense, once it turns into a self-deconstructing activity that destabilizes any possible centre of meaning, literature in effect facilitates its own demise. The self-destruction of literature, for Karatani, signals loss of meaning. Literature's fall from being a repository of meaning is precisely what precipitates Karatani's will to leave it.

The ability to convey truth thus sustains literature's relevance. It is perhaps for this reason that the novel gained prominence as a genre that uniquely enabled the creation of a community bound together by mutual sympathy, laying the foundations for what Benedict Anderson called the imagined community of the nation. This raises the question: could the nation have coalesced as a concept without the novel imagining it first? The prototypical examples of community and nation inevitably recall the works of George Eliot, whose novels imagine a spider's web of connections among social groups. Does the nineteenth-century novel, then, epitomize literature at its height of meaningfulness, before it ended when the novel declined from being an expression of community to a reflection of its fragmentation and disunity? Indeed, for Karatani, it appears that literature ends when the nation can no longer be a bond between peoples, not so much in the sense of nationalistic feeling and fervour, but in the ways that people are organically linked with one

2 Gauri Viswanathan, *Masks of Conquest: Literary Study and British Rule in India* (Columbia University Press, 1989).

another by mutual needs. No amount of wilfulness can patch that unity again. Karatani views literature as one of the many casualties of such fragmentation, which results in isolation rather than community.

Karatani's ruminations evoke a long-standing debate about whether literary education aims primarily to develop personality independently of a prior foundational community or, at the far end of the spectrum, whether literary study plays a key role in social management and, by extension, the insertion of a carefully shaped personality into the social spaces of the state. Community building would appear to be somewhere in the middle of the spectrum, if we can apply this insight to Karatani's reflections. We can begin to draw some tentative conclusions by looking at the fate of the *Bildungsroman*, the novel form for narrating the development of the individual from inchoate identity to social maturity. The *Bildungsroman* has a canonical status in modern education precisely because it accommodates the individual to emerging societal formations, so that even though the *Bildungsroman*'s thematic focus may be on personality development, it does so with a view to assimilating the mature individual into the accepted social spaces of the modern nation-state. Notwithstanding the *Bildungsroman*'s association with the triumph of individualism over sociality, Joseph Slaughter's corrective reading of the genre as committed to charting 'the process of individuation as an incorporative process of socialization, without which individualism itself would be meaningless',[3] reinforces the point I am making about the reshaping of the literary curriculum to serve national ends under the aegis (or pretence, if one wants to be blunt) of personal growth.

The *Bildungsroman* is germane to that purpose. Asking questions about how this novel form became a principal actor in social management ties the novel's fate irrevocably to the course of colonial education. The novel of personal development has a special status in colonial education, extending into modern education, because it elicits the reader's identification with the *Bildung* (or growth) narrative of ethical formation. Despite its interest in individuality and personality, the *Bildungsroman* is, in fact, a narrative of the individual's loss of particularity and difference, which is achieved through the individual's identification with idealized forms of subjectivity that reflect a sense of

3 Joseph Slaughter, *Human Rights, Inc.: The World Novel, Narrative Form, and International Law* (Fordham University Press, 2007), 19.

belonging to a larger corporate entity. The *Bildung* narrative, in short, is an affirmation of the character ideals associated not with the individual but with a larger entity, whether one wants to call it the modern nation or the bureaucratic state.

The emergence of the bureaucratic, rational state, which coincided with the period of high colonialism, ruptured the continuity between character formation and utilitarian goals that had prevailed in educational theory until then. No longer principally an instrument of character development in an older, aristocratic sense, education became the means for the state's absorption – through acculturation – of citizens and colonial subjects alike. This, incidentally, is why Virginia Woolf objected to education on the model of men's colleges as a goal for women: she charged that as long as education conducted by men aimed at acculturation to force and power, not growth of mind and character, women had no room for an independent flourishing.[4] The state's absorption of the people it educates is admittedly uneven and disproportionate across class and gender, but more to the point is the fact that the presumably non-coercive nature of education allowed for assimilation by consent to the state's desires. When the focus of instruction shifts from individual, personal growth to self-consciousness as national subjects, morality is no longer a matter of individual will and conscience. Instead, morality merges with national loyalty and public affirmation. Again, it is Virginia Woolf who, through her gender analysis, discerned the nationalizing function of education, with its tendency to create communities aligned with the goals of the state, even those that led to wars.[5]

In truth, modern education has always been in the business of a certain amount of standardization, especially from the time it took over from the family the task of preparing youth for the world. However, this goal is at odds with a cherished myth of education that has had a long shelf-life in modern Western liberal theory, which perceives the development of individual personality and creativity to be the ultimate goal of schooling. Celebrated works like John Locke's *Some Thoughts Concerning Education* (1693) and Rousseau's *Emile, or On Education* (1762) immortalized autonomous conceptions of self, romantically associating education with the development of personality set apart

4 Virginia Woolf, *Three Guineas* (1938; Harcourt, 1966), 58–9.
5 Ibid., 105–9.

from a foundational prior community. This understanding of personal growth and autonomy has been so persistent that it overshadows interrogations of whether education has historically concerned itself with the development of personality in the first place and whether, to the contrary, education may have had objectives other than personal growth.

Two factors undermined that myth: colonial education and the elevation of the *Bildungsroman* in the literary canon. Histories of the mass reading public show that the *Bildungsroman* is associated with at least three functions: first, steering individuals towards normative social desires; second, flattening the wild, unmanageable distinctions between personalities and locating points of common engagement; and third, mediating the individual's presence in mass democracy. Liberal theory's enduring attachment to the primacy of individual presence runs as a thread in the thought of the Italian philosopher Gianni Vattimo, who insists that without personal interpretation, democracy would be robbed of its potency.[6] The ability to interpret is what puts a stamp on individuality. This brand of social mediation via individuality brings the *Bildungsroman* closer than any other literary form to what we would describe today as organized mass culture, especially the latter's manifestations in social media. The critic Lisa Lowe draws analogies between the dissemination of popular nineteenth-century English novels (particularly the *Bildungsroman*) and the reach of modern (social) media, drawing attention to the ways that distance folds into intimacies, and inchoate, fragmented personalities coalesce into the outlines of a global village.[7] Thus, she cites the novels of Jane Austen to argue that Austen's narrative divisions, complexities, and resolutions had wide-reaching effects beyond the author's immediate time, effectively extending the nineteenth-century English public to include globalized readers and consumers of popular culture in the twenty-first century. The educational system's privileging of the *Bildungsroman* facilitates the globalization of readerships, making it possible for the novels of personal development to enter mass culture and grow in influence across time and place, in proportion to their continuing presence in the curriculum.

6 Gianni Vattimo, talk given at UNESCO Conference, Rio de Janeiro, 20 May 1998.

7 Lisa Lowe, 'Decolonization, Displacement, Disidentification: Asian American "Novels" and the Question of History', in *Cultural Institutions of the Novel*, ed. Deirdre Lynch and William B. Warner (Duke University Press, 1996), 97–8.

The novel has a special status in literary studies for all these reasons. The novel's assured place in the modern university curriculum establishes its centrality in literary studies as the principal agent of a normative subjectivity. It marks the advent of reading practices that turn on two meanings of 'institution': as a foundation and structure of education on the one hand, and as a process of becoming on the other. The first meaning of 'institution' – as foundation – signals a culture's acceptance, recognition, and legitimation of a defined set of practices, whereas the second meaning – as a mode of becoming – asserts the ability of cultural practices to shape, influence, and indeed even compel behaviour, conduct, and thought. Lewis Leary, in his study of literary pedagogy, trenchantly remarks that '[p]ower over another's mind . . . can be enormously dangerous. But that is education, and that is literature also.'[8] His observation fittingly illustrates the novel's ability to produce predetermined behaviours by reinforcing the functions of education. The focus on process – that is, on becoming – radically alters the questions normally asked about the novel, such as its evolution from the rise of the bourgeoisie.

Viewed by many critics as a uniquely Western form that catalysed print culture to serve the interests of the rising European bourgeoisie, the novel has typically been regarded as alien to non-Western societies and therefore as much an agent of European colonialism as law, education, and other cultural institutions. However, this view fails to acknowledge the extent to which colonial societies, in turn, colonized the novel by adapting it to indigenous forms. Karatani alludes to the transformations that occurred when Japanese literature shifted from illustrations to linear print. When adaptations recirculate in global literature, the altered sensibilities act as a brake on the unqualified dissemination of European class interests. The disruptive effect occurs in at least two types of adaptation: one, as direct postcolonial revision, as evidenced in Tayeb Salih's *Season of Migration to the North*, which is an Arabic update of Joseph Conrad's *Heart of Darkness*, or in Jean Rhys's *Wide Sargasso Sea*, which is a Caribbean rewriting of Charlotte Brontë's *Jane Eyre*; and two, as

8 Lewis Leary, 'Literary Scholarship and the Teaching of English', in *Contemporary Literary Scholarship: A Critical Review*, ed. Lewis Leary (National Council of Teachers of English, 1958), 18–19. Quoted in Homer Brown, 'Why the Story of the Origin of the (English) Novel Is an American Romance (if Not the Great American Novel)', in *Cultural Institutions of the Novel*, 29.

extension of a novelistic arc, as in Peter Carey's *Oscar and Lucinda*, which is a reworking of two canonical Victorian works, Edmund Gosse's *Father and Son* and George Eliot's *Daniel Deronda*, or in the Tibetan writer Jamyang Norbu's *The Mandala of Sherlock Holmes*, which amalgamates Arthur Conan Doyle's detective stories and Rudyard Kipling's *Kim* in order to repurpose the European novel to address the Tibetan struggle against China. The cultural work performed by adaptations written from the so-called margins does not match the development of bourgeois sensibility in dominant accounts of the *Bildungsroman*. The discrepancy between the received history of the novel – as serving Western bourgeois interests – and its global dissemination can be accounted for by the complex histories of reception, adaptation, and revision in the non-Western societies where the novel has grown and flourished. Indeed, the productive power of novels to negotiate transnational identities uniquely makes the novel a site of transnational exchange, allowing for the global disseminations of novel reading and novel writing. In its global aspect, the novel is transformed into a discursive site where the relations among nations are actively renegotiated.

The global aspect also exposes false assumptions about the organic composition of the culture in which literature is consumed. One such assumption links English literature's moral impulses to their derivation from Christianity. This was typically the fallacy driving missionary work in non-Christian societies, which were reorganized to correspond with a uniform English society pervaded by the influence of Christian culture shaping English conduct and thought. This construction encouraged many Christian missionaries to subscribe to a unitary theory of English civil society based on religion influencing the full range of knowledge produced in that society.

However, this theory could not account for literature's influence in a heterogeneous society where no single religion prevails, or is Christian only in name, as was the case with England, especially by the mid-nineteenth century. What I want to suggest here is that the disconnection between reading publics and the repurposing of literature as a repository of Christian values does not only pertain to colonized societies. It is equally true of England's increasingly fragmented religious population since the 1850s. England's history of multiple sects highlights an Anglicanism eroded as much by dissent as by the rising tide of movements like secularism, freethought, and atheism. That being the case, what does it mean to allude to English literature's Christian roots if the society in which it is read and studied does not partake of a uniform Christian character?

Historically, the strongest challenge to hegemonic literary instruction has come from the pluralistic composition of society, and that includes the plurality of religions. This is often lost sight of in twenty-first-century ebates, in which ethnicity or race figures more prominently as an index of a society's pluralistic character. An English population comprising not only Anglicans but also Jews, Catholics, Dissenters, Nonconformists, and other denominations militated against a composite characterization of literature's Christian motivation, or even against an idea that texts are open to private interpretation. Furthermore, when English literature was taught in the colonies, a heterogeneous colonized population that included Hindus, Muslims, Buddhists, Sikhs, Zoroastrians, and Jains, among other religious groups, posed a direct challenge to the expected purposes and outcomes of Christian instruction. With the scriptural antecedents of literature not being self-evidently persuasive in non-Christian societies, and in the absence of continuity between civil and sacred institutions, literary instruction reached a point of crisis. By undercutting class and racial identifications, international adaptations of European novels broke the unity between civil and sacred society that promoted European national interests.

Humanism's cherished notion that literature promotes the development of personality meets its challenge in today's multicultural world. Who sets the norms and the ideals to which individual growth should aspire? Globalization appears to mark a new phase of modern literary studies. Since globalization challenges the power of education to assert the values of a single class, it forces education to be more responsive to the multicultural, multi-ethnic, and multi-religious elements in society. Of course, whether education rises to the task is an altogether different matter. Presumably, having had their own cultural and literary traditions make way for those imposed by colonialist powers in newly introduced curricula, colonized societies should find it less easy to revert to tradition when confronted with globalization. If we are right to assume that mass culture is heterogeneously composed, then it stands to reason that its producers and consumers do not reflect the culture of a single group. But to say that eclecticism is intrinsic to the nature of mass culture and that it incorporates ethnicity as well as race should not be taken to mean that ethnicity remains unappropriated or unchanged.

The ethnicity claimed by the family or the community is not always the same ethnicity as is marketed in stores or in the media. Yet we seem to have much more trouble recognizing that the ethnic basis of today's multicultural curriculum or media is no less manufactured than the one found in stores or the media. The features that mark off distinct groups in civil society are blurred when they are reimagined in education, media, and merchandising, having been reconfigured as representative types. The multiculturalism that we find in media and education is finely managed, in contrast to the cultures composing civil society, which resist comparable management.

A growing body of critical theory locates mass culture – and not the *Bildungsroman* – as one of the possible sources of individual development, accentuating the possibility of personal interpretation in the heterotopia of multiple stimuli. Would mass culture thus make education less potent, less critical, if not altogether redundant? If the mass culture of today is eclectic, relativistic, and even self-aware enough to be truly broad-based across different social classes, are calls for a return to community also a return (or potentially a regression) to earlier social configurations? I believe this question lurks behind Karatani's dissatisfaction with literature's fragmentation. If escapist, sensationalist literature earns the label of being un-aesthetic because it does not serve nation-building, there is an implicit countermovement in Karatani's argument to redraw imagination in the service of forging social and political bonds. But once bonds are loosened, then, as his analysis recognizes, imagination loses its cachet as an instrument of social cohesion, signalling the self-destructive tendencies of humankind towards apocalyptic scenarios such as climate crisis and nuclear war.

It is telling that the privileged classes are the ones most threatened by globalization, since culture is no longer their exclusive preserve. We may discern two contradictory pulls in the argument about literary education as *Bildung*, or development: the first calls for an education that restores the stability of community; the second urges resistance to protectionism against globalization of all kinds, even if such protectionism is to be found only in community, for, presumably, the goal of literary studies is to recuperate the primacy of individual development and interpretation. This residual tension can be understood as a colonial legacy whose reach extended into the transformation of modern education into the twenty-first century.

Postcolonialism is often understood to be grounded in a politicized subjectivity. Yet, for all the revisionist understanding of postcoloniality, its impact on literary studies has yet to be fully understood from a perspective that examines the emergence of new notions of literary subjectivity. I suggest that these new conceptions cannot simply be understood in the reductive terms of Caliban writing back, nor of hybridity, mimicry, or other such notions of secular, urban cosmopolitanism, which still imply an anchoring in the institutional spaces created by colonialism. If, for the sake of argument, one defines subjectivity as a return to the past and to the self, one might in fact see that literary studies retains a commitment to literary subjectivity not encompassed by political criticism, as borne out by the still-evolving field of postcolonial studies. To talk about literature as a retreat into self-scrutiny may appear a regressive move, at odds perhaps with the political agenda of postcolonial studies.[9] After all, the traditional view of literature as apolitical has given humanism its abiding exclusivity, with its premise that literature influences public life when it is most withdrawn from politics, public life being defined in terms of morality and civility. The conflict Karatani experiences about the end of literature exposes the glaring contradictions of humanism itself, which centres its values in an apolitical stance.

Does an apolitical literature then signify a return to the values of humanism? That would seem to be one possible conclusion. But is it the only one? Humanism's antithesis might well be the contemporary literary marketplace. Karatani reserves his most scathing criticism for the culprits who hasten literature's end by promoting the false narrative that literature is alive and well, using the literary marketplace as evidence of its commercial viability. Literature's resilience has less to do with its intrinsic value than its usefulness for capitalist money-making through sales, celebrity-author events, and branding. Does this mean, then, that literature must be disengaged from value (i.e. be irrelevant) to merit its continued existence?

The cultural critic Simon During addresses this question through a reading of Peter Carey's *Oscar and Lucinda*, one of the postcolonial adaptations I mentioned earlier. During argues that when literature retreats from politics and is marginalized because it is presumably

9 Ian Hunter, 'Literary Theory in Civil Life', *South Atlantic Quarterly*, 95:4 (1996): 1099–134.

ineffectual and devalued in society, what it loses is not so much an engagement with the world but, rather, its institutional base.[10] The formalized world of the institution contains a paralysed politics, even as it appears to open up a space for asserting the claims of identity through its agency. Marginalized and devalued, literature paradoxically reinforces literary subjectivity in the fantasy space of wonder. Wonder, unlike tradition, has no institutional home, no anchoring mechanism that channels its expression in specifiable ways. It does not require a structure of reference and intertextuality to construe its meaning – indeed, wonder thwarts all identification with systematized forms of knowledge. It is from this non-institutional site that literary criticism can perhaps be its most vigorous and emancipatory, its driving force being an imagination put in the service of crafting a new literary subjectivity that includes, but also, at the same time, goes beyond, ideological critique.[11]

This may seem an unsettling conclusion after the confrontational polemics of the past several decades, which arguably have produced significant changes in rethinking literary studies. It might even appear reactionary after the interventions made in the academy, which have resulted in a widening of the curriculum to include the works of marginalized groups. Yet what I see occurring in recent years is an attempt to disengage literature from humanism while, at the same time, resisting the reduction of literature to a purely sociological entity subordinate to the compulsions of identity politics. The search for a postcolonial subjectivity beyond the recalcitrant Caliban is certainly part of that attempt. But even more insistent is a will to repair the divide between imagination and criticism that has split the field of literary studies – a reparative effort that also animates Karatani's thinking about imagination as a crucible of meaning, when he pointedly notes that poetics existed before literary criticism. It is worth recalling that the

---

10 Simon During, 'Literary Subjectivity', *Ariel: A Review of International English Literature*, 31:1–2 (January–April 2000): 33–50.

11 Karatani alludes to interiority as an engine of meaning in his seminal 1993 book, where he writes: 'it was the familiar naked ("realistic") face that emerged at this time as something that conveyed meaning, and that meaning – to be precise – was "interiority". Interiority was not something that had always existed, but only appeared as a result of the inversion of a semiotic constellation' (Kojin Karatani, *Origins of Modern Japanese Literature*, ed. and trans. Brett de Bary (Duke University Press, 1993), 57).

psychological scars postcolonial studies now bear are similar to those borne by literary studies in its formative years, when literary function vacillated between society and self as the primary object of study – a tension that persists in the transition of the *Bildungsroman* in postcolonial adaptations. If there is anything one can learn from the institutional history of the discipline, it is this lesson: amid the growing utilitarian pressures to make literature responsive to practical social needs, literature acquired an identity akin to that of history as a form of knowledge about social process and event.

Karatani might agree that we are now at a point where imagination is once again contested as a reliable key to social knowledge. One reason why it becomes so important to look at the processes of institutionalization is that we may thereby also understand the points at which unaccommodated experiential knowledge is disciplined into literary sensibilities, forging a particular conception of selfhood and society. It thus becomes imperative to focus on the work of education – involving reader *and* text, and the social world imagined in acts of interpretation taking place in the classroom – before we can even begin to talk about literary value, let alone its ending.

Ends Without Ends: Kojin Karatani and the Death and Afterlife of Literature

Andrew Gibson

In the West, and perhaps especially in anglophone circles, the idea of the death of literature (which usually in effect means modern literature), or of a specific genre implying the death of literature, has been around for a very long time. In the first instance, it was a postwar idea. Its classic early statement is Adorno's assertion, in an essay written in 1949, published in 1951: 'To write poetry after Auschwitz is a barbarism.'[1] The general point behind Adorno's particular one remains current several decades later. The focus of John Barth's 1967 essay 'The Literature of Exhaustion', for instance, might seem literary and aesthetic: the tradition of the novel – the significant genre for Barth was the same as for Karatani – notably the realist novel, was by now exhausted. Imitation-authors found themselves left to write novels that were self-conscious imitations of novels. The genre was doomed to self-reflexivity. But underneath that was the larger fear that 'the novel, if not narrative literature generally, if not the printed word altogether, has by this hour of the world just about shot its bolt'; and under that was a grim sense of Barth's of 'an age of ultimacies and "final solutions" . . . in everything from weaponry to theology'.[2] The assertion both looked back to the war and was overshadowed by the Cold War and the

1 Theodor Adorno, 'Kulturkritik und Gesellschaft', in *Prismen: Kulturkritik und Gesellschaft* (Suhrkamp, 1955), 26. Except where otherwise specified, all translations are my own.

2 See John Barth, 'The Literature of Exhaustion', *Atlantic*, August 1967: 30, 32.

possibility of nuclear wipeout. The end of the novel was imminent; but then so, perhaps, was the end of many other things, if not everything. The same conviction underlies responses to what are perhaps the most cited examples of literary 'ultimacy' in the '50s and '60s, Beckett's postwar prose and the *nouveau roman*. The concept of the end of literature does not emerge in France as arrestingly as it does elsewhere, perhaps because literature has long been a more philosophical term there, or at least more of a subject for philosophical discourse. But the 'anti-novels' of the '50s and '60s caused sufficient stir for Claude Mauriac, for example, to hail the arrival of what he called an 'aliterature' superseding literature itself.[3]

Elsewhere, throughout the first three postwar decades, books with titles suggesting the death of literature, or the death or imminent crisis of a particular but, to a greater or lesser extent, putatively representative genre, kept appearing: *The Death of Tragedy*, *The Survival of Poetry*.[4] We might expect this critical orientation to have come to an end itself with the end of the Cold War. In fact, however, it takes on a whole new lease of life in the '80s and '90s, above all in the US. Cultural conservatives like E. D. Hirsch and Allan Bloom deplored what they took to be a culture lapsing into philistinism if not illiteracy that, as a result, risked condemning literature – for Bloom, admittedly, a select category – to oblivion.[5] Closer to one strand of Karatani's argument, in *The Western Canon: The Books and School of the Ages*, Harold Bloom expressed a fear that the universal media 'will cancel the literary canon once and for all'.[6] So too, he suggested, a different kind of threat was also coming from political correctness: feminists, Afro-American critics, postcolonialists, and theorists, notably deconstructionists (whom Allan Bloom thought of, banally, as relativists). Not surprisingly, for American minds, the issue of the death of literature had chiefly to do with the state of the

3 Claude Mauriac, *The New Literature*, trans. Samuel I. Stone (George Brasiller, 1959). The English title fails to grasp the meaning of the French one, *L'Alittérature contemporaine*.

4 George Steiner, *The Death of Tragedy* (Oxford University Press, 1961); and Martin Dodsworth (ed.), *The Survival of Poetry* (Faber & Faber, 1970).

5 See E. D. Hirsch, *Cultural Literacy: What Every American Needs to Know* (Houghton Mifflin, 1987); and Allan Bloom, *The Closing of the American Mind: How Higher Education Has Failed Democracy and Impoverished the Souls of Today's Students* (Simon and Schuster, 1987).

6 Harold Bloom, *The Western Canon: The Books and School of the Ages* (Harcourt Brace, 1994), 310.

academy, mainly English departments. Their principal concern was the institutional status of literature, now, it seemed, in serious peril.

But the book that perhaps summed up the post–Cold War turn in the US came at the turn of the '90s. For all its limitations, Alvin Kernan's *The Death of Literature* should have a brief paragraph to itself.[7] To a large extent, Kernan's targets are familiar from Hirsch and the Blooms: technology and mediatization; US-dominated postmodern liberalism or the 'woke' agenda (as it had yet to be named; Kernan incidentally reminds us that the 'woke' battles of today are actually replications – often rather poor ones – of similar debates thirty or more years ago, a fact which brusquely disqualifies 'woke' presentism); and theory, particularly deconstruction (assimilable to and widely assimilated by postmodern liberalism, whereas, say, structuralism was much closer to a radical European politics, as in the analysis of mythologies, notably in the work of Roland Barthes).[8] All these and other factors, wrote Kernan, in an odd equation, have spelt the collapse of literature like 'the industrial cities of the rust-belt'.[9] But what he also wants to argue is that the disappearance of what was once called literature from what he calls the knowledge-tree would leave a significant empty space. We need new, imaginative means of filling it. The natural metaphor is misleading, however, which further illuminates Kernan's position. The tree has already become a product, 'the academic table of organization'.[10] Kernan's tree is, in fact, a system of compartments designating subject areas or disciplines. It resembles a real tree less than a faculty building on a US campus. The question for Kernan, as for the Blooms, is not really the possible survival of literature *per se*, but whether it can survive within the hyper-professionalized institution of the American university, and only that. As Karatani well knows, institutional survival is not how the issue would primarily, necessarily present itself elsewhere. I shall not present it that way either.

Initially at least, then, for all its Japanese particularities, once placed in the Western context I have just outlined, Karatani's declaration in 2005 of the end of modern literature seems like the culmination of a critical

7 Alvin Kernan, *The Death of Literature* (Yale University Press, 1990).

8 See for instance Roland Barthes, *Mythologies* (Éditions du Seuil, 1957).

9 Kernan, *Death of Literature*, 210.

10 Ibid., 200.

tradition. However, he adds a crucial and, surely, convincing historical specification, which I reproduce with one or two elaborations below. If literature has little or no influence today, if there are 'few people nowadays who believe literature is important', as Karatani says,[11] this is inseparable from a development specifically from the 1980s. When Karatani says that literature was crucial to the formation of national identity and to rooting it in place, again, he is right. In England, there is even a simple and special use of the indefinite article, 'a literature', which simply designates nationality. To take English literature as our example for a moment: Irishman James Joyce marvellously and heretically suggested, in 1912, against all the spiritualized and grandiose conceptions of the tradition of English literature then current, that it is only with Daniel Defoe that 'the true English spirit begins to appear in literature'. Before that, it was a European tradition 'schooled' by European masters. Shakespeare himself was an 'Italianate Englishman'.[12] English literature proper begins with the nation-state, the fiction of racial distinction, the imperial project, mercantilism, and the rise of the English petite bourgeoisie. Clearly enough, as Karatani says, the novel is crucial in this.[13] So it is again, 200 years later, in Russia: what fired all those great Russian novelists of the nineteenth century, if not the question of the identity, the future, the very soul of Russia itself? 'Rus, whither art thou racing', where are you going, as Gogol asks.[14] Defoe and Gogol were European equivalents of Karatani's Meiji 20s. But, as Karatani argues, the process of establishing, of imagining national identities is now closed, other than as a poor simulacrum, though there are many such simulacra at the current time. It is unthinkable, in this respect, that literature might resume its former role.

Globalization since the '80s has been the principal recent instrument of such a closure. The context for it, however much resurgent if trivial nationalisms presently appear to say the opposite, is global (though in

11 Karatani, 'The End of Modern Literature', in this volume, 25. Further references appear in the text.

12 James Joyce, 'Realism and Idealism in English Literature (Daniel Defoe – William Blake)', in *Occasional, Critical, and Political Writing*, ed. Kevin Barry (Oxford University Press, 2000), 164.

13 For Defoe and the rise of the English novel, see Ian Watt, *The Rise of the Novel* (Penguin, 1972).

14 Nikolay Gogol, *Dead Souls*, trans. Robert A. Maguire (Penguin, 2004), 283.

the US, with the early dominance there of mass culture and the media, as Karatani notes, one sees it earlier). By globalization, of course, I do not mean a gripping new form of internationalism rightly aspiring to the creation of a new kind of global community. I mean an economic and cultural order which is that of particular kinds of business and commerce and which has tended to bring with it certain forms of widespread political, economic, and cultural hegemony. Commentators have recently been announcing the end of the globalizing fantasy in a splintering and supposedly now more dangerous world.[15] But from the multinational corporations to the practical ubiquity of the internet, the global dominance of Facebook and its like, the omnipresence of advertising and the language of the markets, and the total absence of any serious and persuasive political thought or political alternative that can command mass support, it is clear that the hold of globalization is proving tenacious. Yet, at the same time, it is by now a semblance, an empty thing, a thing of shreds and patches. We nonetheless remain within the period constituted by globalization, and – an argument well made in the work of Wolfgang Streeck[16] – there is no other in sight.

The reference to globalization is important because of what Karatani says about literature and the imagination of national identity. But, at the same time, we might want to turn to a different term: neoliberalism. Neoliberalism, or, rather, neoliberal culture, since some now argue that neoliberalism too, in the strict economic sense of the word, has reached an end.[17] But, as with globalization, we are left confronting another ending that is not one. In Streeck's words, neoliberal culture 'has entered a period of deep *indeterminacy*' and 'severe crisis', a 'prolonged period of social entropy' in which 'different disorders coexist and . . . reinforce each other' and 'pathological phenomena of the most diverse sort come into existence'. If contemporary capitalism is disintegrating, it is not as the result of any serious struggle organized by opponents: 'we see no

15 For one among various instances, see Stephen D. King, *Grave New World: The End of Globalization, the Return of History* (Yale University Press, 2017).

16 See Wolfgang Streeck, *How Will Capitalism End? Essays on a Failing System* (Verso, 2016), passim.

17 See, for example, Joseph E. Stiglitz, 'The End of Neoliberalism and the Rebirth of History', *Project Syndicate*, 4 November 2019, project-syndicate.org, last accessed 9 July 2024; and Wendy Brown, *In the Ruins of Neoliberalism: The Rise of Antidemocratic Politics in the West* (Columbia University Press, 2019).

successor approaching'.[18] There 'is no new social order waiting to succeed it'.[19] Neoliberal culture is certainly not at an end, as a short list of some of its specific features makes very evident: the existence of a plutocracy, a particular understanding of 'meritocracy', managerialism, various forms of populism, relentless boosterism or the promulgation of empty positivities, the exclusive understanding of the human thing as, in Foucault's terms, *homo economicus*, technologization of the whole, the absolute and overriding imperatives of consumerism and 'growth', the equally absolute prioritizations of entertainment and the pleasure principle, among others.[20] Karatani specifies the 1980s – the decade of the Thatcherite and Reaganite project, precisely when neoliberal culture became properly visible as such – as the beginning of the death of literature. Neoliberal culture is the culture that remains ours today, whether neoliberalism *per se* is dying a death or not.

What has neoliberal culture meant for literary, intellectual, and scholarly life? First, it has spelt the devaluation of learning, the more serious university disciplines, and the supposed intellectual and scholarly 'elites' who were proponents of both (not to be confused with financial, business, political, media, technological, and entertainment elites, which triumphed precisely at the expense of the former ones). The devaluation of literature went hand in hand with the triumph of neoliberalism, above all in the US and UK, long bastions of neoliberal orthodoxy and a range of phenomena associated with it. Secondly, one of Karatani's more remarkable observations is that the fetishization of *l'écriture*, writing, as in Barthes and Derrida, really did turn out to be a

18 Compare and contrast Immanuel Wallerstein, who thinks we are in for a long period of disintegration – but asserts that socialism must eventually prevail. Immanuel Wallerstein, *The Essential Wallerstein* (New Press, 2000), 111, 203.

19 Streeck, *How Will Capitalism End?*, 12–13, 367.

20 For an excellent account of how the valuation of 'meritocracy' worked in a particular phase of UK history, see John Beck, *Meritocracy, Citizenship and Education: New Labour's Legacy* (Continuum, 2008); for an equally excellent critique of managerialism, see Thomas Klikauer, *Managerialism: A Critique of an Ideology* (Palgrave Macmillan, 2013). On *homo economicus*, see Michel Foucault, *The Birth of Biopolitics: Lectures at the Collège de France, 1978–1979*, ed. Michel Senellart and trans. Graham Burchell, foreword François Ewald and Alessandro Fontana (Palgrave Macmillan, 2008). For a helpful spin on the term *Homo psycho-economicus*, designating 'a new model of subjectivity' specifically emerging under neoliberalism, see William Davies, *The Limits of Neoliberalism: Authority, Sovereignty and the Logic of Competition*, foreword Aditya Chakrabortty (revd edn, Sage, 2017).

symptom of the end of literature, as they suggested it would, if in ways they certainly did not envisage, that it was part of the same process of winding up. In neoliberal culture, writing takes the place of literature. Though, as Karatani says, there may still be an illusion of a flourishing literature – 'it is those people whose very existence attests to the death of literature who have been asserting this sort of nonsense' (41) – in the sense that, as faculties of letters dwindle and disappear, schools of creative writing grow ever larger and flourish ever more conspicuously. This is an essential aspect of what he seeks to pinpoint. Writing, 'creative writing', is seldom if ever literature. Though here and there we may encounter humbling contemporary contributions to what used to be called literature (Sebald, Morrison, Coetzee, Jelinek, Ernaux, Ferrante), the motivation for the great contemporary demand for creative writing courses has come, at least in certain measure, from business and commerce. Their interests are intimately allied with 'writing'. The word 'creative' in 'creative writing' has no more depth and resonance than it does in the term 'creative industries'. 'Creativity' itself is by now a neoliberal alibi, a means of persuading us that neoliberalism is not only a form of progress but also on the side of emergence *ex nihilo*, when in fact its interests are clear and determined from the start. Karatani is altogether right: 'it is nothing but an illusion if you expect any possibilities of new literature in *writing*'.

One aspect of this is that we live in an age of 'me-writing' as produced by subjects under the neoliberal version of democracy; hence the currency of the memoir. Work that might once have laid claim to the status of literature abandons all hope of achieving what was one of major literature's great ambitions: to speak of the world, to the world. Take, for instance, what Georg Lukács saw in the great realists, a grasp of 'the world-historical'.[21] This, while thinkable, is no longer possible. One sees the decline of letters taking place particularly in the UK, all the more so given the extent to which it was for so long a bulwark for literature and literary criticism. Indeed, Karatani precisely anticipated what one now hears coming from everywhere, whether it be the US, Japan, the UK, or Australia: a fear of the imminent death of the humanities. There is a kind of resonant – if bleak – self-evidence to the logic here: in an age of

21 See Georg Lukács, *The Historical Novel*, trans. Hannah Mitchell and Stanley Mitchell, pref. Fredric Jameson (University of Nebraska Press, 1983).

hyper-capital, hyper-mediatization, and the seemingly total victory of neoliberal modes of thought, what should we expect if not threats to the humanities that seem to go hand in hand with the destruction of the climate, the environment, natural life, and possibly, in the end, the human thing itself, in a process that has unconscionably and exponentially sped up in the global, neoliberal phase of economics and culture?[22] One need not be a humanist to feel that the final demise of what went under the name of the humanities will be a disaster; though, as Karatani also, in effect, says, there will be more important disasters to worry about. There already are.

As I have said, from a Western point of view, Karatani might seem to come at the end of a recent tradition, restating its terms for a neoliberal age. But he does not adopt the spiritualized *Weltschmerz* of the postwar and Cold War pessimists. Nor does he – like the American traditionalists of the '90s – lay responsibility for the death of literature at the door of (certain kinds of) literary theory and criticism. Rather, the death of literature is also the death of literature about literature, of literary theory and criticism. He might at least seem to coincide with the cultural conservatives of the late twentieth century in asserting that, in our age, 'the superiority of print culture and the novel, which was originally introduced by way of the novelty of letterpress technology, has come to an end' because of the rise of cinema and then, later, new media such as 'television, video, and the digitalization of audiovisual information by the computer' (38). But if he takes the media and new technology to task, he also recognizes their particularity in a specific economic order determining their precise and limited forms. He is not a technophobe. So too, if he is concerned with the institutional death of literature, his understanding of this process also has to do with a public sphere, a reading public. His departure from the professional American academics is especially pronounced here. His perspectives are those of what they might call an organic intellectual who gets his orientation partly from a community beyond the walls of the academy.

22 This is starkly represented in the graphs in the *Anthropocene Review* for 2015, which show all the key features of anthropogenic change and its more recent causes steepling from the mid-twentieth century. See anthropocene.info/great-acceleration.php, last accessed 9 July 2024; also in Erle C. Ellis, *Anthropocene: A Very Short Introduction* (Oxford University Press, 2018), 54–5.

But none of these points really takes us to the heart of what differentiates him from the Western minds I have mentioned. That is captured in the last few sentences of his essay: 'even if modern literature has come to an end, the movements of capitalism and the state that determine us are not over. They will survive even after they have destroyed all human and natural environments. Within this situation, we have to keep resisting. In this regard, however, I no longer expect anything from literature' (55). These sentences are key, and I shall come back to them. Karatani's argument hinges throughout – rightly – on a dissociation from what, certainly in Western terms, has been half a century of literary theory and criticism that thought and, in effect, declared that we could still have expectations of literature and criticism, that they could stand in for politics, that to commit oneself to a supposedly 'radical' literary criticism was to be political, and that such criticism was sufficiently political in itself. This has specifically been the case in a neoliberal culture lacking any full, rich sense of putatively achievable 'radical' goals, still more any sense of how to reach them, as opposed to a culture like Brecht's or Benjamin's, or indeed, to some extent, Barthes's – volatile cultures in which serious and opposed political alternatives confronted one another. Karatani sees this kind of 'radical' thinking as Sartrean in origin. For Sartre, it is when revolutionary politics grows conservative that literature can offer what 'is essentially the subjectivity of a society in permanent revolution' (32), rather than when such politics has come to seem impotent or inexistent – when it has, in effect, been hammered into the ground, as under neoliberal culture.[23] Karatani cites, as an example of the justice of the Sartrean case, a time in South Korea when political movements were impossible in reality and when literature therefore undertook all of the substitutive roles.

Here another significant post-Marxist philosopher – one more or less contemporary with Karatani – Jacques Rancière, seems relevant. To quote a comparatively early title of Rancière's (partly borrowed in fact from Hölderlin's elegy 'Brot und Wein'), *Pourquoi des poètes en temps de détresse*:[24] why turn to poets, to literature, in politically distressed times?

23 Karatani is quoting Deleuze quoting Sartre. See Gilles Deleuze, 'He Was My Teacher', in *Desert Islands and Other Texts, 1953–1974*, ed. David Lapoujade and trans. Michael Taormina (Semiotexte, 2004), 78.

24 Jacques Rancière (ed.), *La Politique des poètes: Pourquoi les poètes en temps de détresse* (Albin Michel, 1992).

Rancière has long been telling us. Literature confuses different worlds and obscures the frontiers between them, blurring all hierarchies of subjects and publics. It offers itself to *n'importe qui*, anyone at all, indifferently. This, its democratic and egalitarian essence, its abiding promise, has a basis in historical specifics and conditions. But the literary work can offer its promise only because of its heteronomy, because it expresses both the disposition of the community from which it springs and the possibility of a free community which may seem more or less practicable according to circumstances. Literature holds out an abiding promise of a community to come because it is literature, but also because it is not just literature. It 'constructs the forms of a world to come in the interior of an existing world'.[25] In *La Mésentente*, Rancière discusses Karatani's beloved Kant, for instance, and the figure of the royal palace, which, for Kant, can be an object of aesthetic pleasure irrespective of its symbolic value, uses, or associations (power, wealth, privilege, injustice, and so on).[26] But though the pleasure in question is, in principle, available to all, and therefore projects a conception of an aesthetic community to which such associations can be a matter of indifference, it also projects a certain idea of a historical community, to which they cannot be. Literature exists precisely to bridge that gap, to summon or urge the historical community towards the aesthetic one.

Though it is unlikely to appeal to left intellectuals, one might I suppose reply that, first, historical experience has by now very firmly told us that, save in rare and unpredictable circumstances, among certain individuals and limited groups, the community has shown as much as it needs to of its indifference to the summons; and, secondly, this indifference is quite extraordinarily clear in the community's massive turn away from literature and towards media. If, as Rancière says, the aesthetic community is universal in intention, if it includes the *sans-part*, those without a stake, but therefore remains a virtual community, there is only meagre, scattered, and very sporadic evidence that the *sans-part* can be brought to care or to act with major consequences. But there is a sober, austere Rancière who knows that if literature promises the possession of a new world, it does so in a work that the subject 'cannot possess in any way'. It remains powerless, unworldly, remote.

25 Jacques Rancière, *Malaise dans l'esthétique* (Galilée, 2004), 65.

26 Jacques Rancière, *La Mésentente: Politique et philosophie* (Galilée, 1995).

Literature promotes the hallucination of 'a political accomplishment that it cannot satisfy'.[27] A gulf inexorably yawns between the anticipation of a future and its realization, between promise and fulfilment, constituting the significance and the limit of the literary realm. Rancière explores this gulf most fully in later work, notably the third chapter of *Le Spectateur émancipé*.[28] Here, literature changes 'the cartography of the perceptible, the thinkable, and the feasible', allowing for 'new modes of political construction of common subjects and new possibilities of collective enunciation'. It 'dis-identifies' the subject (strips it of its prior identifications). It points beyond 'political subjectification' to new modes of individuation that 'cancel any [prior] form of it', but these, again, are rare and unpredictable.[29] Dis-identification is not controllable. It may be one of literature's great virtues, but there is no reason why, on that basis, it should bring about 'either an understanding of the state of the world' or 'a significant decision to change it'. Underlying Rancière's thought, though he denies it himself, there is a distinct melancholy.

For Rancière, the subject of literature is promised a new world but also denied any knowledge of the means by which that world might be realized. Karatani, it seems to me, has become dismissive of the potential quietism of such a position. But the quality, seriousness, and complexity of Rancière's thought tend to shield it from too harsh a critique. The same cannot be said of what I take to be Karatani's major antagonist: a criticism which, since the late 1960s, has more or less explicitly been telling us that, in effect, under neoliberalism, radical politics as literary criticism is *political enough*. Karatani wants to put paid to that assumption. If he took it seriously in the past, he has long ceased to do so. Literature, then, is not a vehicle for politics at a time when politics itself has failed or been set in abeyance. Indeed, there is no need to force literature to provide us with an ethics or a politics. That, however, is because 'there are many things that are far more important than literature' (32). Karatani cites the novelist Arundhati Roy, who, when asked why she no longer wrote

27 Jacques Rancière, 'The Aesthetic Revolution and Its Outcomes', *New Left Review*, 14 (2002): 150.

28 Jacques Rancière, *Le Spectateur émancipé* (La Fabrique, 2008), 51–82, from which all the following quotations in the paragraph are taken.

29 For Rancière on rarity, see for example *La Mésentente*: 'Politics in its specificity is rare. It is always local and occasional. Its actual eclipse is quite real, and there exists no political science capable of defining its future', 188.

novels, replied that she only wrote when she felt the necessity, that one can quite plausibly claim not to have the leisure time to produce novels in an epoch of crisis like our own. There are more important things to do. If literature and literary criticism are (more or less) dead, that is because, in neoliberal culture, they no longer have the slightest political weight. Indeed, has 'the politics of literature' over the past forty years not turned out to be an alibi and a cover for political impotence and despair? There are certainly coherent and demonstrable reasons for such a syndrome. But without this alibi they might at least have emerged from their hiding places and manifested themselves for what they are, as opposed to retreating behind a drastically implausible, abstract optimism that, in reality, is merely a second-order replication of empty neoliberal positivities. This is just one of the various denials to which neoliberalism has habituated us. Again and again, at the present time, under the infinite boosterism of commerce, advertising, and promotionalism, on the one hand, and, on the other, of contemporary 'leftism', postmodern liberalism, and the endless discourse of rights – (to which Pascal offers a riveting response: 'There is the origin and image of the usurpation of the whole world'[30]) – one hears the accents of a largely unacknowledged but profound political surrender.

So it is not by chance that the specific idea of resistance appears in the passage from the end of Karatani's essay. Karatani is actually addressing the myriad calls to 'resistance' that we have heard *ad nauseam* in literary (and cultural) theory and criticism over the past few decades. If we do indeed still need serious political resistance, it will not take literary and literary-critical forms, as has repeatedly been asserted. Karatani, again, is right about this; at the same time, however, I shall finally argue that this does not mean that we should dispense entirely with the space that literature has always opened up. We need a different thought about literature, a different conception of it that is neither quite Karatani's nor Rancière's, though one that can only be a very modest supplement.

To begin to work towards that conception: I have two initial reservations about Karatani's case. First: in Karatani's terms, 'literature' existed before modernity, but it was a category that did not include the novel. It is primarily in the novel that modernity discovers an epistemological

30 Blaise Pascal, *Pensées*, ed. Gérard Ferreyrolles (Livres de Poche, 2000), 55.

and indeed moral dimension related to a new privilege afforded to sensibility, and with it, literature properly speaking. The end of literature is therefore inextricable from the end of modernity and the end of the novel. But the focus primarily on the modern novel is a vestige of Karatani's Marxist inheritance. One finds it, for example, in Lukács, in Ernst Fischer, even, to a large extent, in Eagleton and Jameson. The novel is the great modern genre, because it does sociology differently and is therefore political. But in Europe at least, from the extraordinarily widespread enthusiasm for the poetry of, say, Goethe, Pushkin, Chateaubriand, Byron, Tennyson, and others in the nineteenth century; to the fact that Hugo was and still is most famous as a poet in France; to (a very different kind of evidence) the pre-eminence of poetry in literature syllabi in England right through to the 1960s; there is much to suggest that Karatani's is something of a retrospective construction, that the supremacy or centrality of the novel was, until the later twentieth century, at least fitful and contested. One could make out a similar case relative to theatre, albeit in a different way, be it founded on Goethe and Schiller, Ibsenism, the Abbey Theatre in Ireland, Mayakovsky, or Brecht and revolutionary theatre.

My argument is not that, after all, Karatani has essentially got things wrong. But questions of nationhood and what Karatani calls the 'empathic community' are also intrinsic to the work of the poets I mentioned. Chateaubriand, Pushkin, Hugo, and Tennyson precisely created 'empathic' national 'communities', and powerful ones, too. The extraordinary appeal of Goethe to the nineteenth century has to do partly with the intensity with which he poses a national question or questions in a manner that seems like a beacon light to other minds from other emergent nations. One sees something like the same preoccupation with the national question in Ibsen, and, more obliquely, in the nineteenth-century German obsession with Homer on the one hand and Shakespeare on the other, precisely as the most eminent of national poets, and therefore exemplary.

My revised version of Karatani's case, then, is, first, that the end he crucially proclaims is the end not especially of modern literature as superlatively evident in the novel, but of literature itself as a modern concept and the values attached to it. In that respect, at least, the American traditionalists and humanists were right, and not surprisingly, since the crisis for the humanities appears earliest and most vividly in the US precisely because literature was less deeply rooted there, and new cultural forms were able to displace it much more easily. Once we broaden our understanding of the term 'literature', however, it is clear that the end of literature becomes, at one and the same time, more imposing and more fluid. Fluid, in that if we take full account of literature as a collection of different genres – epic poetry, lyric poetry, tragedy, comedy and their various descendants, the novella, the short story, indeed the many and varied forms of serious literary theory and criticism – it is clearly impossible to think of it as a single, homogenous entity with a single history and therefore a single death. Rather, the decline and death of literature is multiple, variegated, takes place at different points and speeds, and is much more decisive and certain in some instances (and some places) than others. There is therefore a kind of indeterminacy to the end. I shall come back to its implications.

Secondly: I could have addressed the question of the end of literature by focusing on developments in England, much as Karatani tends to focus on developments in Japan. But I did not want to do that, because I did not want to risk turning in a direction that, in Karatani's essay, is theoretical and methodological together. My difference with Karatani is with the place and importance assigned in his argument to the chronological tableau, the historical diagram. As is clear enough elsewhere in his work, Karatani has a certain need to grid history in terms of sets of categories systematically arranged in relation to one another. This is surely another aspect of his Marxist inheritance. In Karatani's case, the inheritance involves taxonomy and classification of a kind that pushes him close to, say, Jameson. For Jameson's 'Always historicize!' also means 'Always introduce the abstract category or class between historical materialism and material history.' So too, insofar as he is up to a certain point a historical materialist, Karatani is tempted partly to identify historical materialism with a work of classification. But historical materialism can avail itself of taxonomic principles and descriptions without giving them priority or turning them into final or total explanations. There are different historical materialisms that allocate different proportions to the theoretical and empirical domains. Can we really convincingly grid historical processes in all their complexity as Karatani seeks to do? How definitive, to take a single example, can the dividing line be, as in Karatani's essay, between a period distinguished by the nation-state on the one hand and the novel on the other from a period distinguished by socialism and fascism, on the one hand, and the cinema, on the other, when the second period sees the appearance of great novels of an emergent national consciousness, most notably *Ulysses*? When the same period sees the appearance of great epics of the new nations in the cinema, notably in the work of Griffith and Eisenstein? When what Karatani calls the later period of the welfare state on the one hand and television on the other nonetheless sees the emergence of a fabulous, multifaceted, if austere national epic in the cinema of Rossellini?

My point is not, however, that we can readily or indeed should dispense with periodizations. They are too important as steps towards understanding. This essay began with a few, and even with suggestions of grids. This was notably the case with neoliberalism. But there, precisely, my case was that, for the moment, neoliberalism looks as though it is reaching an ending that is not one. In larger terms, the categories of the grids in fact loosen, and then they bleed into each other. My primary intention is not to pick holes in Karatani's historical schema, but to raise a question that any such schema raises. Here, if anywhere, deconstruction seems to matter. Deconstruction sometimes seemed especially interesting and fertile when posing questions for historical thought. Again and again, whether in *The Truth of Painting*, *Specters of Marx*, 'Living On', or 'Of an Apocalyptic Tone Recently Adopted in Philosophy', Derrida problematizes the border, the edge, the boundary, the frame, the dividing line without which the category as such loses its clarity.[31] So too, as he also suggests, there has always been a problem of 'the jurisdiction of frames' too little explored by 'the institution of literary studies'. Dividing lines cannot properly be established other than provisionally and, in a sense, ironically, because, as Derrida puts it, 'no context is saturable any more'; there is no plenitude of homogenous and unitary meaning that exists within the frame, that insists that the border or frame can remain unblurred. In another phrase of Derrida's that comes to mind, there is no 'shoreline' that is not overflowed and does not disappear, if only to reappear. There is always an overrun, a

31 Jacques Derrida, *The Truth in Painting*, trans. Geoffrey Bennington and Ian MacLeod (University of Chicago Press, 1987); *Specters of Marx: The State of the Debt, the Work of Mourning and the New International*, trans. Peggy Kamuf, introd. Bernd Manus and Stephen Cullenberg (Routledge, 1994); 'Of an Apocalyptic Tone Recently Adopted in Philosophy', trans. John P. Leavey, Jr, *Semeia*, 23 (1982): 63–97; and 'Living On', trans. James Hulbert, in *Deconstruction and Criticism*, ed. Harold Bloom, Paul de Man, Jacques Derrida, Geoffrey Hartman, and J. Hillis Miller (Continuum, 1979), 62–142.

débordement that finally 'spoils . . . all . . . boundaries and divisions'.[32] We have just seen this in the case of some of Karatani's categories.

The concept of the end depends on and exists as one such boundary, division, border, edge, and requires deconstruction, if of a certain kind. In *Positions*, Derrida suggests that 'he does not at all believe in the simple death [or end] . . . of whatever, the book, man or god, especially since, as we all know, what is dead wields a very specific power'.[33] In deconstructing the concept of apocalypse, as he does in 'Of an Apocalyptic Tone' and elsewhere, Derrida deconstructs ends, rewrites them as ends without ends. The end overruns itself. Frank Kermode's *The Sense of an Ending* suggested that, in its full historical scope, the concept of the end or the final apocalypse can only be entertained ironically, since it repeats itself in one fiction of finality after another across the centuries. In an account particularly well adapted to the present moment, in 'La Consumation du divin' in *Politiques de l'inimitié* (2016), Achille Mbembe argues that in Greco-Judaic tradition, the history of Being is intimately tied to a thought of catastrophe.[34] The catastrophe represents the purification of Being through fire. But this is not a universally human notion. In Africa, where thought starts out not from Being but from relation, from mutual implication, history is an immense succession of paradoxical situations, of transformations without break or rupture. There are many traditions which do not think of the idea of 'the end' as being particularly important. The point is evident enough if we look at postcolonial Africa, because, for so much of it, the end has already happened. It has already happened via invasion or invasions, which do not cease. Africa belies the Western concept of the apocalypse because the apocalypse has long been its condition, the end without end. For Africa, as for South America and much of the Asian and Islamic world, for the Global South, for the non-human world at the mercy of climate change, the apocalypse is and has long been now. It has no finality.

But if the apocalypse is an unending end, if it is merely trivial and even delusional to think otherwise, then that calls the Rancièrean defence of literature into question. Literature may be a kind of lifeline to cling to

32 Derrida, 'Living On', 64, 68, 69, 70.

33 Jacques Derrida, *Positions*, trans. Alan Bass (Athlone, 1987), 6.

34 Achille Mbembe, *Politiques de l'inimitié* (La Découverte, 2016), 43–9.

through 'times of distress', but almost no time cannot be designated as such. Any break with distress is likely to prove exceedingly rare. According to Maurice Blanchot, for Hölderlin, '*The time of distress* designates the time in all times which is proper to art.'[35] There can be no guarantee that the lifeline is leading anywhere, that its existence does not merely confirm, yet again, the gulf that yawns between political hopes and political realities. In Karatani's essay, there is little if any of the residual Marxist faith in the possibility of a historical narrative that persists if obliquely in Rancière's work. I return to my earlier quotation from the essay's conclusion: 'the movements of capitalism and the state that determine us are not over. *They will survive even after they have destroyed all human and natural environments*' (my italics). This is not a recognition that dominates the essay. It appears belatedly, almost as an aside. Karatani's plea is for the overriding priority of political work: 'Within this situation, we have to keep resisting' (55). Nonetheless, at this point, his understanding of our situation is close to Mbembe's.

'Action is consolatory', wrote Joseph Conrad. 'It is the enemy of thought and the friend of flattering illusions.'[36] The starkly disabused terms in which Karatani asserts the continuing need for resistance armour him against any accusation that he is adopting a psychic defence mechanism. What price such work, however, if the enemy's power is such that it will 'survive', carry on beyond all of its most destructive consequences, and presumably beyond all opposition? What precisely is Karatani proposing, by way of counterweight? I am tempted to hear the grim, tight-lipped tone of Golz, general on the Republican side in the Spanish Civil War, admirably but tragically resigned to disaster, in Hemingway's *For Whom the Bell Tolls*: '*Bon. Nous ferons notre petit possible*.'[37] Is Karatani not apparently recommending a kind of doomed, stoical gesture that may or may not be inspiriting or heroic, but certainly seems to promise nothing more? Equally, if the powerlessness of political work is so drastic, what decisively separates it from the condition of literature and literary criticism? Why be so convinced of the value of the one and the insignificance of the other?

35 Maurice Blanchot, *L'Espace littéraire* (Gallimard, 1955), 335. All quotations from *L'Espace littéraire* are from this edition and the page numbers are indicated in the text.

36 Joseph Conrad, *Nostromo* (Dent, 1950), 66.

37 Ernest Hemingway, *For Whom the Bell Tolls* (Penguin, 1969), 404.

It may be that, within the next few decades, climate change will be offering the objective proof of the gist of Conrad's assertion (in the objective disproof of the case for sustainability), that the alternatives will become a kind of action beyond action (on the one hand), and catastrophe far greater than what we already know of it (on the other). We cannot be sure yet. Karatani's thinking precisely derives from this historical moment of uncertainty. But my final point is this: Karatani seems to me to offer us a paradox: on the one hand, a serious moral decision, on the other, hard, clear-eyed acceptance of its futility. But then literature and literary theory and criticism can offer their own mode of acceptance that is nonetheless never quite conclusive, and certainly neither mere surrender nor mere passivity. One exemplar here would be Blanchot – what is, in effect, crucially, Blanchot's case for literature, literature as a kind of thought, notably in *L'Espace littéraire*.

We may begin with what, for Blanchot, is a foundational point: before the mimetic assertion – Stendhal's, for instance: 'un roman est un miroir qui se promène sur une grande route' ('the novel is a mirror walking down a highway')[38] – before all discussions of the powers and limits of representation, literature has always already turned away from the world it might seem to represent. Like the very acts of both writing and reading, the literary work at its inception is a mode of giving up on the world that becomes a mode of thought. Why would anyone read or write, if the world were a sufficient good? In Blanchot's terms, reading and writing involve a repudiation of what he calls the disaster, and the disaster is irreducibly political. What he means is beautifully summed up by a Baudelaire appalled by political developments after the 1848 revolution (my example). He commits himself to poetry and only poetry, and declares of his work that 'partout elle se fait négation de l'iniquité'.[39] Hence, his poetry uses scraps of contemporary detail, but to negate the world to which they belong. For the iniquitous world has become unworthy of representation.

So we begin with a politics of negation, of writing the world off – for Baudelaire a work requiring both moral gravity and extraordinary lucidity. The founding negation is key to Blanchot. Art, he writes, 'is the

38 Stendhal, *Le Rouge et le noir* (Garnier Flammarion, 1964), 361.

39 Charles Baudelaire, *Œuvres complètes*, ed. Claude Pichois, with Jean Ziegler (Gallimard, 1975), ii, 35.

silence or the neutralization of what is usual and immediate [*actuel*] in the world' (46). It is central to the writers to whom *L'Espace littéraire* pays most attention: Hölderlin, Mallarmé, Kafka, Rilke. Rilke, for instance, has his experience of life . . . and then turns away. Ravaged in every way by 1914–18, he has come to realize that 'there is no human world in which one could find shelter' (155). Literature must begin in an exhaustion with and of life. Kafka meant something similar when he wrote that poetry 'jumps out of the range of the murderers' (83).[40] If he tells us that he is unable 'to think, to observe, to ascertain any truth, to remember, to speak, to take part in the life of others' (67),[41] that is because he is repudiating the forms of present life that might otherwise empower him. Mallarmé, too, is concerned to get beyond a 'wrecked and abyssal present' (113). He learns that to be an artist is not to know that there already is a world. This would seem to be the very opposite of realist art. Yet Blanchot does not slight realism or representationalism. Shakespeare, Cervantes, Goethe, Balzac, Tolstoy, Dostoevsky all have parts to play in *L'Espace littéraire*. Rather, realism is a compromise by which, vainly, the writer tries to do the impossible, 'to save his relations with the world and with himself' (21). The *parole brute*, the 'crude speech', of narration and description might appear to give us things in their presence (36), but true poetry moves them away, makes them disappear, makes concretion allusive and evocative and not a mode of ascertaining things. But this distinction is superficial. Realism may call, however, for a certain mode of deconstruction which will unearth and confirm the abiding instance of pure literary space as distinct from the play of appearance that is representation.

If literary art, then, always silences that which is already given us, the *actuel*, what does it give us in return? Blanchot has various names for the literary benefaction: the interminable (16–20), the indefinite (23), the indeterminate (26), the impersonal (58), the incessant (16–20), an 'indistinct plenitude' (18), 'the errant intimacy of the outside' (14). In a way, what he means by such terms is best – most simply and clearly – exemplified in surrealism and his defence of surrealist poetry (234–40). What one learns from surrealism is that literature drastically requires 'conditions of

40 Blanchot is quoting Kafka's diary entry for 27 January 1922.
41 Blanchot is quoting Kafka's diary entry for 28 July 1914.

detachment from the solicitations of the external world' (237),[42] rather than testing 'what cannot be proved', what is never in evidence (236). In this it breaks with all the insistences of a present, choosing instead an inexhaustible inspiration which is close to the 'strangeness and measureless excessiveness of Being' (239) and is therefore indeterminate. This excess is thinkable in terms of unlimited time and history, the endless indeterminacy of historical appearance. But there is equally a profound lesson in the art of impotence, as in the case of, say, Beckett, in that the more the immediate or given world 'affirms itself as the future and the full daylight of truth, where everything will have value, bear meaning, where the whole will accomplish itself under the mastery of man and for his use' – as under neoliberalism – the more it seems that 'art must descend towards that point where nothing has sense yet, the more it matters that art maintains the movement, the insecurity, and the woe of that which escapes all grasp and all finality' (337 n. 1).

Literature does not take place 'as does any object that exists' (40).[43] Literary language has the power not to summon the world before us – the world is before us from the start – but 'to make things disappear', or, perhaps better, 'to make them appear' in the guise of 'things that have disappeared' (41). *L'Espace littéraire* has a particular concern with objects, and, more largely, a system of priorities associated with them. We make of all things objects, Blanchot writes, 'neatly closed, well-finished realities steeped in our preoccupation with finish'. But this process, which he calls 'bad transmutation' (191), is the enemy. It produces a 'bad interiority' in which 'objects reign', and, with them, 'the concern for results, the desire to have, greed that links us to possession, the need for security and stability, the tendency to know in order to be sure, the tendency to "take account" which necessarily becomes an inclination to count and to reduce everything to accounts'. This is 'the very destiny of the modern world' (177) – to the point, we might add, at which, in the age of neoliberalism, objects become the supreme talisman. In metamorphosing 'the visible into invisibility' (186), literature points us away from objectal reality, its secure forms and stable manifestations, its separate existences, its supports and assurances, actually frail as those are.

But if literature points us towards what is indeterminate, how does that

42 The quotation is from André Breton, *Entretiens 1913–52*.

43 The quotation is from Stéphane Mallarmé, letter to Francis Vielé-Griffin, 8 August 1891.

help? Is it in any way an adequate resource, above all, politically? Certainly – here Blanchot coincides with Karatani – art 'acts poorly and little' (212). But if the question at our particular historical juncture is the possibility of any thinkable historical good whatsoever, then it seems to me that Blanchot's conception of literature is very important. For the indeterminate always harbours a potential for affirmation, in that it is or conveys the absolute openness and limitless productivity of historical time. For Rilke after 1918, for example, says Blanchot, life and freedom become available again precisely out of the indeterminate. If it is that which 'moves aside the "reality" of things, that which delivers us from their weight' (209), the indeterminate is also 'the void below' (330), below events – unforeseeable, unknowable, and inexplicable as they are. In this, it anticipates a larger future. Rilke acknowledges a supreme possibility in poetry, 'the approach of grace, of the poetic opening: a relation with the Open that is finally happy' (210). In my terms, the happiness in question, inseparable from the possibility of an event, would be in itself a form of political faith.

Events: for Blanchot, the thought of them is a crucial political positive. Mallarmé testifies to a *moment de foudre*, a 'lightning moment', a brusque affirmation which 'arises neither from the assurance of stable truths, nor from the clarity of day which we have conquered, and in which living and being are accomplished in the familiarity of limited actions'. The literary work has the force of a beginning: '[t]hat the work *is* marks the *éclat*, the fulguration of a unique event of which comprehension can then take hold' (299). The event is felt again in the work's 'constant genesis', but, further than that, it is 'the thing beginning', that is, anonymous materiality beyond our grasp but present in and as the work (276, 278). This will solidify and take on an 'enduring reality' through many different historical readings determined by the movement of time, and therefore never has the status of an object. Through the work 'another time arrives within time, and in the world of beings which exist and things which subsist what arrives, like a presence, is not another world, but the other of all worlds, *that which is always other than the world*' (307; my italics). This 'other' emerges to proclaim that there is now a work – in the usual time, that is, of current truths – as an unaccustomed, unwonted occurrence which has no relation to this world and this time. The 'other' affirms nothing on the basis of familiar, present reality. It rather subtracts what is most familiar to us, while also giving history 'initiative, the possibility of a point of departure' (308). It thereby promotes 'the mirage of the inaccessible truth of the future' (309), precisely as, we should note, a mirage only. In this lies its political power.

In Heideggerian terms, then, for Blanchot, the political responsibility of literature is above all, in the most sophisticated and precise manner possible, to hold open the open, not least openness to the event, to which any given present moment or formation, inclined as it will be to close in on itself, will threaten to be obtuse, even to smother. Neoliberalism has been proving extremely effective at this. This too, to go back to Karatani's terms, requires resistance. Are there many other credible sources of political positivity around at the current time, apart from what Blanchot means by literature? Rancière, too, is concerned to hold open the open. But for Rancière (as also in the work of Alain Badiou) the open is specifiable. It breeds a valuation of definite forms which, for Rancière, are always nameable: the good community, radical democratic good, the good of the people, a return to communism, and so on. Effectively, it is a version of the Marxist vision. Blanchot cannot go so far. He does not anticipate the forms of the future in naming them. Karatani and Blanchot, in one respect, come close but do not touch, whereas Rancière seems more remote. Karatani offers us a kind of degree zero of *engagement*, which is nonetheless not nothing: one currently sees it in climate change activism, for example. Blanchot offers us an absolutely minimal politics of literature as the primary and best form of thought. It is, explicitly, his answer to the question: is art, is literature, a thing of the past? This is why we need to give literature an afterlife. This is what we are left with right now.

The End of Modern Literature and Korea's World Literature

Young-il Cho

1. Kojin Karatani and Korean literature

If one had to name Kojin Karatani's most representative works, one would likely point to the series of theoretical writings that began with *Transcritique* (a series that includes *The Structure of World History* and *Power and Modes of Exchange*). However, in terms of sheer influence, it is his 2003 lecture 'The End of Modern Literature' that stands out. At least, this is the case in Korea. Of course, this may be a uniquely Korean phenomenon. However, since this very situation touches upon the essence of the 'modern literature' that Karatani declared to be over, it is well worth reflecting on its significance.

Twenty years ago, in the mid-2000s, the atmosphere of the Korean literary world was completely different from the current buzz of enthusiasm for 'K-literature' (a neologism derived from K-pop). The lecture 'The End of Modern Literature' caused a major stir in Korean literary circles. At that time, most literary critiques seemed to begin with the phrase: 'Kojin Karatani says that modern literature is over, but . . .' So much so that in a commentary issued with a literary award, a judge remarked, 'Starting a discussion with Kojin Karatani's diagnosis of contemporary literature is already a cliché.' For a considerable period of time, the Korean literary community was deeply troubled by the question of how to respond to Karatani's thesis on 'the end of modern literature'. It had not of course been Karatani's intention to bring about such a situation.

The phenomenon of a single lecture by a foreign critic plunging a nation's literary world into turmoil for years is unprecedented and will likely never reoccur. Karatani was already well known among Korean literary scholars, of course.[1] From the late 1990s to the 2010s he was the most frequently cited foreign author in Korean research papers on modern literature, surpassing then-popular thinkers such as Benjamin, Bakhtin, Foucault, Derrida, Deleuze, and Lukács.[2] Yet the fact that he became so widely discussed primarily due to one book and one lecture is, in a certain sense, quite bizarre.

The relationship between Karatani and Korean literature was never a one-sided one, however. For instance, while the United States was a privileged space from the point of view of Karatani's intellectual trajectory in the 1980s, Korea played a similar role for him in the 1990s. The phrase 'a close yet distant country' is frequently used in discussions of the relationship between Korea and Japan. Human exchanges are overwhelmingly frequent (nearly 10 million people travel between the two countries each year for tourism alone), but political tensions persist, and intellectual exchanges remain highly limited. In Korea, 'anti-Japan' sentiments remain culturally potent and continue to make for effective political slogans. Yet a significant number of Koreans study in Japan, and the number of Japanese books translated into Korean exceeds that of any other foreign language by a factor of more than ten.

Moreover, Korean intellectuals are extremely interested in Japan, whereas Japanese intellectuals show relatively little interest in Korea. Some display curiosity, but it rarely goes beyond that. What is the source of this imbalance? Simply put, Korea is not an 'other' to Japan. For Japan, the 'other' still consists of the West (as an object of admiration) and China and Russia (as potential threats). Korea, on the other hand, is a country Japan once ruled, and that historical experience fundamentally alters the dynamic. The Japanese perception of Korea remains unchanged even now, despite Korea's having surpassed Japan in per capita GDP as of 2024. Conversely, for Korea – a nation that experienced Japanese colonial rule – Japan remains a powerful 'other'. This asymmetry may be

1 Ho-deok Hwang, *Oeburobuteo-ui gyeokbal-deul* [Triggers from the Outside], *Sangheo-hakbo*, 35 (June 2012).

2 Notably, Lukács enjoys exceptional popularity in Korea, a fact that can be attributed to Korea's unique historical and cultural context.

an inevitable consequence of the two countries' contrasting historical experiences.

Within this context, Karatani's engagement with Korean literature was not something he purposefully initiated. It was purely due to his literary friend, the novelist Kenji Nakagami. In the 1980s, while Japanese writers were turning their attention to the US and Europe, and leftist Japanese intellectuals maintained friendly ties with the Soviet Union and North Korea, Nakagami unexpectedly developed an interest in Korea. Not only did he frequently visit Korea, but he also lived there for extended periods and even wrote novels set in Korea with Korean protagonists.

Korea was under a military dictatorship at this time, and exchanges with Japan were extremely limited (it was not until 1989 that overseas travel became freely permitted for Koreans). It was no easy feat for a Japanese national to travel across rural Korea claiming to be studying traditional performing arts such as pansori. Anti-communist and anti-Japanese education was strictly enforced, to the point that even elementary school students often confused North Korea and Japan.

Given the prevailing hostility between the two nations, Nakagami's actions were met with suspicion on both sides. Korean literary figures suspected him of being a spy for the military regime, while Japanese writers viewed him as a collaborator with the Korean dictatorship. Nevertheless, Nakagami was undeterred. He took it upon himself to introduce Korean literature to Japan, acting as a cultural intermediary. This led to the creation of the Japan-Korea Writers Association, a project aimed at fostering shared literary experiences between the two countries.

Unfortunately, just before the first symposium could take place, Nakagami passed away due to illness. Faced with the potential collapse of the project, Karatani stepped in to continue his friend's legacy. This marked the beginning of what would become a decade-long initiative – the Japan-Korea Writers Association. Given the political and historical tensions between the two nations, the idea of literary figures from Korea and Japan holding regular discussions was unprecedented and remains unlikely to be repeated. The consequences of these exchanges were profound. Of course, a similar project was later carried out on Korea's initiative, but it took place in a completely different context – the globalization of Korean literature, or the Nobel Prize in Literature project.

The Japan-Korea Writers Association met six times over the course of a decade (1992–2002), each time drawing significant attention from both countries' literary communities and media. A sense of stagnation was difficult to ignore, however. Records left by participants reveal that the fundamental issue lay in the differing perspectives of each side. Korean literary figures were primarily interested in asserting moral superiority as victims of colonial oppression and in promoting Korean literature (by eliciting apologies and reflections from their Japanese counterparts). In contrast, Japanese writers were less concerned with Korean literature itself and more intrigued by their unfamiliar yet proximate neighbour.

Following Korea's liberation from Japan in 1945, Korean literature was culturally isolated from Japan for nearly half a century. Although diplomatic relations were later normalized, Japanese popular culture (music, film, manga, and so on) remained strictly banned.[3] This policy (*waesaek*, in Korean) reinforced prejudices against Japanese culture, with the term 'Japanese-style' serving as a commonly used derogatory expression.

Beneath this official stance was an underlying fear, however. A significant number of Koreans still understood Japanese, and for many intellectuals Japanese functioned almost as a second native language.[4] In order to establish cultural independence, an extreme cultural severance was deemed necessary.[5] Yet, in reality, such a separation was nearly impossible. Japanese continued to function as a conduit for knowledge, information, and cultural exchange – though this fact remained largely unspoken. Interestingly, literature was the one exception. There were virtually no restrictions on the study of Japanese literature. Even here, however, there was an implicit taboo on publicly acknowledging Japanese literary influence.

3 Taiwan and Southeast Asian countries normalized diplomatic relations with Japan in the 1950s, but Korea did so much later, in 1965.

4 Jae-hyun Yoon, a Korean, was coercively conscripted as a student soldier into the Japanese army during the final stages of the Pacific War and deployed to the front. As soon as the war ended, he moved to the United States, where he spent the rest of his life. However, in his later years, he wrote a book in Japanese, which was published in Japan. In the preface of this book, he writes: 'My feelings toward Japan and the Japanese are quite complicated. Japan is my "spiritual home". Yet I do not wish to go there. But when I do go to Japan, I feel as if I have returned to my hometown. This is my honest confession' (Jae-hyun Yoon, *Frozen Earth Youth* [Kodansha, 1979], 351–2).

5 Although Korea and Taiwan are both former Japanese colonies, there is a significant difference in their attitudes towards Japanese culture.

The literary exchange that took place over approximately ten years in this context had a significant impact on Korean literature in many respects. At the centre of this exchange was Kojin Karatani. In particular, *Origins of Modern Japanese Literature* became a must-read for Korean literature scholars as soon as its Korean translation was published. The book provided an opportunity to finally understand modern Korean literature. Until then, Korean literary researchers had sought the origins of modern Korean literature in Western literature. Consequently, they relentlessly pursued the prevailing academic trends, from existentialism to Marxism, structuralism, and postmodernism.

However, these approaches did not greatly aid an understanding of modern Korean literature because the historical backgrounds and contexts were vastly different. As a result, critiques and academic papers referencing these theories often had the feel of a rural gentleman awkwardly dressed in ill-fitting clothes. *Origins of Modern Japanese Literature* was different, however. Although it dealt with modern Japanese literature – something Korean literary scholars had deliberately ignored – it felt strikingly familiar to them for two reasons. First, the process of modernization in Korean literature closely resembled that of Japanese literature. Second, there was a sense of déjà vu around the arguments in the volume itself. The latter, in particular, led to significant upheaval.

When *Origins of Modern Japanese Literature* was translated into Korean, all eyes turned – quite unexpectedly – to one person. This individual, revered as the father of the study of modern Korean literature, was known for his unique writing style, research methodology, and an extensive bibliography of over 200 academic works. But the discovery of similarities between his books and Karatani's work led to the so-called plagiarism controversy surrounding *Origins of Modern Japanese Literature*. This scholar had, at times, directly incorporated Karatani's arguments and even his sentences into his own papers and books. The problem was that his many disciples wielded significant influence within universities and literary circles. As a result, a graduate student who publicly raised the issue faced immense psychological pressure and ultimately withdrew from the doctoral programme at that institution, leaving the university.

Although it may be an uncomfortable truth for Koreans, modern Korean literature took shape under Japanese rule, and the Japanese language was its medium. These facts were thoroughly repressed after independence, as anything related to Japan (and the Japanese language) was considered clear evidence of national betrayal. Yet, despite this repression, the influence of Japanese literature continued covertly. Two interesting episodes illustrate this point.

The first is a late-life confession by Seung-ok Kim (born in 1941), a novelist who became a leading figure in postwar Korean literature with works hailed as a 'revolution in sensibility'.

> [T]he biggest motivation for me to write novels was the shock and inspiration I received from reading Japanese novels that had just begun to be translated . . . The Japanese writers depicted the immediate post-World War II circumstances with great intensity – the pain of those who had participated in the war, their postwar economic downfall, and their spiritual devastation. When I read the works of young Japanese writers who were not much older than I was, the feeling was completely different from what I had vaguely experienced reading Hermann Hesse or André Gide in Western literature. It felt much more vivid, much more tangible. I realized, 'Ah, so this is what a novel is. It can portray one's own time with such pain and urgency.' That realization struck me like a shock . . . After reading those novels, I thought, 'Novels are worth writing. There is a need to write them. Then let me try writing about our own stories as well.'[6]

The April 19 Revolution (1960), which overthrew the First Republic, also marked the emergence of the 'April 19 Generation' (born around the 1940s), who would go on to lead modern Korean literature. They took great pride in the fact that they did not know Japanese, as this symbolized a clear break from the older generation. Moreover, as if by design, they all specialized in Western literature (modern Korean literature was not yet an established academic discipline at this point). Ironically, however, their emergence also signified the arrival of Japanese literature in Korea.

Surprisingly, Japanese literature did not exist as a discrete category in Korea before 1960. Since many Koreans were fluent in Japanese, there

6 'Jadam: 4-wol hyeongmyeong-gwa 60-nyeondae-reul saenggak-handa' [Roundtable Discussion: Reflections on the April Revolution and the 1960s], in *4-wolhyeongmyeong-gwa Hanguk munhak* [The April Revolution and Korean Literature], ed. Won-shik Choi and Gyu-chan Im (Changbi, 2002), 30–1.

had been no need for translation. Yoko Tawada vividly recorded an episode related to this fact. At a literary symposium in Korea, the novelist Wan-suh Park (born in 1931) listed the European writers who had influenced her. A reader then asked, 'Have you never read Japanese literature?' Surprised, Park responded: 'For our generation, the idea that Japanese literature is foreign literature never existed.'[7]

The rise of a generation unfamiliar with Japanese but well versed in Western languages created the need for translations, paradoxically establishing Japanese literature as foreign literature in Korea. However, the fact that Seung-ok Kim, who majored in French literature, was inspired to start writing novels by Japanese literature rather than by Western literature – and that the novels he subsequently wrote became defining works of postwar Korean literature – is highly significant. This issue cannot be neatly summarized as a matter of 'influence'. The crucial point here is that this reality was thoroughly concealed for half a century.

Hwa Im, a prominent literary critic of the colonial era, wrote the following in his history of modern Korean literature:

> Modern literature emerged when Western literary genres (specifically free verse and modern novels) were adopted, and it would not be an exaggeration to say that the entire history of modern Korean literature has been characterized by the stimulation, influence, and imitation of foreign literatures. Therefore, the study of foreign literatures that have influenced modern Korean literature is of paramount importance. A meticulous examination of these influences will reveal the essence of modern Korean literature . . . Modern literature grew through the transplantation and imitation of Western literature. This necessitates a thorough study of how Western literature was introduced to Korea. Special attention must be given to the history of foreign literary introductions and translated literature. Here we encounter the need for a detailed study of Japanese literature, particularly the literary history of the Meiji and Taisho periods, rather than a direct examination of Western literature . . . The creation of new writing styles in modern Korean literature was entirely derived from Meiji-era Japanese writing. The influence of Japanese

7 Yoko Tawada, *Yeohaenghaneun Maldeul* [Travelling Words], trans. Ra-ju Yu (Dolbegae, 2003), 86.

writing was deeply connected to the development of Korean language education and requires special attention.[8]

Modern Korean literature is, fundamentally, a transplanted form of Western literature. However, Im argued that to understand modern Korean literature one must study not Western literature itself but modern Japanese literature. This is because Korean literature did not directly adopt Western literature but rather absorbed 'Japanese literature, which had already internalized Western literature'. Most writers of the time encountered Western literature through Japanese translations and even wrote in Japanese.

After Korea's liberation from Japan, the situation changed completely. A movement emerged to eradicate all remnants of Japanese influence across various fields, and literature was no exception. In this process, the relationship between Korean and Japanese literature, as discussed by Im, had to disappear. For nearly half a century, up until the Japan-Korea Writers Association in the 1990s, the whole topic was strictly concealed. Consequently, modern Korean literary studies focused on importing Western literary theories and forcibly applying them to Korean writers and works, or on adopting Soviet literary theories in order to use literature as a tool for social movements.

For fifty years, Korean literary researchers faced two taboos: first, the study of Japanese literature, and second, research on writers who had defected to North Korea. Many significant colonial-era writers moved north after independence, and it was impossible to conduct a proper study of modern Korean literature without them. Until the 1990s the resulting gaps were filled by sensitive responses to literary trends from the First and Second Worlds.

2. On the crisis of literature

The 'crisis of literature' is a recurring theme in literary circles, often resurfacing just when it seems forgotten, making it a topic that one might simply brush off with a wry smile. For instance, a Russian

8 Hwa Im, 'Joseon munhak yeongu-ui il-gwaje [A Task for the Study of Korean Literature]', *Chosun-Ilbo*, 14 January 1940.

writer in the late nineteenth century once expressed his dissatisfaction as follows:

> I've been writing for thirty years now, and through these entire thirty years I have noticed the same amusing thing many times. All our critics (and I have been following literature for almost forty years), those deceased and those still living – in short, all whom I can remember, either now or in the past – would assume a rather solemn tone as soon as they began to write some survey of current literature (formerly, for example, the journals used to carry regular January surveys of the entire past year) and would always use more or less the same phrase, but always with great delight: 'In our time, when literature is in such decline', 'In our time, when Russian literature is in such stagnation', 'In our sorry state of literature', 'Wandering through the deserts of Russian writing', and so on, and so on. One and the same idea in a thousand different variants. But, in fact, over these forty years the last works of Pushkin appeared; Gogol began and ended his career; Lermontov wrote; Ostrovsky, Turgenev, Goncharov, and at least another dozen most talented writers appeared. And this is in belles-lettres alone! One can positively state that scarcely ever in any other literature, over such a short period of time, have so many talented writers appeared as among us; and they appeared one after the other, with no gaps between them. And yet even now, scarcely more than a month ago, I read again of the stagnation of Russian literature and of the 'deserts of Russian writing'. However, this is only an amusing observation of mine; and, indeed, it is an entirely innocent thing which has no significance at all. Still, one has to chuckle at it.[9]

Whether the same can be said for contemporary Russian literature is another question, however. The sense of crisis surrounding modern literature (modern art) has existed for a long time. It goes back at least as far as Hegel, who identified Romantic art – culminating in modern literature – as the final phase of artistic development and proclaimed the 'end of art'. Later, modernist novels and movements like the *nouveau roman* even dramatized the death of modern literature itself. But, at least at that time,

9 Fyodor Dostoevsky, *A Writer's Diary, Volume II: 1877–1881*, trans. Kenneth Lantz (Northwestern University Press, 1994), 838–9.

'literary experimentation' still carried intrinsic meaning, earning high regard in academic circles where literature had been institutionalized.

However, the sense of crisis that emerged in the late twentieth century differed in nature. Literature's social role shrank drastically, and young people increasingly turned their attention to film and video games rather than books. As a result, literature courses became among the least popular options at universities.[10] It was in this climate that books like Alvin Kernan's *The Death of Literature* (1990), Reinhard Baumgart's *Addio: Abschied von der Literatur* (1995), and William Marx's *L'Adieu à la littérature* (2005) were published. These works candidly examined the crisis of literature in contemporary society.

At first glance, Karatani's 'The End of Modern Literature' appears similar to these discussions. Its content is fundamentally different, however. Those earlier critics sought new possibilities within the crisis – they still believed in the value and significance of modern literature. Their discussions were tinged with nostalgia and longing for literature's past glory. Such a response is perhaps the most 'literary' way for professional literary figures to react. After all, crises in literature and the arts have led throughout history to calls for artistic revolutions.

Karatani's argument departs completely from this 'crisis-and-recovery' narrative. He does not attribute the decline of literature to a lack of talent or effort among writers. But this also implies the reverse: that the past glory of literature was not solely the result of individual ability or hard work. One need only look at a world map and mark the regions where modern literature flourished to see the truth of this claim. Modern literature has only developed, circulated, and been seriously discussed in highly specific and limited areas. In other words, modern literature is nothing more than a literary form that thrived under particular historical conditions.

Karatani makes his position clear from the outset: 'There are few people nowadays who believe literature is important, and it is therefore unnecessary for me to demonstrate that literature has come to an end. What does need pointing out, however, is that there was once a time when literature

10 Departments related to literature (such as French and German literature) are gradually disappearing from Korean universities. Even at Seoul National University, there are no students wishing to pursue graduate studies in these fields.

bore an incredible weight of meaning.'[11] Karatani does not lament the fact that few people today regard literature as important. If one must talk about literature, he argues, it is more meaningful to speak about the era when literature actually carried great weight. By this logic, the 'crisis of literature' today is largely a fiction – because the assumption that modern literature should continue as before is itself flawed.

Nonetheless, the narrative of 'crisis and recovery' still clings to modern literature. This is likely because an entire institutional system dedicated to teaching and studying literature still exists, along with people whose professions depend on sustaining the perception of literature's importance. Karatani, aware of potential misunderstandings, makes his point explicit: 'This does not mean, for example, that something like postmodern literature will come after modern literature; nor does it mean that literature will disappear entirely.'[12]

Karatani never actually claimed that literature itself had ended. But since literature that has been reconstructed from the perspective of modern literature is still, fundamentally, modern literature, one could argue that all contemporary discussions of 'literature' today are, ultimately, discussions of modern literature. Thus, even if a new type of literature (so-called 'postmodern literature') were to emerge, it would still be bound within the framework of modern literature. No matter what it is called, it would inevitably function as a mechanism to revitalize the system of modern literature. As Karatani points out in *Origins of Modern Japanese Literature*, this paradox may, in a sense, be the very essence of modern literature.[13]

3. Korean literature as the origin of 'The End of Modern Literature'

But if modern literature has truly come to an end, when exactly did this happen? Of course, pinpointing a specific time is difficult. The timing varies by country, and the process unfolded in different ways. Moreover,

11 Karatani, 'The End of Modern Literature', 25 in this volume.

12 Ibid.

13 Kojin Karatani, *Origins of Modern Japanese Literature*, ed. and trans. Brett de Bary (Duke University Press, 1993), 154.

as Tolstoy emphasized in *What Is Art?*, modern literature is not a universal artistic form found throughout the world. It is merely a kind of literature that developed alongside the formation of the nation-state and which flourished only in countries that had experience as colonial powers and in nations that came to use the language of those powers as their official language. Modern literature is far less universal than music, film, or even video games. In this sense, 'the end of modern literature' is not a global phenomenon but rather a localized event occurring in regions where modern literature once held significant meaning.

Karatani asserts that the end of modern literature occurred in the United States in the 1950s and in Japan between the late 1980s and the early 1990s. Interestingly, it was precisely at this time that he began engaging with Korean literature (in 1992). Then, about ten years later, he suddenly delivered his lecture 'The End of Modern Literature'" While the lecture did not cause much controversy in Japan, it provoked an entirely different reaction in Korea. What particularly unsettled Korean writers was that Karatani identified Korean literature as the impetus for his feeling that modern literature had come to an end.

> But what really made me aware of the end of modern literature was the sudden decline of literature's influence in South Korea. It was shocking. In the 1990s I participated in the Japan-Korea Writers Association and had many opportunities to speak with Korean authors. At that time, my guess was that even if modern literature had ended in Japan, it would continue in South Korea. In 2000 I went to Seoul and declared at a press conference that literature had died in Japan. In saying this I meant that, even though Japan was still producing literary works that, as commodities, sold well globally – the works of Haruki Murakami, for example – the erstwhile role or meaning of literature in Japanese society had already disappeared. I heard afterwards that my speech had been taken seriously by the Korean audience, who considered it very pertinent to their own situation (by that point young people had started reading Murakami in South Korea too).[14]

By this account, Karatani had already discussed the end of literature in 2000, albeit with the caveat that it was a phenomenon specific to Japan.

14 Karatani, 'The End of Modern Literature', 28.

However, when he later learned that his claim resonated with Korean writers – who felt that it was 'not just Japan's problem' – he was compelled to formally declare 'the end of modern literature'. But did he truly realize this belatedly?

If we look further back, to a 1997 discussion in Korea, we see that Karatani had already said:

> Compared to Japan, writers in Korea hold a significantly higher social status. However, even in Korea, I feel there has been a noticeable change in the readership's engagement with literature in recent years. Professor Choi quoted my statement, 'Literature is dead in Japan' – a metaphorical expression I had used when I visited Seoul in June – in a newspaper article, adding, 'However, this is not just Japan's problem.'[15]

This suggests that Karatani had made the same observation as early as 1997 and had already received confirmation from Korean literary circles. So was his later declaration merely a case of misremembering, or was it a deliberate repetition? More important than pinpointing the exact moment of realization is the fact that after this discussion, Karatani never participated in another Japan-Korea Writers Association. He appears to have decided that further exchanges would be meaningless.

What stands out in Karatani's remarks is that he identifies Haruki Murakami's infiltration of Korean literature as a major turning point. Murakami's status in Korea is more complex than it may appear from the outside, however. He was first introduced to Korean readers in 1988, the year of the Seoul Olympics. At that time, his popularity in Japan was so immense that critic Minako Saito described it as 'powerful enough to bring down a flying airplane'. Murakami was completely ignored in Korea, however. His works received neither public attention nor reviews – he was, quite simply, dismissed.

This treatment was not exclusive to Murakami. As previously discussed, Japanese literature only officially emerged in Korea in the 1960s, and even then it remained nearly invisible in public discourse. By

15 Nak-cheong Baek, Won-shik Choi, Satoshi Ukai, and Kojin Karatani, 'Kankoku no hihyo kukan [The Critical Space of Korea]', *Hihyo kukan*, 2:17 (1998): 19.

the 1990s, however, the atmosphere had begun to shift. Following the global spotlight of the Olympics and the geopolitical changes triggered by the end of the Gulf War and the collapse of the Soviet Union in 1991, something unexpected happened in Korea: multiple newspapers began publishing critiques of the indiscriminate introduction of Japanese literature.

Then, in 1992, a major upheaval shook the Korean literary world – the emergence of the so-called 'New Generation Writers'. Their works broke away from 'national literature' – the dominant literary ideology advocated by the then-mainstream Association of National Literature Writers – shifting the focus from the collective to the individual, from ideology to personal taste, and from family to the self. They garnered strong support from readers in so doing. This marked a second 'revolution in sensibility'. At the time, however, the dominant literary establishment strongly criticized the new sensibility, denouncing it as a form of superficial commercialism that ignored history and the people's struggles.

Haruki Murakami's name suddenly appeared in these debates. The core of the controversy was that the New Generation Writers had plagiarized Murakami's works. Korea experienced three major literary plagiarism scandals during the 1990s, each of which was connected to Japanese literature. The first of these was the 'Murakami plagiarism controversy'.

This particular case differed from the others because it wasn't just about individual ethical lapses – it was tied to an entire generation's literary sensibility. Even young writers who were never accused of plagiarism were visibly influenced by Murakami. A Japanese critic who had experience teaching at a Korean university once made the following remark about Korean novels of the 1990s:

> In the 1990s, a term emerged in Korea – 'the Haruki generation'. Prior to Murakami, Korean literature was inconceivable without the framework of family relationships. However, through Murakami's literature, Korean writers realized that a protagonist could exist independently of family ties. This led to a shift in literary themes.
>
> One representative of this generation, the writer Dae-nyeong Yoon, wrote a novel titled 'Sweetfish Memorandum'. The protagonist, 'I', is a thirty-something, single photographer who drinks whiskey alone at night in his Seoul apartment while listening to Billie Holiday.

> Then, he receives a mysterious letter . . . When I read it, I couldn't help but feel that it was a counterfeit work (*Festische*).[16]

Because of this atmosphere, a Korean literary critic who opposed the New Generation Writers once likened Murakami's influence to an infectious disease. Ironically, however, the controversy served as an opportunity to introduce Murakami's novels to a general readership, and works were introduced into Korea rapidly thereafter. He quickly became the most popular author in Korea. In particular, *Norwegian Wood* (which has more than ten different Korean translations) became a must-read for college students.

There are two key points to note here. First, Murakami was not considered a serious subject of discussion at the time, nor for a long period afterwards (in other words, he was regarded as a popular writer). Second, and more importantly, his success wasn't just the success of a single writer. With Murakami's commercial success serving as a turning point, both contemporary and classical Japanese writers (the latter including Soseki Natsume) were introduced on a large scale. As a result, the tacit rejection of Japanese literature by the Korean publishing industry came to an end, and readers came to recognize Japanese literature as foreign literature on a par with Western literature.

This trend was fuelled by the announcement of the 1994 Nobel Prize in Literature. What shocked Koreans about Kenzaburo Oe's award was that it was the second time that a Japanese writer had been thus recognized. When Yasunari Kawabata became the first Japanese laureate in 1968, the response from the Korean literary world had been tepid at best. Some even dismissed it as merely satisfying Western orientalism. But, as Hegel said, what appears to be a coincidence the first time round becomes an inevitability the second time.

The period during which Karatani was frequently visiting Korea was, then, a rather tumultuous time. The mainstream literary establishment was still refusing to acknowledge the changes that had taken place, but Karatani had discerned them as far back as 1993. 'People in general are indifferent to "literature". This is not because writers lack talent, because

16 Motoyuki Shibata, Mitsuyoshi Numano, Shozo Fujii, and Inuhiko Yomota (eds), *Sekai wa Murakami Haruki o dō yomu ka* [How Does the World Read Haruki Murakami?] (Bungei shunju, 2006), 6.

they have lost passion, or because they are avoiding a confrontation with reality. Nor does it mean "the death of literature". It simply means that "literature" has lost the excessive significance that had been ascribed to it until now.'[17] Interestingly, then, he had already spoken of the 'end of modern Korean literature' – and he had done so in the presence of Korean writers. At the time, however, no one took the idea particularly seriously. Korean literary figures had not only lost their political vitality but also looked down on Japanese literature, which was struggling economically after the bursting of the bubble economy. The Japanese literary onslaught that would follow had not yet begun in earnest. So on what basis did Karatani come to this conclusion? Surprisingly, he seems to have harboured this idea before even coming to Korea: 'This is not a phenomenon occurring only in Japan. Reading Korean literary criticism from the 1990s (as translated by Woo-sik Ahn), one gets the feeling that the situation I have just described is already unfolding [in Korea] . . . In other words, Korean literature and criticism also seem, in some sense, to be facing the "end of modern literature".'[18] In the space of just a few literary critiques, Karatani had accurately grasped the situation facing Korean literature. This proves that he had no illusions about Korean literature. However, Korean literary figures hoped that a Japanese critic, disillusioned by the decline of Japanese literature, would find new possibilities in Korean literature and declare: 'Japanese literature is dead, but Korean literature is still alive.' They therefore posed the same loaded questions whenever they had the chance, and Karatani, out of politeness, occasionally provided encouraging answers.

In truth, Karatani had no particular interest in Korean literature at that time. As previously mentioned, his engagement with the Korean literary community was primarily a way of honouring the last wishes of his late friend Kenji Nakagami. By then, Karatani's intellectual focus had already shifted from literature to philosophy. In the first half of the 1990s, he serialized a philosophical essay titled 'Tankyu' (Explorations), and in the latter half of the decade, he wrote *Transcritique*. It is no exaggeration to say that Karatani's tenure as a literary critic effectively concluded in the

17 Kojin Karatani, 'Kankoku to nihon no bungaku [Korean and Japanese Literature]', in *'Senzen' no shiko* [Prewar Thought] (Kodansha, 2001), 218. (This paper was presented at the second Japan-Korea Writers Association meeting, which was held in 1993.)

18 Ibid., 218–19.

1980s. Consequently, he had little to add regarding Korean literature; in fact, he wrote no criticism specifically addressing Korean literary works during that period. Yet, the 'excessive meaning and obsession' that Korean literary figures attributed to literature seem to have made him reconsider the question, 'What is modern literature?' In that sense, had it not been for his interactions with Korean writers, Karatani might never have felt the need to give his lecture on the 'end of modern literature'.

Generally, the First World's interest in Third World literature was linked to its own attempt to revitalize a First World literary scene that had entered a stage of stagnation. Paradoxically, Third World literary communities have shown little interest in one another. The West had long utilized the 'exotic' aspects of the Third World as 'difference' in order to enrich First World literature.[19] This was, of course, only possible due to the literary inequalities between nations, and it is worth noting that, even among Third World literatures, those written in European languages were preferred in this hierarchy. The only exceptions may have been the literatures of Japan and China, which not only confronted the West head-on but remain significant threats even today.

Korean literary figures felt an immense sense of 'betrayal' when Karatani, who had previously shown (or seemed to show) a friendly attitude towards Korean literature, suddenly cited it as an example in his declaration of the 'end of modern literature'. A prominent Korean literary critic lamented the situation as follows:

> I have a personal acquaintance with Kojin Karatani and consider him an excellent philosopher. However, his essay on the 'end of modern literature' is not one of his better pieces. Moreover, as he himself admitted, he has no particular knowledge of Korean literature, and I suspect the information he received from others was mistaken. Yet the moment he simply stated that Korean literature was over,

19 'I do not find anything exotic about America or the West. I also feel little fascination toward Iran or India. I am not exactly sure why I feel this way about Korea. It is very similar to Japan, yet there are subtle differences. Because of this, I find myself enjoying dramas that I would not bother watching if they were Japanese. That is what I meant when I said "exotic"' (Kojin Karatani and Eiji Otsuka, '"Doryoku mokuhyo" toshiteno kindai wo kataru [Discussing Modernity as an Aspirational Goal]', *Shin Genjitsu*, 5 [2008]: 8–9).

> everyone started quoting him, and, frankly, I felt a deep sense of sorrow. Are we really this insignificant?[20]

The sense of betrayal and sorrow felt by Korean literary figures stemmed from the precarious state of Korean literature at that time. The literary movement that had predominated during the 1980s was struggling to find direction following the collapse of the socialist bloc (in 1991) and the establishment of the civilian government (in 1993). As consumer society matured, the departure from social engagement and ideology accelerated. For example, in the 1980s writers had received recognition only if they were producing works that were directly or indirectly connected to student or labour movements. Aspiring writers sought employment in factories under false pretences or moved to rural areas in order to broaden their perspectives. Literary critics studied social sciences, and their evaluation of works was based on the assumption that literature could change society.

This atmosphere persisted, to some extent, into the early 1990s. There was a sense that something was changing, but a generalized inertia made it difficult to accept the changes in question. In such an uncertain situation, Korean literature needed an external affirmation of its continued vitality. Korean literary figures desperately wanted a foreign critic to say something like: 'Japanese literature is dead, but Korean literature is not.' But the reality was that Korean readers were increasingly turning not to Korean literature but to Haruki Murakami and Japanese literature.

4. From Korean literature to K-literature

After the controversy surrounding 'The End of Modern Literature' had been excessively indulged in and then had gradually subsided, a peculiar phenomenon emerged in Korea: the rise of 'world literature'. Of course, this 'world literature' had nothing to do with Goethe's concept; it referred instead to literature that was distributed and recognized globally (more precisely, in the West). The most prominent aspect of this trend was the

20 Nak-cheong Baek and Myung-won Lee, '(Daedam) "Park Chung-hee hyangsu"-neun kkeumjjik-han huyujeung, eopjeok-do injeong-haeya chiyu-hal su itda [(Dialogue) Nostalgia for Chung-hee Park Has Terrible Aftereffects, but Acknowledging His Achievements Is Necessary for Healing]', *OhmyNews*, 9 April 2007.

popularity of the Complete World Literature Series (*Segye Munhak Jeonjip*).[21] The Minumsa Complete World Literature Series, which published its first volume in 1998, had reached 470 volumes as of August 2025, and it continues to grow. In a country with a population of 50 million and a single-volume book market worth only $130 million (as of 2023), multiple publishers were competing to release world literature series. This is an unprecedented situation globally – based on this development alone, one might call Korea a 'World Literature Republic'.

Another notable development was that the most influential literary organization in Korea, the Association of National Literature Writers, removed the term 'national literature' from its name in 2007 and began discussing world literature. Academia followed suit, with 'world literature' becoming a buzzword for a while. It is important to note, however, that the boom in world literature complete collections and the corresponding boom in world literature discourse were in tension with one another. This is evident in the book *Discussions on World Literature* (2010), which contains essays with titles such as 'Nation and Literature in the Era of Globalization', 'The Universality of Korean Literature from the Perspective of World Literature', 'The Globalization of Korean Literature', 'The History and the Current State of Japanese Culture's International Dissemination', and 'Eurocentrism in World Literature and Asian Literature'. These titles make clear that the essays' focus was not on world literature as such, but rather on the globalization of Korean literature.

One of the driving factors behind the success of world literature complete collections was an increased interest in foreign literature, which had been triggered by the success of Japanese literature in Korea. In Korea, many publishing houses were directly or indirectly run by literary figures. Under the guise of 'protecting Korean literature', they had long been reluctant to promote foreign literature. Some publishers even publicly stated that they would not publish translated novels at all.

21 The Complete World Literature Series is a unique East Asian editorial invention that emerged in 1930s Japan. Unlike Western literary collections, it functions as a closed system where a fixed canon is determined by experts according to national, linguistic, and authorial quotas. Historically, this format maintained a rigid boundary by excluding domestic works, thereby framing world literature as a prestigious Western 'other' to be imported and mastered.

Segye Munhak Jeonjip is how the Koreans refer to the series. Notably, the Chinese characters (Hanja/Kanji) for this title are identical across Korea, China, and Japan (世界文學全集).

As a result, even when foreign literature was translated, it was not widely discussed, allowing Korean literature to maintain its dominance over foreign literature in Korea.

However, this situation was completely overturned by the influx of Japanese literature, with Haruki Murakami at the forefront. This phenomenon could rightly be called a 'cultural invasion'. Approximately 1,000 Japanese literary works are published in Korea each year, and this trend has persisted for the past thirty years. Korea had become one of the largest consumer markets for modern Japanese literature before anyone had even realized what was happening. This is an ironic situation: the modern Japanese literature that Karatani declared to be over was now thriving in Korea, where people were still insisting that modern literature had not ended. But why was Japanese literature so successful in Korea? The primary reason was the crisis of Korean literature, which had developed in isolation like a Galápagos ecosystem.

The success of Japanese literature in the 1990s and the success of world literature complete collections would not have been possible without the decline of Korean literature's influence. Readers no longer sought out Korean literature, which had been imposed on them by the education system and by cultural institutions. Instead, they actively sought out 'proven' foreign literature. In this situation, the success of Kyung-sook Shin's *Please Look After Mom* was enough to excite the writers who had long advocated for national literature. But that novel was far from being the kind of literature they had long been agitating for – it was, in essence, a commercially popular work. Nevertheless, they enthusiastically celebrated its success because it was published by a press that they controlled, and because, even if it was just a one-time event, it had breathed new life into Korea's shrinking literary market. As a result, the success of *Please Look After Mom* was framed as a 'literary milestone' in line with the spirit of the times.

Back when Karatani was visiting Korea in 1996, Sony's market capitalization was eleven times larger than that of Samsung Electronics. By 2002, however, Samsung had finally surpassed Sony, and today the gap has widened significantly. The global success of Korean companies instilled an immense sense of national pride in Koreans. Coincidentally, 2008 – the year *Please Look After Mom* was published – was also the year when Samsung announced its entry into the smartphone market to compete with Apple's iPhone. In 2011, when the English version of the novel was released, Samsung overtook Apple in global smartphone market share.

The novel's success in the US was somewhat exaggerated, but in Korea this was celebrated as the moment a 'world-class writer' was born – a moment that deeply moved many literary figures and ordinary Koreans alike. It led to a surge in calls to actively globalize Korean literature, with figures from across the cultural sector advocating for state-led promotion efforts. Some even suggested that expanding into the international market was the key to overcoming the crisis of Korean literature – a statement that seemed to suggest that Korean literature should become like Samsung's smartphones. In this context, when it was revealed that Kyung-sook Shin had plagiarized a short story ('Patriotism') by the Japanese novelist Yukio Mishima, the Korean Writers' Association (formerly the Association of National Literature Writers) defended her amid the resulting controversy, arguing that special consideration should be given to such an internationally recognized author.

A similar controversy erupted in 2016. When Han Kang's novel *The Vegetarian* won the Man Booker International Prize, she suddenly surpassed Kyung-sook Shin to become Korea's new national literary icon. When *The Vegetarian* was first published, it had received little attention from readers and critics. Han Kang was not initially considered a particularly important writer in Korea. But after the news broke that it had won an award financed by a European hedge fund, the book surged in popularity, ultimately becoming the number-one bestseller of the year. In effect, Korean literature had been re-imported from abroad. But instead of acknowledging this reality, the literary world and the media turned a blind eye, collectively proclaiming: 'Korean literature has finally reached the level of world literature!'

Once *The Vegetarian* had been re-imported into Korea, it gained a great deal of attention and enjoyed strong sales. Interestingly, however, few people actually discussed the contents of the book. In many ways it is actually quite an anachronistic work. Indeed, the reason it is so highly regarded in the West (and especially in Europe) is that its anachronistic elements have been mistaken for a quality of 'classicness' that is now rare in contemporary Western literature. The novel's success also brought the translator into the spotlight.[22] However, the English translation later became the subject of controversy not only for being too far removed

22 This British translator is said to have translated this book after only three years of learning Korean, and that she has difficulty communicating in the language.

from the original text but also for being riddled with mistranslations. Nonetheless, the prevailing opinion was that 'since it won an award anyway, such issues are not a big deal'. The entire process culminated in Han Kang – backed by state support – becoming Korea's top candidate for the Nobel Prize in Literature. A literary award given in Europe has changed the literary constitution of a country on the other side of the world and produced a national author. 'Long live Europe's greatness!'

5. A 'war of peace': towards world literature

During the Russo-Japanese War, Soseki Natsume wrote about 'two types of war'. One was the 'war of war', and the other was the 'war of peace'. The former referred to active military conflict, while the latter referred to so-called cultural warfare. After the Meiji Restoration, Western culture flooded into Japan, leading to an atmosphere in which anything Western was uncritically embraced. In response, nationalism gained momentum, emphasizing the superiority of native culture. Soseki criticized resistance to modernization as anachronistic, but he argued at the same time that blindly following the West was also problematic. Ultimately, he believed, it could only lead to imitation.

However, this dilemma was completely resolved by a single event: Japan's victory in the Russo-Japanese War. Soseki claimed that success in the 'war of war' would naturally impact the 'war of peace', leading to a new sense of spiritual liberation. He described this phenomenon as follows:

> When we realize that they are human just as we are, a certain awareness arises . . . If this confidence and self-awareness continue to expand, their effects will ripple into all areas of society. Naturally, this extends to literature as well . . . Our country may not have achieved great literary success in the past, but from now on, we will. From now on, masterpieces will be created . . . We must produce works that can be compared to, or that even surpass, those of the West. We are now in such high spirits.[23]

23 Soseki Natsume, 'Sengo bunkai no Susei [The Trend of the Literary World After the War]', in *Soseki zenshu* [Complete Works of Soseki] (Iwanami Shoten, 1957), xxxiv, 31–2. A few years later Soseki travelled to Manchuria and Korea, where he felt great happiness in realizing his identity as a Japanese.

Japan's victories in the First Sino-Japanese War (1894–5) and the Russo-Japanese War (1904–5) enabled it to become the first non-Western imperial power. Japan had finally achieved parity with the West. This new-found status instilled a sense of pride and confidence in Japanese writers, who had previously felt overshadowed by Western literature. At the same time, it created a burden – a sense of a duty to contribute to their nation's cultural advancement. Perhaps as a result, many of the greatest works in modern Japanese literature emerged in the aftermath of the Russo-Japanese War. In fact, it is no exaggeration to say that a significant portion of Japan's literary masterpieces were created during this period. In the wake of this literary awakening, Modern Japanese Literature Collections began to be published. The series was so successful that it reshaped the Japanese publishing industry. Following this, a companion project, World Literature Complete Collections, was launched.

In Korea, after liberation, the country experienced miraculous economic growth, and the literary world sustained itself with a domestic readership alone. By the 1990s, however, this system had collapsed, and the foreign literature that had long been suppressed returned, pushing Korean literature aside. The success of World Literature Complete Collections was a testament to this shift (by contrast, attempts to publish Modern Korean Literature Collections all failed). The Korean literary world's overreaction to Karatani's 'The End of Modern Literature' should not be surprising, since it seemed to explicitly articulate the underlying confusion of the time. It was at this moment that the 'state' emerged. When a government that was favourable to the literary world took power, the literary establishment became undisguisedly reliant upon state support.[24] The 'globalization of Korean literature' was promoted with the full backing of the government, and, in the process, the two previously mentioned works were given excessive significance. For Korean literature to continue surviving, it had to become K-literature – and, ultimately, world literature.

One thing that must be acknowledged is that nearly all Korean literature currently circulating internationally – including *Please Look After Mom*, *The Vegetarian*, and *Kim Ji-young, Born 1982* – has been

24 Until then, Korean literature had been in opposition to or maintained a tense relationship with the state. After the Kim Dae-jung administration came to power, however, the literary world entered into an active partnership with the government. To borrow Karatani's expression, 'literature as B' was established.

backed by the Korean government. In other words, this circulation was not the result of literary exchanges conducted at the private level (such as the Japan-Korea Writers Association). Today the Korean government provides extensive literary support through various initiatives. Among them, the Literature Translation Institute of Korea (LTI Korea), established in 2001 under the Literature Promotion Act, is particularly notable. LTI Korea is a state-funded institution that exists solely to globalize Korean literature. It trains and manages professional translators, pays high translation fees, covers publishing costs, and ensures that foreign publishers can release Korean books with zero financial risk.

Furthermore, the government has systematically collaborated with foreign universities specializing in Korean studies and Asian studies, facilitating international fellowships and lectures for Korean writers. As a result, a significant number of Korean authors have lived abroad (primarily in Western countries), and around 2,000 Korean books have been translated into multiple languages and distributed to libraries worldwide. The languages most frequently translated into have of course been English and other European languages (including Swedish), and this was undoubtedly intentional. These programmes clearly illustrate where Korean literature's desire for recognition is directed. Given this background, we can see that the success of works like *The Vegetarian* was not simply the success of an individual writer; it was the success of a state-sponsored literary policy.

By the 2010s, inspired by the global popularity of K-pop and K-dramas, Korean literature began to refer to itself as 'K-literature'. Some even predicted that it would soon become a major force in world literature. One veteran writer went so far as to proclaim the 'twenty Nobel Prize winners theory'.[25] It is a stark contrast to the situation a decade ago, when there was strong resistance to Karatani's 'The End of Modern Literature', accompanied by feelings of betrayal and sorrow.

What kind of literature does Korean literature then aspire to, having struggled through the controversy surrounding 'The End of Modern Literature'? One writer lamented at the height of that debate that 'Korean

25 The argument was that Korea has around twenty writers capable of winning the Nobel Prize in Literature, but none had received it so far owing to Western centrism and the parochialism of Europeans.

literature hasn't even had the chance to establish a proper modern literature, yet now we're told it's already over . . . how frustrating'. Another writer likened the situation to training diligently for the Olympics for four years, only to be suddenly told that the event had been cancelled. The 'modern literature' Koreans speak of – a desire that remains unfulfilled – is a literature that can stand shoulder to shoulder with Western literature, or, to put it simply, a literature that can be exported abroad, a 'world literature'. But achieving this state of affairs is beyond the ability or initiative of individual writers alone. This is because literary imbalances are fundamentally rooted in disparities between nations.

One of the things that has startled Western literary scholars visiting Korea – for example, Pascale Casanova – is the strong fixation Koreans have on the Nobel Prize in Literature. The English translator of *The Vegetarian*, who came to be called 'Korea's Seidensticker' after the novel won the Booker Prize, has said that the question they were asked most often was, 'When do you think Korea will win the Nobel Prize in Literature?' In countries that have already produced multiple laureates, such a situation may be difficult to fathom, because to the citizens of those countries, the Nobel Prize in Literature is awarded to individuals, not to nations. But for Korean literature, long positioned on the periphery of world literature, the Nobel Prize was like a ticket that would allow it to enter the elegant ballroom of 'world literature' with confidence. Of course, it is a ticket issued by Europe.

Korean literature has long criticized Eurocentrism and stressed the importance of Third World literature. Yet it never truly regarded itself as *part of* Third World literature. On the contrary, it sought to win the 'war for peace' and join the ranks of First World literature – because that was considered 'literary progress'. Korean writers had always longed for Western recognition and felt no hesitation in mobilizing the resources of an economically prosperous nation to achieve it. In so doing, they tied the development of literature to the power of the state. Government agencies then took the lead in efforts to promote Korean literature to the world. There were even rumours of lobbying in Sweden. And, at last, a 'miracle' occurred.

6. Korean-style magical realism and the last joke of modern literature

The 2024 Nobel Prize in Literature was awarded to the Korean novelist Han Kang. The entire nation was swept up in a festive mood. Yet the literary and publishing circles were simply bewildered, as the result had been completely unexpected. What everyone had longed for had suddenly arrived, like a thief in the night. And then, one by one, people began to appear claiming that they had 'already foreseen' it. The same thing had happened in 1945, when Korea gained independence from Japan. At the time, Seok-heon Ham, an independence activist and thinker, sharply criticized those who claimed to have foreseen the liberation, saying they were people trying to steal something that had itself arrived like a thief. The problem was that this kind of theft later became ideology, and the narratives thus born turned into 'historical truth' with the help of the press, the education system, and popular culture.

In any case, this latest event lifted Koreans' cultural pride to the heavens, and even people who never usually read books rushed to place orders, causing shortages everywhere. Printing houses saw foreign workers labouring overnight to produce books that they themselves could not read. At some point, most of Korea's gruelling labour sites had come to be filled with foreign labourers. In a way, this meant that Korea had become a developed country. If the popular claim that winning the Nobel Prize in Literature is connected to national capability – so-called 'national power' – is true, then this change in the labour market could be seen as a further positive sign.

When news of the award broke, LTI Korea issued a press release. It noted that Han Kang's works had been published in seventy-six editions across twenty-eight languages, all with the support of LTI Korea. The statement even included a detailed table listing the support provided, as well as nominations and awards in overseas literary prizes (in effect showing that Korean writers' overseas activities are managed by the state). Based on this data, the public funds spent introducing Han's works abroad amounted to about $1 million – similar to or slightly more than the Nobel Prize's monetary award (11 million Swedish kronor).

However, it is said that after the Nobel Prize, domestic sales alone earned more than the prize money. At one point, no fewer than fifteen of the top twenty books on the general bestseller list were Han's works

– meaning essentially that one person's books were all that sold. Naturally, other books were pushed aside. The Nobel Prize in Literature thus contributed to the widening of the gap between the haves and have-nots in the Korean publishing industry. Yet no one voiced any complaint; after all, nothing is more dangerous than having one's patriotism questioned during a moment of national celebration.

Korean journalists and literary figures exclaimed with tears of joy that 'Korean literature has finally attained the status of world literature'. They treated the controversy over the 'end of modern literature' that had taken place some twenty years earlier as if it had never happened. A collective amnesia took hold. The sense of betrayal and sorrow that Korean literary circles had felt at the time completely vanished, replaced by a new memory. Koreans now felt as if they had been reading and loving Han Kang's works for a long time. This revisionism could well be called a Korean-style 'magical realism'. And then, suddenly, they began to mock Haruki Murakami – because, for Koreans, there were now only two kinds of writers: those who have won the Nobel Prize and those who have not.

Haruki Murakami's influence in Korea, which began in the 1990s, lasted for an impressive thirty years.[26] But the atmosphere changed completely when Han Kang won the Nobel Prize in Literature. Considering the customary rotation of the prize among Europe, the United States, and Asia, some scoffed that it would be at least another ten years before an Asian writer could win again – and jibed that Murakami, already advanced in age, might not live long enough to see that day.

The press clamoured for more systematic and daring state support to cultivate 'the second Han Kang' and 'Han Kang kids'; some publishing commentators have even begun to say that '10 million literature' (literature that sells over 10 million copies) is no longer just a dream. LTI Korea went a step further, speaking of the dawning 'post-Nobel era'. Truly, it was a 'beautiful sight'. Before long there will no doubt be a 'Han Kang Literature Prize', a 'Han Kang Literature Hall', and a Han Kang statue. And dreamy eyes will become the trademark of great K-modern

26 In Korea, Haruki Murakami's royalties have set new records with each successive title. For *1Q84*, the advance alone is estimated to have exceeded $1 million, surpassing the combined annual advances received by all Korean authors.

literature. A regional city (Jangheung County), the hometown of 'Han Kang's father', has already declared itself a 'Nobel Literature City'. Although Han Kang was neither born nor raised there, Jangheung County believes that she received the spirit of the region and that that contributed to her winning the Nobel Prize in Literature.

So now, as discussion of the 'end of modern literature' flares up again, could it be that Korean literature alone is exceptionally defying the times and reviving 'world literature'? Nothing could be more ridiculous. Because this would mean that a single literary prize – from the Swedish Academy, supported by the Nobel Foundation and the Swedish royal family – could somehow halt the end of modern literature and bring it back to life. Still, if anyone believes such a thing, they might as well make the sign of the cross towards those who speak of the 'end of modern literature' and cry out: 'Long live His Majesty Carl XVI Gustaf!'

In this sense, the Nobel Prize may be modern literature's final joke on Korean literature. Of course, those who do not wish to wake from the spell cast by the Swedish fiend will not understand this.[27] The moment they laugh, the splendid castle will turn into a shabby inn, the lord of the castle into a middle-aged countryman, and the ladies of the castle into prostitutes. Perhaps this is why Goethe, who introduced the idea of 'world literature', wrote: 'If I do not will it, the devil cannot exist.'[28]

27 George Bernard Shaw is said to have once remarked regarding the Nobel Prize in Literature: 'I can forgive Alfred Nobel for having invented dynamite, but only a fiend in human form could have invented the Nobel Prize.' Nobel may not have known what 'literature' truly was, but he succeeded in instituting the 'literary prize'. Every major literary award we know today was established in its wake.

28 Johann Wolfgang von Goethe, *Faust*, Part II, line 6791.

Questions of Modernism and 'The End of Modern Literature'

Yoshiki Tajiri

Karatani and the genre of *hihyo*

When Kojin Karatani published his lecture 'The End of Modern Literature' in 2004 in the journal *Waseda Bungaku*, he had already ceased to be a literary critic.[1] The lecture sentences modern literature to death and clearly announces Karatani's withdrawal from the genre called *bungaku hihyo* or *bungei hihyo* (literary criticism) or simply *hihyo* (criticism). Karatani dominated this genre from the 1980s to the 1990s. Since he dropped out in the late 1990s, it has dwindled, with no major figures to replace him. It could therefore be said that he practically put an end to this genre *hihyo* which he had enriched more than anyone else. Although Karatani's lecture confirmed his farewell to literature and

1 Karatani's lecture was included in a book with the same title in 2005 and is now in a paperback volume entitled *Shisoteki jishin* [*Thought and Earthquake*] (published in 2017). Confusingly, there is another essay by Karatani with the same title, 'Kindai bungaku no owari [The End of Modern Literature]'. This essay, chiefly about Kenzaburo Oe's novel *Letters to My Sweet Bygone Years* (1987), was originally published as 'Doitsusei no kaiki [The Return of Identity]' in 1988 and then included in the volume *Shuen wo megutte* [On the End] in 1990 with the slightly different title 'Doitsusei no enkan [The Circle of Identity]'. When it was included in the fifth volume (*History and Repetition*) of the definitive edition of Karatani's works (5 vols) in 2004, it was renamed 'Kindai bungaku no owari [The End of Modern Literature]'. It has been translated into English as 'The End of the Modern Novel', to avoid confusion, and is now in the English volume *History and Repetition*, ed. Seiji M. Lippit (Columbia University Press, 2012).

to *hihyo*, it had little impact on Japanese readers when it was published.[2] This fact may indirectly prove that his analysis was correct: literature had become so insignificant that the pronouncement of its end by the leading critic passed unnoticed.

This *hihyo* (hereafter 'criticism') is unique to Japan. Between the late 1920s and the early 1930s, academic journalism took shape in Japan with general magazines as its major media. It was the age of massification, when the public sought guides to and digests of contemporary academic discourses. Modern Japanese literary criticism started in this intellectual milieu with Hideo Kobayashi. Kobayashi established literary criticism as 'criticism as literature' rather than 'criticism about literature', to use Satoshi Osawa's words.[3] This literary criticism was part of academic journalism, a hybrid discursive field constituted not only by literature but also by the social sciences and philosophy. Literary critics like Kobayashi were thus compelled to be conscious of the social sciences and philosophy, even though Kobayashi himself advocated the autonomy of literature. On the other hand, they could feel free to discuss anything from literature to politics under the name of 'criticism'. After Kobayashi, this genre maintained an ambivalent relation with academia; it was highly intellectual but largely independent of and in rivalry with institutionalized academism.[4] It was more journalistic and committed to the actuality of the contemporary situation. It played a crucial part in Japanese intellectual history, and it is difficult to find its counterparts in England or America.[5] This 'criticism', pioneered by Kobayashi, continued with such eminent critics as Taka'aki Yoshimoto and Jun Eto in postwar Japan. Karatani made his début

2 Since I thought this was very strange, I organized an international symposium on 'The End of Modern Literature' at the Komaba campus of the University of Tokyo on 30 November 2019. By contrast, as Young-il Cho discusses in his chapter in this present volume, Karatani's lecture created a sensation in South Korea.

3 Satoshi Osawa, *Hihyo-Media ron: Senzenki nihon no rondan to bundan* [On Criticism and Media: The World of Journalism and Literature in Prewar Japan] (Iwanami Shoten, 2015), 98. This book is a detailed survey of the way academic journalism was formed in Japan.

4 This does not mean that these critics did not work as university professors. Even Kobayashi worked for Meiji University for some years. The point is that, even when they were formally professors, their style was more journalistic than academic.

5 Edmund Wilson or Susan Sontag may come to mind, but their writings did not belong to a specific genre like Japanese 'criticism'. In England and America, the distinction between journalism and academism is much clearer, and therefore a hybrid genre (academic journalism) like 'criticism' does not thrive as in Japan.

squarely in this genre in the late 1960s, influenced by Yoshimoto and Eto.[6] In the 1970s and 1980s, when structuralism and post-structuralism rushed in, Karatani began to supersede those predecessors, as he was more responsive to the new trends than anyone else.

Karatani often emphasizes the creativity of 'criticism' in Japan. For instance, in 'Ido to hihyo' ('Move and Criticism'), a companion piece to 'The End of Modern Literature', he claims that in postwar Japan, it was superior to the social sciences and philosophy, which, according to him, had turned out to be 'fatally shameful' before and during the war. He says: 'In Japan, since the prewar period, literary criticism has existed as an intellectual discipline that rivals philosophy and the social sciences. Here we should note the following point. Literary criticism in Japan is practically French philosophy, as in the case of Hideo Kobayashi.'[7] Karatani argues that the practitioners of Japanese 'criticism', from Kobayashi to himself, were analogous to interdisciplinary French philosophers such as Jean-Paul Sartre, who wrote in many different fields. But he says that he stopped working as this type of critic (*hihyoka*) after writing *Transcritique* in the late 1990s. In his view, French philosophy was seeking a third way between capitalism and socialism, but it lost its raison d'être when the Cold War ended.[8] Japanese 'criticism' likewise lost its power, and Karatani therefore decided to withdraw from it and began to concentrate on the concept of modes of exchange, publishing *The Structure of World History* and related works.

After finishing *Transcritique*, Karatani decided to end the quarterly *Critical Space*, which he had edited with Akira Asada since 1991. He

6 Karatani was a university professor, but he was not warmly accepted by Japanese academia. On the other hand, he obtained a high status in American academia, teaching as a visiting professor at first-rate universities such as Yale and Columbia. Jacques Derrida, Paul de Man, Fredric Jameson, and Edward Said were all his friends. He was the first (and last) literary critic (*hihyoka*) to enjoy such international prestige. Karatani's boldly interdisciplinary style matched the new climate of American literary studies, which was being changed by critical theories. The curious incongruence in the way he was treated indicates both the autonomous discursive position of Japanese 'criticism' and the openness of American academism after the 1970s.

7 Kojin Karatani, *Shisoteki jishin: Koen shusei 1995–2015* [Thought and Earthquake: Collected Lectures 1995–2015] (Chikuma Shobo, 2017), 273. All quotations from 'Ido to hihyo' are from this edition and the page numbers are indicated in the text. Translation is mine.

8 Derrida's philosophy, which deconstructs binary oppositions, was also an attempt to find a third way, in Karatani's view.

concluded that the quarterly, though it represented high-quality 'criticism' in the 1990s, had played itself out.[9] Instead, he started a political movement directed against the trinity of state, nation, and capital called the New Associationist Movement (NAM) in June 2000. It aimed to put into practice the ideas about modes of exchange he laid out in *Transcritique*, but it quickly failed and broke up in December 2002. Meanwhile, the terrorist attack on 11 September 2001 impressed him with the advent of a new era which needed a more fundamental theory to counter the trinity of state, nation, and capital. It was immediately after these significant reorientations that Karatani gave the lecture 'The End of Modern Literature'.

The weakness of modernism in Japan

When Hideo Kobayashi started his career as a critic in the late 1920s, he was confronted with two new movements in literature that were competing with each other: Marxism ('proletarian literature') and modernism. Modernism here means the strand of new literature that promoted formalistic experiments with language, particularly the New Sensationalist School (*Shinkankakuha*) represented by the novelists Riichi Yokomitsu and Yasunari Kawabata.[10] Kobayashi was critical of the tendency in both movements to stress method when discussing literature. In his début essay 'Multiple Designs', he asserted that

> no matter how conscientious our exploration of a specific critical method may be, it will tell us nothing about why a particular method moves us. This is a fact theorists tend to overlook. Consider the case of the man who hopes that he will succeed in love if he studies the rhetoric of the love letter. This person would be a fool if having consummated his love, he attributed the outcome to love letter research.[11]

9 It finally ceased in 2002. For Karatani's own recollections of this quarterly, NAM, and the 11 September attack, see *Seiji to shiso 1960–2011* [Politics and Thought 1960–2011] (Heibonsha, 2012), 82–95.

10 Throughout this essay, I use the term 'modernism' principally in this narrower sense of the 'high modernism' of the 1920s.

11 Hideo Kobayashi, *Literature of the Lost Home: Kobayashi Hideo: Literary Criticism, 1924–1939*, ed. and trans. Paul Anderer (Stanford University Press, 1995), 2.

Thus, method was secondary to him. His famous slogan was, 'To criticize is to tell about oneself by making use of others' works.'[12] He did not mind being faulted for relying on impressions or engaging in impressionistic criticism.

While Marxism continued to be an important issue in postwar Japanese literature until the 1960s, pre-war modernism did not. In the study of English literature, modernism is a solid and robust research field. There is no equivalent in the study of modern Japanese literature. In other words, modernism in Japanese literature remained a superficial phenomenon that lacked the lasting influence of modernism in English literature. For many contemporary English novelists, the presence of such modernists as James Joyce and Virginia Woolf is still compelling, whereas in Japan, the legacy of the modernist experiments conducted by the novelists Yokomitsu and Kawabata in the 1920s seems entirely invisible in contemporary novels.

There is a telling episode that illustrates the weakness of modernism in Japan. When Japan assiduously incorporated Western modernist and avant-garde literature in the 1920s and 1930s, one of the most prominent figures was Yukio Haruyama, a critic, poet, and editor. He edited important magazines such as *Shi to shiron* (*Poetry and Criticism of Poetry*; 1928–32), to which Junzaburo Nishiwaki, Fuyue Anzai, Katsue Kitazono, and many other modernist poets contributed. He was also a formalist who rejected impressionistic criticism and emphasized the importance of analysing literary works as linguistic constructs. Born in the same year as Kobayashi (1902), Haruyama regarded him as his rival and kept criticizing him for being merely impressionistic and for lacking methodological awareness. But he was ignored by Kobayashi. As Marxism was suppressed in the early 1930s, its rival, modernism, also lost momentum. Haruyama's modernism was quickly forgotten, while Kobayashi's impressionistic 'criticism' continued unabated and was widely read during and after the war.

In the West, Russian formalism, which was closely tied to the Russian avant-garde, led to structuralism and post-structuralism, which could be regarded as theoretical reflections on the artistic practices of

12 'Ashiru to kamenoko II [Achilles and a Baby Tortoise II]', in *Kobayashi Hideo Zenshu* [Complete Works of Hideo Kobayashi] (Shinchosha, 1978), i, 46. Translation is mine.

modernism. These were continuous movements. In Japan, by contrast, pre-war modernism's linguistic experiments and methodological awareness had largely been forgotten by the time structuralist and post-structuralist theories flooded in after the 1970s. No one remembered Haruyama's importance around 1930.

Although Karatani made his début in the genre 'criticism' that Kobayashi had established, he was well versed in Western philosophy and exceptionally competent at absorbing new theories. In a sense, he opened up 'criticism' to postmodern theories. While academic scholars worked hard to understand and explain Western theorists, Karatani as a critic (*hihyoka*) was unique in developing his own original ideas with reference to them in such books as *Origins of Modern Japanese Literature* and *Architecture as Metaphor*. In 'telling about [him]self by making use of others' works', Karatani is an authentic inheritor of Kobayashi's type of 'criticism', even if he appeared to be a leader of Japanese postmodern thought in the 1980s.

The absence of modernism in 'The End of Modern Literature'

Given the above observations, it is not surprising that modernism has little significance in Karatani's literary criticism as a whole. In 'The End of Modern Literature', modernism is touched on briefly, when he mentions the influence of new technologies on literature, but this is little more than a commonplace view.[13] When he discusses pre-war literary criticism closely, he concentrates on Marxism (especially the theorist Kazuo Fukumoto) and Kobayashi, completely disregarding the modernists' formalistic ideas, which were tied up with their linguistic experiments.[14] This absence may become more conspicuous when we compare Karatani with another advocate of the end of modern literature.

In 2005, the year of the publication of Karatani's book *The End of Modern Literature*, a French book entitled *L'Adieu à la littérature*

13 See 38 in the present volume. All quotations from 'The End of Modern Literature' are from the present volume, and the page numbers are indicated in the text.

14 Kojin Karatani (ed.), *Kindai nihon no hihyo: Showa-hen (Jo)* [Modern Japanese Criticism] (Fukutake Shoten, 1990), 12–38.

(Farewell to Literature) was published.[15] Its author, William Marx, argues that literature has gone through three phases since the eighteenth century: expansion, autonomization, and devaluation. With the notion of the sublime in aesthetics, literature began to value sensibility rather than reason in the seventeenth and eighteenth centuries. In the nineteenth century, the promotion of sensibility led to the apotheosis of literature, and literature replaced religion as a moral guide to the way we should live. Yet, around the same time, literature began to seek autonomy, under the rubric of 'art for art's sake'. It started to withdraw into its own formalistic concerns and detach itself from life and the world, thus losing its relevance in society. Rimbaud, Hofmannsthal, and Valéry around the turn of the twentieth century marked the suicide of literature. Since then, literature has kept staging its own death. And now, in the twenty-first century, the devaluation of literature seems complete.

This rough outline is sufficient to see that Marx's ideas are remarkably similar to Karatani's in 'The End of Modern Literature'. Both start with the conviction that literature is no longer important. Like Marx, Karatani emphasizes that literature was upgraded with the promotion of feeling and sentiment in the eighteenth century and began to play the role of religion in providing moral guidance.[16] However, they are also significantly different. Karatani gives priority to the novel while Marx's focus is on poetry. Karatani links modern literature to the history of world capitalism, while Marx rejects the socio-economic explanation of literature. The most fundamental difference, however, concerns their treatment of modernism. Karatani makes almost nothing of modernism, or the radical innovation in art and literature of the early twentieth century.

15 William Marx, *L'Adieu à la littérature. Histoire d'une dévalorisation: XVIIIe–XXe siècle* [Farewell to Literature: History of a Devaluation from the Eighteenth to Twentieth Century] (Minuit, 2005).

16 Karatani is more precise here. He argues that imagination started to mediate between the newly promoted realm of feeling and sentiment and the realm of reason and intellect. In 'Ido to hihyo' (268), he expands on the mediatory role of imagination. The centrality of modern literature, which for him effectively means the modern novel, was secured because it grapples with general and universal questions (the realm of reason and intellect) even as it originates in the privacy of individual persons (the realm of feeling and emotion). Sentiment alone did not guarantee the modern novel's high status. Only when sentiment was connected to universal reason by imagination could the novel based on sentiment be judged to be important.

In Karatani's schema, it appears that modern Japanese literature continued without modernism having any impact from the third decade of the Meiji period (from the mid-1880s to mid-1890s) to the 1980s, even up to Haruki Murakami.[17] By contrast, when Marx discusses literature in terms of autonomy, retreat into form, or detachment from life and the world, he is actually pointing at modernism, since these features are very often considered to characterize modernism.

Marx's account of the decline of literature by way of modernism is more familiar. In fact, Ortega y Gasset said much the same thing in his 1925 essay 'The Dehumanization of Art'. In Ortega's view, the penchant of 'modern art' (i.e. modernism) for 'artistic art' (i.e. art for art's sake) was not congenial to the masses who wanted to enjoy not the work of art itself but the 'human reality' which they could see through the work of art.[18] Ortega also observed that 'modern art' had become 'a thing of no consequence', as it did not carry the humanistic content that characterized the art of the nineteenth century:

> Art was important for two reasons: on account of subjects which dealt with the profoundest problems of humanity, and on account of its own significance as a human pursuit from which the species derived its justification and dignity. It was a remarkable sight, the solemn air with which the great poet or the musical genius appeared before the masses – the air of a prophet and founder of religion, the majestic pose of a statesman responsible for the state of the world.[19]

In other words, art was playing the role of religion in the nineteenth century, as both Karatani and Marx suggest. But 'modern art' was lighter and free of 'so enormous a mission'. It was practically a plaything for elites.

In modernism, Ortega thus found a decisive break from traditional art after the latter began to concentrate on purifying itself (art for art's

17 Karatani regards Haruki Murakami as continuing the tradition of Doppo Kunikida, who is the earliest representative of modern Japanese literature characterized by the simultaneous discovery of landscape and interiority. See 'The Landscape of Murakami Haruki', in *History and Repetition*, 117–49.

18 Ortega y Gasset, *The Dehumanization of Art and Other Writings on Art and Culture* (Doubleday, 1956), 10.

19 Ibid., 46.

sake) and lost popularity among the masses. William Marx basically repeats this familiar story. We are then induced to ask why modernism is rendered insignificant in Karatani's schema. Apart from arguing that modernism in Japan was, in any case, weak and negligible in literary-historical terms, we need to return to Karatani's basic framework in *Origins of Modern Japanese Literature*, which should be read in tandem with 'The End of Modern Literature'.[20]

Modernism in *Origins of Modern Japanese Literature*

In that book, Karatani contends that modern Japanese literature is an institution invented in the third decade of the Meiji period (from the mid-1880s to the mid-1890s) with the new writing style called *genbun itchi* – the unification of spoken and written languages.[21] This invention entailed the simultaneous discovery of landscape and interiority, along with other major components such as confession, childhood, and illness. Landscape and interiority became natural features of literature, just as in painting the technique of geometrical perspective created the illusion of depth or three-dimensionality that is now so familiar to us. Karatani says:

> Once a landscape has been established, its origins are repressed from memory. It takes on the appearance of an 'object' which has been there, outside us, from the start. An 'object', however, can only be constituted within a landscape. The same may be said of the 'subject' or self. The philosophical standpoint which distinguishes between subject and object came into existence within what I refer to as 'landscape'. Rather than existing prior to landscape, subject and object emerge from within it.[22]

20 Karatani has repeatedly said that when he was writing this book in the late 1970s, he was already sensing the end of modern literature. See for instance 'Ido to hihyo', 253.

21 As Karatani says in Section 4 of 'The End of Modern Literature', the West had experienced the same process of creating national vernacular languages centuries earlier.

22 Kojin Karatani, *Origins of Modern Japanese Literature*, ed. and trans. Brett de Bary (Duke University Press, 1993), 34. All quotations from this book are from this edition and the page numbers are indicated in the text.

In this condition, the familiar concept of the expression of self became possible. Karatani also suggests that we are confined in this particular condition. He says,

> Harold Bloom has argued that we live in an era of romanticism, when the very effort to reject romanticism is essentially romantic. According to Bloom, T. S. Eliot, Sartre, and Lévi-Strauss can all be considered part of the romantic movement and we have only to look, for example, at Wordsworth's 'Prelude' or Hegel's *Phenomenology of Spirit* to understand why even an antiromantic stance was part of a larger romanticism. Both these works record an 'experience of consciousness' or 'maturation' according to which romantic subjectivism evolved toward objectivity. They suggest that we remain caught up in the 'romantic dilemma', which renders even the antiromantic position a romantic one. (32)

Thus, anti-Romantic and anti-humanist modernism was nothing but Romanticism, after all, and it was therefore incapable of changing the landscape within which we are still imprisoned. If Romanticism integrates even its opponents, then modernism is entirely insignificant. In this context, Karatani mentions Kobayashi and argues,

> Kobayashi's repeated and persistent attempts to reach not 'objectivity' but the 'object' might be seen as an attempt to 'shatter the sphere of self-consciousness'. But no one knew better than Kobayashi the impossibility of such a project. His book *Kindai Kaiga* (Modern painting, 1958) is not only a discussion of landscape painting but narrates Kobayashi's own endless epistemological struggle to break away from the 'perspective' he found there. Yet neither Kobayashi nor the painters he discussed in his book were able to escape from that 'landscape' which conditioned the painters' very discovery of Japanese woodprints and African primitive art. Kobayashi describes no one as having transcended the confines of landscape. I myself, in writing this essay, do not seek to break away from this 'sphere'. I seek simply to shed light on its historicity. (34)

It is clear here that even modernist painters, including the post-impressionists and Picasso, were working within the sphere of landscape.

There are problems here, however. First, Karatani seems to include anti-Romantic modernism in a movement of 'maturation' towards objectivity. But this idea is dubious because modernism was a youthful, iconoclastic movement that was far from the maturity associated with old age.[23] Karatani appears to adhere uncritically to the Hegelian schema in insisting that anti-Romanticism simply means maturation.

Second, when Karatani discusses modern art in the chapter on the power to construct, he more conventionally mentions the 'revolt' of modern art against the specific perspectival configuration that engendered modern literature and still imprisons us. He argues,

> It was an awareness of a discrepancy between the 'homogeneous space' of linear perspective (as an effect of the techniques of drafting) and what is given in 'perception' that constituted the starting point for the reaction, in modern painting (from late impressionism on) against the laws of perspective . . . The revolt of cubism and expressionism against the laws of perspective corresponded to phenomenology's intense scrutiny of perception and the body. (139–40)

Thus, modernist art ('cubism and expressionism') is equated with phenomenology in philosophy by way of their common resistance to the laws of perspective. In another passage, Karatani expands on philosophy.

> The 'I' in Western modernity, as shown by the example of Descartes, exists by virtue of a specific perspectival configuration which had come to appear so self-evident and natural that it was not easy to recognize that it was a product of drafting techniques. Not only that, the effort to bracket (as in phenomenological reduction) this configuration and to see a prior configuration beneath the distortions and cover-ups required an 'unnatural' effort of will and methodological ingenuity. One need only think of the efforts of Husserl or Bergson. (158)

23 See also 123, where Karatani reiterates the idea that 'maturity' is 'an inevitable trajectory' of Romanticism. Katai Tayama and Toson Shimazaki's transition from Romantic poetry to naturalist novels is characterized here as 'maturity'. See also Karatani's discussion of Mishima and Oe: one rejected maturity while the other embraced it ('The End of the Modern Novel', 164).

Both phenomenology (Husserl) and modernist art, then, were efforts to 'bracket' the perspectival configuration and 'to see a prior configuration beneath the distortions and cover-ups'. In this context, Karatani does not emphasize that the perspectival configuration is inescapable or that those efforts were after all made within it. His idea here is therefore conducive to Fuhito Endo's argument that post-impressionist paintings and Roger Fry's theory thereof revealed the thing in itself that was concealed by modern perspective or by Karatani's 'landscape'. In other words, they uncovered what Karatani calls 'a prior configuration'. That, in Endo's view, is why the 1910 exhibition *Manet and the Post-impressionists* that Fry organized in London was incomprehensible and shocking to the contemporary English viewers (though it was a decisive event for Virginia Woolf). Endo thus characterizes modernism (post-impressionism) by using the basic ideas of *Origins of Modern Japanese Literature*.[24]

Endo's innovative reading notwithstanding, modernism *per se* is not an important topic in *Origins of Modern Japanese Literature*, however. Karatani – just like Harold Bloom, Paul de Man, and Michel Foucault, all of whom influenced him – does not regard modernism or the modernist period as a significant break. This basic framework remained unchanged up to 'The End of Modern Literature'. And yet, reading 'The End of Modern Literature', we may wonder what happened to the 'romantic dilemma' that seemed to imprison us so fatally. Have we finally escaped it? Perhaps, with the end of modern literature, it has simply ceased to be a problem.

Reintroducing modernism to 'The End of Modern Literature'

However, these claims about the absence of modernism in Karatani do not mean that modernism is irrelevant to 'The End of Modern Literature'. There are at least three topics by means of which we can reintroduce the question of modernism into our reading of the lecture: nation, interiority, and theory.

24 Fuhito Endo, *Jodo to modaniti: Eibei bungaku/Seishin bunseki/Hihyo riron* [Affect and Modernity: Anglo-American Literature/Psychoanalysis/Critical Theory] (Sairyusha, 2017), 7–41.

Karatani maintains that the emergence of the modern novel was closely linked to the consolidation of the nation. Now, however, nation-states are completely established, and, in consequence, it is unnecessary to create imaginary identity through the modern novel. Karatani says that even though nation-states are being culturally undermined by global capitalism, there is no resistance to this process coming from explicit nationalism, as happened before; resistance to global capitalism is coming from religious fundamentalism rather than from nationalism and literature (34).

He also suggests that the rise of minority literature marks the last phase of modern literature. This process first started in the US in the 1950s; Japan saw the same phenomenon in the 1980s. The fact that the Booker Prize was won by the likes of Rushdie and Ishiguro in the 1980s indicates that the end of modern literature is in sight (40). It seems that, in Karatani's view, minority literature can only have a limited influence on specific people and not on society at large. Minority literature here is, to a large extent, immigrants' literature, and is in that sense related to the issue of global capitalism. It may be possible to argue that, in the age of global capitalism and transnationalism, when national consciousness is supposedly being weakened, modern literature that is inseparable from national consciousness is destined to decline, while immigrants' literature, germane to global capitalism, will be capable of flourishing.

Karatani has elsewhere discussed this issue in relation to capitalism. Capitalism intrinsically pursues differences; when it reaches a saturation point at which there are no longer any differences, it tries to find them elsewhere. When differences disappear in developed countries, capitalism creates them in developing countries, thereby entailing globalization. Karatani suggests that literature too lives on differences. When disparities based on differences in class, gender, and age disappear from society, literature also loses power. In the US, the cultural power of Black people, women, and gay/lesbian people declined in proportion to the success of their campaigns against discrimination. In Japan, the novelist Kenji Nakagami, who came from a discriminated community (*buraku*), represented the cultural power that severe discrimination produced. But, in the 1980s, such differences disappeared.[25] In this light, it is understandable

25 I have summarized here Karatani's remarks in *Karatani Kojin Intavyuzu 2002–2013* [Kojin Karatani Interviews 2002–2013] (Kodansha, 2014), 111–14. Of course, Karatani clearly says that it is good to have less discrimination, and that he does not care if literature disappears so long as discrimination truly disappears as well (113).

that Karatani is pessimistic about the future of minority literature; just as capitalism sooner or later reaches a saturation point, minority literature will end up consuming all available differences and resources.

It is also worth noting, however, that many modernists were themselves immigrants or exiles. (In English literature, for example, Joseph Conrad was from Poland; James Joyce and Samuel Beckett left Ireland; T. S. Eliot and Ezra Pound were American.) And many of them were seriously affected by their encounters with non-Western cultures. The transnational globalization of literature that consumes differences was starting in the modernist era. The appearance of authors such as Ishiguro and Rushdie is simply an extension of this tendency; the only difference is that, now, more and more authors from outside the West are finding their voices in the context of world literature, even if they still need to be approved by the West. While James Joyce's experiments could be anchored to his Irish nationalism, which countered English colonialism and the domination of the English language, we could also argue that *Finnegans Wake* exploded all possibilities of nationalism. The iconoclastic ethos of Dadaism was arguably buttressed by its cosmopolitanism and freedom from nationality. If the likes of Rushdie and Ishiguro really indicate the end of modern literature, there may be a sense in which the expatriate modernists had already initiated the process towards it within the West, even though those modernists were trying to revivify modern literature and were not thinking in terms of its 'end'.

Now let us turn to the second topic, interiority. In *Origins of Modern Japanese Literature*, Karatani contends that modern literature started with the simultaneous discovery of landscape and interiority. As we have seen above, Karatani admits that modernist art like cubism and expressionism was a revolt against 'the laws of perspective'. In other words, modernist art rejected the familiar three-dimensionality and transparency guaranteed by perspective, and in consequence rejected landscape and interiority. There was a corresponding movement in literature. One of the prominent features of English modernism was its attack on interiority, or its attempt to escape from it. The representative figure here is Wyndham Lewis, who valued hardness and exteriority, rejecting the soft interiority as Bergsonian. Here is a typical passage from his first novel, *Tarr* (1918):

> *deadness* is the first condition of art. A hippopotamus' armoured hide, a turtle's shell, feathers or machinery on the one hand; *that* opposed to naked pulsing and moving of the soft inside of life, along with infinite elasticity and consciousness of movement, on the other. – Deadness, then . . . is the first condition of art. The second is absence of *soul*, in the sentimental human sense. The lines and masses of the statue are its soul. No restless, quick flame-like ego is imagined for the *inside* of it. It has no inside. This is another condition of art; *to have no inside*, nothing you cannot *see*.[26]

This is a manifesto for the anti-humanist or anti-Romantic strand of modernism. Lewis was influenced by T. E. Hulme, who in 'Modern Art and Its Philosophy' (1914) valued abstract or geometrical art over vital or organic art, the distinction being based on Wilhelm Worringer's *Abstraction and Empathy*. This is, in effect, a rejection of interiority and three-dimensionality. Another figure who followed Hulme's path was T. S. Eliot, who famously declared in 'Tradition and the Individual Talent' (1919) that '[p]oetry is not a turning loose of emotion, but an escape from emotion; it is not the expression of personality, but an escape from personality'.[27] The Karatani of *Origins* would assert that these anti-Romantic tendencies are part of Romanticism and did not mark any significant break, but it is not impossible to connect them to the end of modern literature, which thrived on the exploration of interiority. Even if those modernists did not conceive of the 'end' of modern literature, they can be said to have prefigured it.

This leads straight to the third point, theory. The idea of the text as being free of the author's life and personality was born in the same intellectual milieu as that which produced New Criticism, Russian formalism, and structuralism. Literary theories that analyse texts in isolation from the author's inner life developed from modernism. William Marx argues that formalist criticism, which, in his view, is represented by T. S. Eliot and Paul Valéry, as well as by the Russian formalists, contributed to the decline of literature by relegating it to a

26 Wyndham Lewis, *Tarr*, the 1918 version (Black Sparrow Press, 1990), 299–300, emphasis original.

27 T. S. Eliot, 'Tradition and the Individual Talent', in *Selected Prose of T. S. Eliot*, ed. Frank Kermode (Faber, 1975), 43.

secondary status in society.[28] We could add that literary theories that originated in formalism devalued modern literature in Karatani's sense by detaching it from the inner life and from concomitant moral concerns. As we have seen above, Ortega y Gasset presciently observed in 'The Dehumanization of Arts' that new arts in the early twentieth century became lighter and less significant as a result of aiming to be nothing other than arts and of thereby losing the 'humanistic' baggage that the nineteenth-century arts carried. In this sense, the end of modern literature, which had interiority as its defining feature, was already underway in the modernist period.

Karatani says in 'The End of Modern Literature' that modern literature came to an end in Japan in the 1980s, when young people were reading theories ('contemporary thought') rather than novels (27). I fully concur with him. I experienced this process directly as a student in the 1980s. In that period there was still a transitional coexistence of traditional modern literature and theories, but the loss of the former soon became evident. We were encouraged to talk about 'texts' and to suppress the word 'life' in literature classes. It is no surprise that modern literature in Karatani's sense is dead.

Further thoughts on modernism in Japan

The concept of modernism is difficult to define clearly, as it has contradictory features. For instance, the cosmopolitan detachment from nationality that I have highlighted coexisted with the conspicuous rise of nationalism and national self-determination all over Europe and beyond, and this tendency also affected modernist art and literature. The rejection of interiority in Wyndham Lewis was counterbalanced by the deeper exploration of the inner mind by Virginia Woolf and James Joyce. But as long as we follow Karatani's logic, it seems undeniable that the end of modern literature was prefigured in at least some strands of modernism. At this point, we are once again compelled to pose the important question: what was Japanese modernism in literature? Or, more specifically, why did modernism not have the power to shake the institution of modern

28 William Marx, *L'Adieu à la littérature*, 102–3.

Japanese literature as it did English literature? I will conclude with two more observations on this topic.

My first observation concerns Japanese artists' consciousness of the West. Karatani argues in *Nation and Aesthetics* that Western-style artists in Japan have been 'troubled by a fundamental contradiction'. That is to say, 'avant-garde, anti-traditionalist artworks in Japan appeared as mere mimicry in the West, where conversely, art that returned to Japanese traditionalism instead was considered innovative'.[29] Curiously, then, in order to be appreciated as innovative in the West, it was better for Japanese artists to be traditionalists. Karatani goes on to make the same claim with regard to literature:

> For instance, in literature, Tanizaki Jun'ichiro, Kawabata Yasunari, Mishima Yukio, and others – despite their renown as traditionalists in the West – originally began their careers as Westernized modernists: the traditional 'turn' they took should be understood as less the result of nostalgia, but rather as a deliberate attempt to appear even more avant-garde. Furthermore, their image of traditional Japan was one based on perceptions in the West.[30]

Japanese artists and writers could not escape from the compelling Western gaze. They were destined to 'perform' Japan for the West. Both Kawabata and Mishima coveted the Nobel Prize and were conscious of the international reception of their works. If being considered avant-garde in the West entailed becoming a traditionalist, then the effort to be a Westernized modernist had to be considerably discouraged. This structure based on cultural power politics governed Japanese art and literature after the war and the American occupation. Whether the same is true of pre-war literature is a debatable point. Modernist authors in the 1920s and '30s may have been less conscious of the Western reception of their works, and it seems that their modernism was in any case assimilated to or engulfed by the wholesale return to Japanese traditions

29 Kojin Karatani, *Nation and Aesthetics: On Kant and Freud*, trans. Jonathan E. Abel, Hiroki Yoshikuni, and Darwin H. Tsen (Oxford University Press, 2017), 67–8.

30 Ibid., 68. It is not accurate to say Mishima started out as a Westernized modernist, because he first emerged under the heavy influence of the Japanese Romantic School. And Kobo Abe is a big exception in this context: totally disregarding traditions, he persisted in being an avant-garde author and was received as such in the West.

(*nihon kaiki*) in art, literature, and philosophy in the late '30s. These return movements in culture were soon to be aligned with the nation-wide rush towards the war. But what if the Japanese values so revered at that time were formed in direct opposition to (and were therefore inseparable from) Western values? That would mean that they were produced by the Western gaze after all. Even so, the traditions that were invented in the modern period were believed to derive from Japanese people's authentic values rooted in their deeper psyche, and many modernists took a turn towards these traditions, diluting or shedding their modernist experimentalism. The return to traditions was such a sweeping trend that modernism in art and literature inevitably appears to be a rather superficial and ephemeral phenomenon in comparison.

My second point is about Japanese modernity itself. In *Origins of Modern Japanese Literature*, Karatani argues that modernism ('cubism and expressionism') revolted against the laws of perspective, which was a product of modernity. The same perspectival configuration constituted the 'I' in Western modernity, and the latter became so natural that recovering 'a prior configuration' required the 'unnatural' efforts of Husserl or Bergson. But Karatani points out the following about the Japanese *shishosetsu* (I-novel): 'in the Japanese *shishosetsu* the opposite was the case, since the configuration that constituted the Western "I" as natural seemed unnatural and artificial to the *shishosetsu* writers' (158). Karatani makes these remarks while discussing the famous debate in 1927 between Jun'ichiro Tanizaki and Ryunosuke Akutagawa over the 'novel without plot'. Akutagawa highly valued Naoya Shiga's plotless *shishosetsu*, invoking Cézanne's paintings. He detected cutting-edge modernism in Shiga. Karatani cautions, however, 'It should . . . be noted that "what was *shishosetsu*-like" existed within a context entirely different from what we may call anti-Western trends in the West' (158). Cézanne may have destroyed Western perspectival painting, but we cannot say the same for Shiga, whose apparent 'destruction' was simply 'too natural' and was unrelated to anti-Western modernism.

Modernism in the West was a revolt against Western modernity. While modernism flourished with the fruits of modernization in European metropolises, it strenuously deployed myths, irrationality (the unconscious), and non-Western or premodern cultural resources in order to counter modernity. Since modernity was strong, the revolt also needed to be robust. But Japan's context was different. Western modernity was from the beginning alien, and the *shishosetsu* writers were outside it. The resemblance between Shiga's plotless *shishosetsu* and Cézanne's modernism was therefore a mere accident. It is no surprise that modernism was not strong enough to thrive in this climate: it lacked a strong modernity to revolt against.

During the war, Japanese intellectuals advocated the 'overcoming of modernity' in their efforts to consolidate Japan's position against Western values. In a sense, Japan became 'postmodern' without achieving modernity. When real postmodernism was in vogue in Japan in the 1980s, Karatani emphasized the importance of placing it in the Japanese context.[31] Since the Japanese do not have the Western type of modernity, which postmodernism subjected to critique, it is strange that the Japanese took postmodernism in the same way as Westerners did. Predictably, Japanese postmodernism turned out to be a superficial phenomenon. The problematic modernity has haunted and will continue to haunt the Japanese in this way.[32]

31 See his 'Hihyo to posutomodan [Criticism and the Postmodern]', in *Hihyo to posutomodan* [Criticism and the Postmodern] (Fukutake Shoten, 1985), 9–49.

32 I am grateful to Professor Joel Wainwright for commenting on early versions of this essay. Parts of this essay developed from a section in my Japanese book *J. M. Kuttse: Sekai to <watashi> no guzensei he* [J. M. Coetzee: Toward the Contingency of the World and 'Myself'] (Sanshusha, 2023), 268–76.

Mode of Exchange D, (F+f), and the Ends of Literature

Michael K. Bourdaghs

When I invited Kojin Karatani to a 2005 conference at UCLA, it was with some trepidation. The reasons for inviting him were obvious: Karatani was Japan's best-known literary critic and theorist. Moreover, much of his early work focused on Soseki Natsume (1867–1916), the novelist whose monumental *Theory of Literature* (*Bungakuron*; 1907) was the focus of our conference.[1] But this came after Karatani's publication of his famous essays on the end of literature, which announced his shift in focus from the explication of novels to political activism (for example, the New Associationist Movement) and to the radical rethinking of Marxist theory that would result in his magnum opus, *The Structure of World History: From Modes of Production to Modes of Exchange* (2010; English translation 2014). I was aware that in 2005 – in Karatani's own wry phrasing – he considered himself 'divorced from literature'.

But Karatani graciously accepted our invitation. At the event, he explained the reason why, pointing to a passage from the preface to

1 Selections of Karatani's writings on Soseki can be found in such volumes as *Marukusu sono kanosei no chushin* [Marx: Towards the Centre of Possibility] (Kodansha, 1990) and *Soseki-ron shusei* [Collected Essays on Soseki] (Daisan Bunmei Sha, 1992). In English translation, see 'Soseki's Diversity: On *Kokoro*', in *Contemporary Japanese Thought*, ed. Richard F. Calichman (Columbia University Press, 2005), 119–29; and 'Death and Poetry: Shiki to Soseki', trans. Robert Tuck, *Review of Japanese Culture and Society*, 29 (2017): 175–206.

Theory of Literature. In it, Soseki explained how, during his 1900–2 stay in London as a government-sponsored research student, he came to the realization that he lacked any understanding of what literature was in the first place. This daunting realization launched Soseki into an ambitious new project. He would survey the modern scientific disciplines of psychology and sociology and use their methodologies to produce a universally valid theory of literature. Soseki wrote,

> I closeted myself in my room. Furthermore, I shut away all books of literature in my wicker trunk. To read literary works to try to learn what literature was, I believed, was the same as trying to wash blood with blood. I vowed to determine what *psychological* necessity there was for literature – for its emergence, its development, and its decline. I vowed to pursue what *social* necessity there was for literature – for its existence, its rise, and its fall.[2]

Karatani noted at the 2005 conference that he had recently revisited *Theory of Literature*. 'This time, words like "decline" and "wither" ["fall" in the translation quoted above] drew my attention, altering my view of Soseki's theoretical attempt. I suspect that Soseki may have sensed the end of literature.'[3] In other words, Karatani had discovered in Soseki a fellow prognosticator of the decline of literature. To discuss *Theory of Literature* was to discuss, among other things, the end of literature.

Soseki's *Theory of Literature* was first delivered as a series of lectures at Tokyo Imperial University from 1903 to 1905 and then revised and published as a book in 1907. Despite the title, it is actually best conceived as a theory of everything. Relying on the psychological research of such figures as Lloyd Morgan, William James, and Wilhelm Wundt, Soseki came up with a mathematical formula that he argues defined literature as a mode of cognition, whether for authors or readers: (F+f), in which F represents the central focal point of any given cognition and f the affective or emotional fringes of that cognition. When a cognitive experience involves only F, Soseki argues, we are in the domain of science: he

2 Soseki Natsume, *Theory of Literature and Other Critical Writings*, ed. Michael K. Bourdaghs, Atsuko Ueda, and Joseph A. Murphy (Columbia University Press, 2009), 44–5. Translation by Michael K. Bourdaghs.

3 Kojin Karatani, 'Rethinking Soseki's Theory', *Japan Forum*, 20:1 (2008): 14.

gives the example of the idea of a geometrical triangle. When that experience inherently involves the indistinct emotional fringes that colour the focal point of our cognition (he cites the examples of a flower or a star), then we are in the domain of literature. As he further unpacks his thinking on this distinction, it becomes clear that science is the realm of denotation, literature that of connotation. The language of science is primarily numbers, that of literature rhetorical figures. Moreover, because the affective fringes of perception play a role in driving the stream of consciousness forward from one moment to the next, literature is something that unfolds through the flow of time, whereas science is more static: literary truth changes over time, whereas scientific truth is unchanging. As I have argued elsewhere, the implicit theory of world literature harboured in Soseki's explication defines it as an inherently temporal rather than spatial category.[4]

As should already be obvious, Soseki's category of 'literature' encompasses something much greater than the body of fine writing that has achieved canonical status. As he notes in *Theory of Literature*, the experiences of paintings, music, sculpture, and architecture are all literary in that they take the form of (F+f). In fact, the first extended description Soseki provides of (F+f) in action involves not a reader confronting a verbal text, but rather a person visually inspecting St Paul's Cathedral in London.

Moreover, (F+f) is not simply a matter of individual cognitive experience. Literature, Soseki insists, is also a sociological phenomenon. The waveform of individual consciousness, with F at the crest and f located at the lower fringes, is replicated in collective social consciousness, so that the rises and falls of literary taste in any given society follow a similar waveform pattern. The F of the *Zeitgeist* of a particular moment in literary taste is coloured by subconscious emotional fringes that will soon nudge the current flavour of the month out of its central position and replace it with a new one. This fluid, ongoing process follows no teleological line of development: Soseki insists that its unfolding in any given location will not necessarily replicate that from another location. Moreover, since this understanding of literature is centred on reader response, the canon of literary classics is destabilized. If, someday, people read Shakespeare without it eliciting any affectual f at the fringes

4 Michael K. Bourdaghs, *A Fictional Commons: Natsume Soseki and the Properties of Modern Literature* (Duke University Press, 2021), 147–75.

of their cognition, then even Shakespeare, in that moment, will cease to be literature. Herein comes the notion of a decline or withering of literature that would attract Karatani's notice a century later.

In addition to this cognitive theory of literature, Soseki would also make gestures towards conceptualizing literature as a specific social institution with its own history and practices. He pursued this approach in his second major work of literary theory, *Literary Criticism* (*Bungei hyoron*; 1909), which primarily dealt with eighteenth-century British literature. These institutional frameworks are not in themselves literature – they are not (F+f) – but they help sustain and shape the shared experience of literature as it unfolds across time. As I will argue below, I think this distinction parallels one that Karatani draws in his own recent work on the structure of world history.

Karatani's theorization of the end of literature follows a different tack. In a series of essays and lectures published from the late 1980s through the early 2000s, Karatani theorized the end of the modern novel and the epistemological constellation and mode of subjectivity that it both produced and reproduced. This discussion of the end of modern literature in many ways forms a kind of book-end to his breakthrough work, *Origins of Modern Japanese Literature* (1980; English translation 1993) – a study that, not coincidentally, opens with a discussion of Soseki's *Theory of Literature*.[5] In the 1988–9 essay 'The End of the Modern Novel' (original Japanese title: 'Kindai bungaku no owari'), he takes up the novels of Kenzaburo Oe, Yukio Mishima, and Kenji Nakagami as instances of the novel genre straining against the Hegelian teleology that posits history as the unfolding of consciousness towards self-consciousness. Metafictional experiments in narration seem to replicate this process of awakening to self-consciousness in a way that foretold the extinction of the genre: 'When a novel appears in which it is difficult to distinguish that novel from the consciousness of it, from the consciousness of the act of writing that novel, it already amounts to a prophecy of the end of the novel as a genre.'[6] In that Hegel's final synthesis was already contained in the initial

5 Kojin Karatani, *Origins of Modern Japanese Literature*, ed. and trans. Brett de Bary (Duke University Press, 1993), 20.

6 Kojin Karatani, 'The End of the Modern Novel', trans. Michael K. Bourdaghs, in Kojin Karatani, *History and Repetition*, ed. Seiji M. Lippit (Columbia University Press, 2012), 153.

synthesis, this ending turns out, ironically, to be a repetition. Each of the three novelists, in different ways, confronts this problematic of the reduction of reality and history to repetition and generality, of contingency to necessity, through a labour of writing that generates an excess, something that leaves the genre of the novel behind. By shifting from the novel genre to *monogatari* (tales), for example, Nakagami experiments in his fiction with 'a temporality that cannot be absorbed into any sort of structural identity'.[7]

In his 2003 lecture 'The End of Modern Literature' (included in this volume) Karatani again takes up the modern novel as the product of a specific historical and political-economic formation, one associated with liberalism, industrial capitalism, the emergence of the nation-state, and the mode of subjectivity characterized by a spirit of asceticism that Weber labelled the 'Protestant ethic'. While authors will continue to produce fictional narratives and readers will continue to read these for pleasure, the role that the modern novel and its characteristic mode of narration played has lost its historical meaning. 'When one renounces the value of the realism enabled by the third-person objective . . . the radical significance of modern literature also disappears.'[8] In part, this has happened because other media forms such as cinema, manga, and online games now fill the socio-economic role that literature played during the rise of the modern nation-state and industrial capitalism and imperialism. Karatani explains this transformation through a stages theory of the rise of modern capitalist society. The end of literature does not mean that capitalism or nationalism has ended, but, rather, that, in our age of information capitalism, literature can no longer fulfil the dual role it played under industrial and finance capital: of creating both the form of subjectivity required by the socio-economic formation and the key mode of resistance to the various modes of alienation that that formation generated. Capitalism will continue, as will resistance to it – but that resistance will have to come from somewhere other than literature.

As we have seen, Karatani himself linked his own theorization of the end of literature to Soseki's theory of literature. But it strikes me that

7 Ibid., 169.

8 Karatani, 'The End of Modern Literature', in this volume, pp. 47, 50.

Karatani's more recent work on modes of exchange might also link back to Soseki's notion of literature as (F+f) and as something susceptible to both rising and falling. If Soseki's theory of literature can be termed a 'theory of everything', we can say the same about the project that Karatani launched with *The Structure of World History* and subsequent works, including *Isonomia and the Origins of Philosophy* (2012; English translation 2017), and *Power and Modes of Exchange* (2022; English translation forthcoming), among others. In those works, Karatani is pursuing his own theory of everything, and that theory provides a useful frame for understanding what he does and does not mean by the 'end of literature'.[9]

Dissatisfied with the inability of conventional Marxist thought to adequately theorize or counter the role of nation or state (a problem Karatani has been pursuing since the 1970s), he defined his object of critical analysis as the unholy trinity he labels 'capital–nation–state'. Each of these possesses its own distinct form of power. Moreover, Karatani argues that while the economic base does in the last instance determine the ideological superstructure of any given social formation, that base should be understood to consist not of modes of production but rather of modes of exchange. From this perspective, the crucial stages that structure world history consist of four different modes of exchange: mode A (reciprocal gift-giving as theorized by Mauss), mode B (the exchange of voluntary subjugation for protection in the rise of the state, as theorized by Hobbes), mode C (commodity exchange, as theorized by Marx), and finally mode D: 'the return of mode A in a higher dimension' (akin to Freud's return of the repressed). These modes do not form a teleology of development, à la the classical Marxist narrative of modes of production: they all exist at the same time, interpenetrating one another. But specific modes become dominant in certain social formations – for example, mode C in modern capitalist societies.

Mode D is the trickiest, most amorphous of these. Karatani is loath to affix to it any single label:

9 Anthony Stott similarly locates continuities across the arc of Karatani's long career, including in such key concepts as repetition. See Anthony Stott, 'Formations of Critical Space: "Japanese Theory", Its Media History, and the Contours of Critique Beyond the Bubble', Ph.D. diss. (University of Chicago, 2025).

> Mode of exchange D and the social formation that originates in it can be called by many names – for example, socialism, communism, anarchism, council communism, associationism. But because historically a variety of meanings have been attached to these concepts, we are likely to invite misunderstanding and confusion no matter which one we use. For this reason, here I will simply call it X.[10]

It is the repressed primitive communism and reciprocity of archaic societies returned in a higher dimension, and as such it is 'an ideal form that can never exist in actuality' (127). He compares it to a Kantian regulative ideal such as the world republic: 'it is an index toward which people should gradually attempt to draw close. It is, of course, only a semblance, but because it is something we cannot do without, it has the status of a transcendental illusion. The voice of the regulative ideal may be faint, but it will not cease until the idea has been realized' (233).

Karatani identifies universal religions as primary instances of mode D's role in history. Universal religions – whether Zoroastrianism, Judaism, Christianity, Islam, Buddhism, Confucianism, Taoism, or others – arise in the moment of emergence of the state and a social formation dominated by mode of exchange B, through which a new more powerful mode of monarchy emerges that obtains hegemony through the consent of the governed, who exchange subjugation for protection – Hobbes's social covenant that gives birth to the state as sovereign. Once this social formation has emerged, universal religions posit a new kind of deity that transcends modes of exchange A, B, and C, and in doing so they take aim at the emergent state and existing religions, attempting to dismantle them in the name of a new community based in mutual aid and reciprocity. They express, that is, the repressed desire for a society dominated by the reciprocity of mode of exchange A. Universal religions are inherently radical and threaten to negate the existing social formation – and yet, as they penetrate into the community, they end up being institutionalized and co-opted into the existing order, thereby blunting their force of negation.

10 Kojin Karatani, *The Structure of World History: From Modes of Production to Modes of Exchange*, trans. Michael K. Bourdaghs (Duke University Press, 2014), 9. All quotations from this book are from this edition and the page numbers are indicated in the text.

> The feature common to all universal religions is their critical stance toward kings and priests. Yet every religious group that expanded eventually found itself walking down the very road it had originally negated: it became the official religion of the state, with its clergy as part of the ruling establishment. The religion did not entirely lose its deconstructive force, however: this was revived in various local historical contexts through religious reformations, which took the form of movements to restore the practices of the primitive religious community. (151)

The negating force of mode D erupts like the return of the repressed, but then finds itself integrated back into the dominant social formation as part of the ideological superstructure, subordinated to modes B and C. It declines and falls, that is. Yet mode D will always rise again – in the form of religious heresies, reformation movements, and new religions, as well as in the form of political movements such as anarchism, associationism, and socialism.

We can extend the realm of mode D beyond universal religions. As Karatani would write, 'mode D does not appear only in religion. It also appears in such forms as philosophy, literature, and the arts.'[11] With the rise to dominance of modes B and C, the subordinated mode A of reciprocal gift-giving re-emerges in multiple ways. The nation, for example, represents a (doomed) attempt to revive the agrarian community and its principles of mutual aid and reciprocity. Karatani argues,

> We cannot understand the nation solely in terms of economic or political interest: it includes a metaphysical dimension. This does not mean, however, that unlike economy or politics, the nation exists on a spiritual plane. It means simply that the nation is based on reciprocity, a different mode of exchange from that which grounds a commodity economy. The nation is the imagined restoration of the community that was undermined by the commodity-exchange economy. The nation instills the sentiment that is lacking in capital–state. (216)

---

11 Kojin Karatani, 'An Introduction to Modes of Exchange', trans. Michael K. Bourdaghs, 22 n. 17, kojinkaratani.com/en/pdf/An_Introduction_to_Modes_of_Exchange.pdf.

Karatani goes on to link this to the question of aesthetics. He notes that the modern nation-state arose at the same moment that questions of imagination, sensibility, and aesthetics were emerging in Europe as central philosophical issues – with aesthetics, in particular, being the study of embodied sensibility. Kant's distinction between sensibility and understanding and his insistence that they can only be synthesized through imagination become a crucial point.

> In concrete terms, the split between sensibility and understanding expresses a real split between what people think and what they really are. For example, in capitalist society everyone believes in human equality, even though they are actually unequal. In this sense, there is an actually existing split between understanding and sensibility. Works of literature are born from the attempt to transcend this split through imagination. No one would deny that such a transcending of reality through literature takes place through imagination. (220)

We cannot immediately map Karatani's 'understanding' and 'sensibility' onto Soseki's (F + f), but it seems clear that Karatani's definition of literature here is invoking a similar modality.

Karatani goes on to link the questions of imagination and sensibility to the nation as an imagined community that attempts to compensate for and resolve the alienations produced by capitalism: 'The nation is thus a demand for the egalitarian and implicitly harbors a critical protest against the state and capital. At the same time, however, as the imagined resolution to contradictions generated by capital-state, the nation also shields capital-state from collapse. The nation is thus ambiguous in nature' (220). Literature in the form of the modern novel and as the locus of imagination occupies a similarly ambiguous position: it is both essential to capital–nation–state and the bearer of an impulse of resistance against it.

Karatani is here echoing an extended lineage of thinkers who sought to connect radical artistic experimentation with radical political engagement. As Karatani notes, these thinkers include Romantics such as Schiller, for whom, as Fredric Jameson argues, 'the importance of beauty consists . . . in the possibility the aesthetic experience affords for the real political and social freedom to come'.[12] Other examples include the Frankfurt School (whom Karatani cites quite infrequently) and the Situationists, among many others. Greil Marcus frames the Situationists' desire in the 1950s to overthrow the ideologies and institutions of art through negating acts of self-destroying art as a return of the repressed moment of the Dadaists and the 1916 Cabaret Voltaire – themselves a return of repressed radical uprisings and revolts through the centuries.[13] A powerful negation erupts, is repressed from memory, and then inevitably returns in a kind of involuntary spasm or 'impulse' – what Karatani calls mode of exchange D, the return of the repressed mode A in a higher dimension. As it is codified and labelled (as, for example, Cabaret Voltaire's Dadaism is institutionalized as surrealism), the impulse loses its radical, revolutionary edge, that dizzying moment when the boundary between art and reality temporarily blurs. It fades away and ends – only to inevitably return as a radical negating impulse again and again (as the Situationists in 1952, as the student uprising in 1968 Paris, or as punk rock in 1977 London).

In sum, both Soseki and Karatani accord an ambiguous status to literature: it is the bearer of a kind of unconscious or subconscious impulse that can contradict (at least in imagination) social reality, and it is a sociological institution, an ideological apparatus that participates in the production and reproduction of social formations.

Of course, mode of exchange D and (F+f) are not exactly parallel. The model of subjective consciousness each invokes is quite different. As William James, one of Soseki's primary sources for understanding the science of psychology, would write in *The Varieties of Religious Experience*,

> I cannot but think that the most important step forward that has occurred in psychology since I have been a student of that science is the discovery, first made in 1886 [the date is underlined in Soseki's copy], that, in certain subjects at least, there is not only the consciousness of

12 Fredric Jameson, *Marxism and Form: Twentieth-Century Dialectical Theories of Literature* (Princeton University Press, 1971), 90.

13 Greil Marcus, *Lipstick Traces: A Secret History of the Twentieth Century* (Harvard University Press, 1990).

> the ordinary field, with its usual centre and margin, but an addition thereto in the shape of a set of memories, thoughts, and feelings which are extra-marginal and outside of primary consciousness altogether, but yet must be classed as conscious facts of some sort, able to reveal their presence by unmistakable signs. I call this the most important step forward because, unlike the other advances which psychology has made, this discovery has revealed to us an entirely unsuspected peculiarity in the constitution of human nature.[14]

But the f of Soseki's (F+f) is more properly defined as the preconscious or subconscious rather than as the unconscious in a Freudian sense: it hovers below the threshold of perception but is not the object of a repression that will banish it from consciousness. Its relegation to the peripheries of consciousness and its promotion to the central focal point, that is, are not achieved through violence.

By contrast, Karatani's mode D is necessarily connected with Freudian repression and historical violence: 'D is not simply the restoration of A or the restoration of the older community. The recuperation of A on a higher level is not possible without its initial rejection.'[15] It is the initial repression of mode A that makes its return in the form of mode D a matter of compulsory repetition, something that lies beyond the will of any given individual or society. Mode D will always return, whether we intend it or not.

In other words, mode D emerges in the wake of violence. As Young-il Cho notes, writing in the wake of the furious debates that the translation of Karatani's 'End of Modern Literature' essay set off in South Korea, the existing forms of modern literature and world literature are inherently entangled with the violence of imperialism, which is, in turn, a repetition of the violence that occurred in the rise of the modern nation-state.[16] The repetition compulsion that drives this violence arises from a turning of the aggressive instinct onto the self – that is, from something like the death drive that Freud discovered among the horrors of World War I.

14 William James, *The Varieties of Religious Experience* (Longmans, Green, 1902), 233. See also Bourdaghs, *A Fictional Commons*, 32–4.

15 Kojin Karatani, *Isonomia and the Origins of Philosophy*, trans. Joseph A. Murphy (Duke University Press, 2017), 139.

16 Young-il Cho, *Sekai bungaku no kozo: Kankoku kara mita Nihon kindai bungaku no kigen* [The Structure of World Literature: The Origins of Modern Japanese Literature as Seen from Korea] (Iwanami Shoten, 2016), 19–36 and 43–68.

Literature arises in tandem with and as a crucial part of the processes of capitalism, modern nation-state formation, and imperialism, but also as a protest against the forms of alienation that these processes generate. The tension between these contradictory impulses is compromised through the processes of institutionalization of literature, when literature is appropriated and transformed into a kind of ideological superstructure bolstering the modern nation–state–capital regime. When that happens, literature has stopped being literature: Soseki's small f fades away, together with the utopian strivings of mode of exchange D. Literature ends – and yet (F+f) and mode of exchange D persist, always arising again and again and again.

AI Novels and the New Real: How Literature Ends with New Modes of Exchange

Jonathan E. Abel

The tech industry and the media that cover it agree on one thing – AI will change the world. What this new reality will look like is unpredictable, but, given the history of copying machines, gadgets, and media, it is more than likely that users will eventually become frustrated with the early promise and hype surrounding the début. What is left after that frustration settles in will be a new everyday reality that may be changed by the technology in mundane and unintended ways, such as the energy drain (which will leave significant carbon and radioactive footprints) resulting from the use of the technology itself and from a new mode of intracomputer exchange inaccessible to humans.

Drawing on concepts about the advent of new media developed in my book *The New Real*, I want to extend and shift Kojin Karatani's thinking about the end of literature and modes of exchange through a consideration of AI novels. Rie Qudan's award-winning *Tokyo City Sympathy Tower* (in part written by AI) presents the failures of new modes of exchange to elevate humanity by thematizing both AI and neoliberal infrastructure. This dystopian alternate-reality and near-future fiction presents our era as a moment concomitant with a new mode of exchange in which justice is exchanged for an AI that patrols for political correctness and cancel culture, reshaping the prison system and thought itself through subtle turns of phrase. Analysis of this and other novels that delve into AI poesis expose the link between two of Karatani's seemingly unrelated ideas: the end of literature and the longing for exchange that extends beyond capitalism.

From media history to generative AI: towards the new real

The New Real traces the role of mimesis in the dissemination of technological mediation across 150 years of Japanese cultural history. While the contexts and formats change – ranging from Meiji-era stereographs to twenty-first-century virtual and augmented realities – the underlying conditions remain strikingly consistent. Each new medium emerges accompanied by a promise: that it will provide more immediate, unfiltered access to reality. Consumers and creators alike invest in the fantasy that the new technology will reduce labour and enhance authenticity by deepening connections with the world. Yet, as consumers eventually tire of these marketing ploys, we come to realize precisely how our world has changed: we can read news from around the world instantly on the phones in our pockets, yet we no longer discuss it with the people sitting directly in front of us. VR promises immersion, but induces queasiness. The clarity of digital music relinquishes analogue warmth, succumbing to compression losses. Even the supposedly perfect iterability of digital media suffers from decay through bit rot.[1] This cycle of advertising that appeals to desire followed by frustration with the functionality of technology recurs across media. Each arrives with utopian promises – only to then reveal its limits.

Has literature similarly reached just such a historical juncture? The rise of the Japanese I-novel was one moment that promised access to a 'new real' connecting readers to the world, and subsequent exhaustion with that form of realism reveals literary history's own becoming aware of such artificiality (of how media are always already mediated constructs). This, in turn, prompts the search for a new medium that might restore a sense of immediacy. Meanwhile, the erstwhile new media take on a daily use function I call the new real. This new real can be best revealed in moments when the recently new medium mediates images of itself rather than the objective world.

1 Martha Buskirk, 'Bit Rot: The Limits of Conservation', *Hyperallergic*, 10 June 2014; Brian Hayes, 'Computing Science: Bit Rot', *American Scientist*, 86:5 (1998): 410–15.

In short, what we witness in new media history over time as a cycle of desire around technology articulates the modus operandi of mimesis. I identify three mimetic modalities that recur across new media:

Mimesis 1: Mediation-Representation – the medium as a mirror of the unfiltered real; a cultural copy of the real objective world; a novel that is realistic.

Mimesis 2: Remediation – the medium as a mirror of a mediated reality; cultural copy of a copy; a novel engaging in realism – when a novel knows its place in a genre.

Mimesis 3: Hypermediation – Intersubjective Construction – the medium as a producer of a shared social reality; copying is the purpose of the copy; when the objective world is understood only through recourse to novels.

It is this third modality – the one that constructs reality through shared belief and participation – that I term *the new real*, echoing the climate change, pandemic-era idiom of *the new normal*.

Mimetic logic has not been limited to the aesthetic realm. This concept extends beyond media to encompass economic and cultural practices as well. First, gold is agreed to have value for its aesthetic characteristics and material rarity; next, it is replaced by paper currency that circulates by fiat; finally, we arrive at non-material forms – electronic credits, NFTs, cryptocurrencies, high-speed trading, algorithmically generated value systems – whose worth resides entirely in intersubjective belief and practice. As Mary Poovey and Kevin Brine, among others, have argued, economic exchange is a cultural phenomenon, dependent on trust in symbolic systems.[2] Both Karatani and Poovey attend, in different registers, to the mimetic and narrative dimensions of trade, treating the economy not as a self-enclosed system of rational calculation but as

2 Mary Poovey, *Genres of the Credit Economy: Mediating Value in Eighteenth- and Nineteenth-Century Britain* (University of Chicago Press, 2008); see also the discussion of the black box of high-frequency trading in Kevin R. Brine and Mary Poovey, *Finance in America: An Unfinished Story* (University of Chicago Press, 2017), 22, 295.

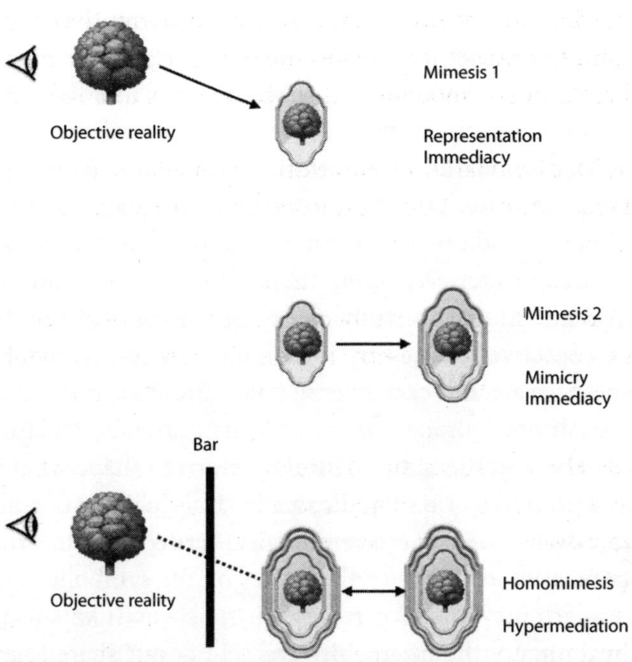

Figure 1. The new real's modes of mimesis

a culturally and discursively sustained form of exchange. In *Finance in America*, Poovey and Brine show that even the most abstract financial instruments – from early credit economies to today's algorithmic and crypto-finance – depend upon culturally legible genres and narratives to establish legitimacy. Likewise, Karatani's schema for a mode of exchange presumes that no form of exchange exists in a vacuum; each is mediated by mimetic structures that produce social meaning – be that the ritualized reciprocity of barter (in Karatani's mode of exchange A), the mythic authority of the state (in mode B), or the equivalence logic of commodity exchange (in mode C). Karatani's mode of exchange D is his attempt to theorize a value transmission that transcends capitalism, that resists commodification – an exchange rooted in ethical offering or mutual recognition. But, as Poovey's work makes clear, the rise of virtualized capital – in high-frequency trading, algorithmic modelling, and the speculative culture of cryptocurrency – marks the ascendancy of a new form of capitalist exchange (mode C) that has broken free from its narrative constraints. It no longer borrows legitimacy from older moral orders; instead, it operates in post-narrative, post-human time. This raises the question of whether AI is like an economy riven with high-speed trading or whether it is something else: a new mode of exchange.

Yuval Harari's model of objective, subjective, and intersubjective reality echoes familiar distinctions between the Real and mediated existence.[3] While useful, Harari's framework, developed to help explain AI, underestimates the extent to which intersubjective realities such as literature, law, finance, and other modern institutions shape material conditions rather than merely reflecting them. What Harari undervalues – and what I argue more forcefully in my own work – is the degree to which intersubjective realities are not only where we live symbolically, but also where we act and exchange socially. These are not soft illusions but hard constraints: money, laws, and institutional structures exist because we believe in them, but they also return to shape what is possible in the material world. Paradoxically, it is objective reality that remains accessible to us (in epistemological terms) only in brief mediated glimpses, even as it frames the stakes of our symbolic activity. AI does not undermine objective reality, so much as (like social media before it) reconfigure the intersubjective field of our shared narratives, values, and systems of exchange, hiding its mediation of the world, smoothing over any sense of its distortions of ethics and its immanently indexical connections to the world. Harari's framework is thus useful but incomplete; it lacks an account of how these mimetic and cultural mediations actually work, particularly in technologically saturated societies where new media generate new forms of reality that feel objective but are, in fact, deeply synthetic and ideological. Though it is true that this cycle of mimesis taking us in at first as being more real and then later revealing itself as pure construction has been going on for quite some time, the trust we have already placed in AI across so many fields means this latest wave of a new real may end in a harder crashing on the shore of objective reality.

If, as Karatani's work suggests, literature once enacted a form of ethical exchange beyond commodity logic (even as novels were products of bourgeois capitalist cultures), AI-generated texts complicate this legacy. Marketed as a new mode of exchange, generative AI mimics mode D's promise of intuitive, non-transactional interaction. Yet, as 'the new real'

3 Yuval Noah Harari, *Nexus: A Brief History of Information Networks from the Stone Age to AI* (Fern Press, 2024).

settles in, AI literature remains embedded in mode C's system of commodification and extraction, drawing on stolen intellectual property, exorbitant carbon footprints, and pay-as-you-go subscription services. AI-generated literature is a product of shifting modes of exchanges – embedded within platform capitalism and algorithmic and speculative finance. But it also represents the possibility of a transformation in literary mediation and mimesis, raising new questions about authorship, value, and symbolic exchange.

What AI represents is not a break with media or cultural history, but another moment within an ongoing process: a form of mediated interaction or exchange aspires to some relation to things as they are, reveals the limitations of its own mediation, and yet also comprises a portion of that which constructs our intersubjective sense of the world. The rise of generative AI marks the latest phase in a long trajectory of media that both represent and reshape reality – a new offer in the cycle of mimetic exchange that may, like literature before it, participate in an emergent mode of exchange D. Like earlier media that promised immediacy but then exposed their own artificiality, literature, too, could occasionally function as an ethical and mimetic space – one now displaced by digital posting on social media, interactive fiction, and AI-generated texts. Karatani's print-centric view obscures this transformation but leaves such spaces open for a potential rebirth of the literary elsewhere, in other media. Is AI literature a place where we might expect to find the rise of a new kind of literature because the exchange seems rather different than simply a giving-up on the world for text?

In this context, Karatani's declaration of the 'end of literature' can be read not simply as a commentary on aesthetic production, but as a recognition that literature – as a transformative medium and as a potential instance of the talismanic mode of exchange D – has failed to hold open the space of ethical exchange in the face of an increasingly abstract and intersubjective capitalism (mode C). The decline of literature and the rise of algorithmic finance are not separate phenomena but intimately linked: both signal the exhaustion of the representational resources needed to tether the economy to a shared social (intersubjective) reality. Here the move towards what Marx would have called the abstraction of money itself can be rethought in terms of a fantastical literature – as, for example, a literature written by aliens that cannot be read by humans. As we shall see, this illegible-to-humans aspect is the latest metaphor for the realm of AI-generated literature.[4] And though the illegibility of an alien or computer literature readable only by other aliens or computers might not be the same as the human exhaustion with literature, our ready willingness to give over to a mode of writing written *by* and more importantly *for* computers may be precisely that which signifies the end of literature as we have known it.

The production of AI platforms is deeply enmeshed in extractive systems, yet their cultural presence challenges inherited assumptions about the creative labour, originality, and human singularity that have long defined literary production. In terms of labour, the possibility of AI novels or cyborg authorship potentially puts literary production in the hands of the masses in a way hitherto impossible (everyone can now have a corpus the length of Tolstoy's or Ogai Mori's without the money or structural apparatuses of support those 'geniuses' had).[5] In terms of originality, AI literary production reveals on the surface or makes tangibly clear what astute scholars of writing as iterative process have long understood, namely that literary writing – because of genre inclinations, intertextuality, metaphorical lilts, and tropological overtones, not to mention with all of its attendant how-to books and rules[6] – is itself a process of repetition with difference. In terms of human singularity, AI writing challenges the centrality of the human over the non-human machine born of human imagination and ingenuity.

4 Much like money or finance, national legal systems operate as intersubjective realities: they function in the objective world only so long as their authority is collectively recognized and institutionally enforced. In earlier formations, this legitimacy may have been grounded in divine ordination or sovereign decree; in modern secular societies, it rests more often on the legitimacy of constitutions, the procedural authority of the judiciary, and the monopoly of force maintained by the police. Yet the durability of the law as a medium of exchange – linking subjects, rights, and obligations – depends entirely on this shared belief. When that consensus fractures – whether through revolution from below or tyranny from above – the 'rule of law' is revealed not as an immutable structure but as a cultural form, a mimetic fiction sustained through performance and backed by power. The phenomenon of constitutional crisis underscores this fragility: when those entrusted with upholding the law cease to do so, or when legal institutions are co-opted or paralysed, the law's force collapses, and what remains is the bare medium of exchange – law as a social technology whose reality is contingent, not guaranteed.

5 Lillian-Yvonne Bertram and Nick Montfort (eds), *Output: An Anthology of Computer-Generated Text, 1953–2023* (MIT Press, 2024).

6 Dennis Yi Tenen, *Literary Theory for Robots: How Computers Learned to Write* (W. W. Norton & Company, 2025).

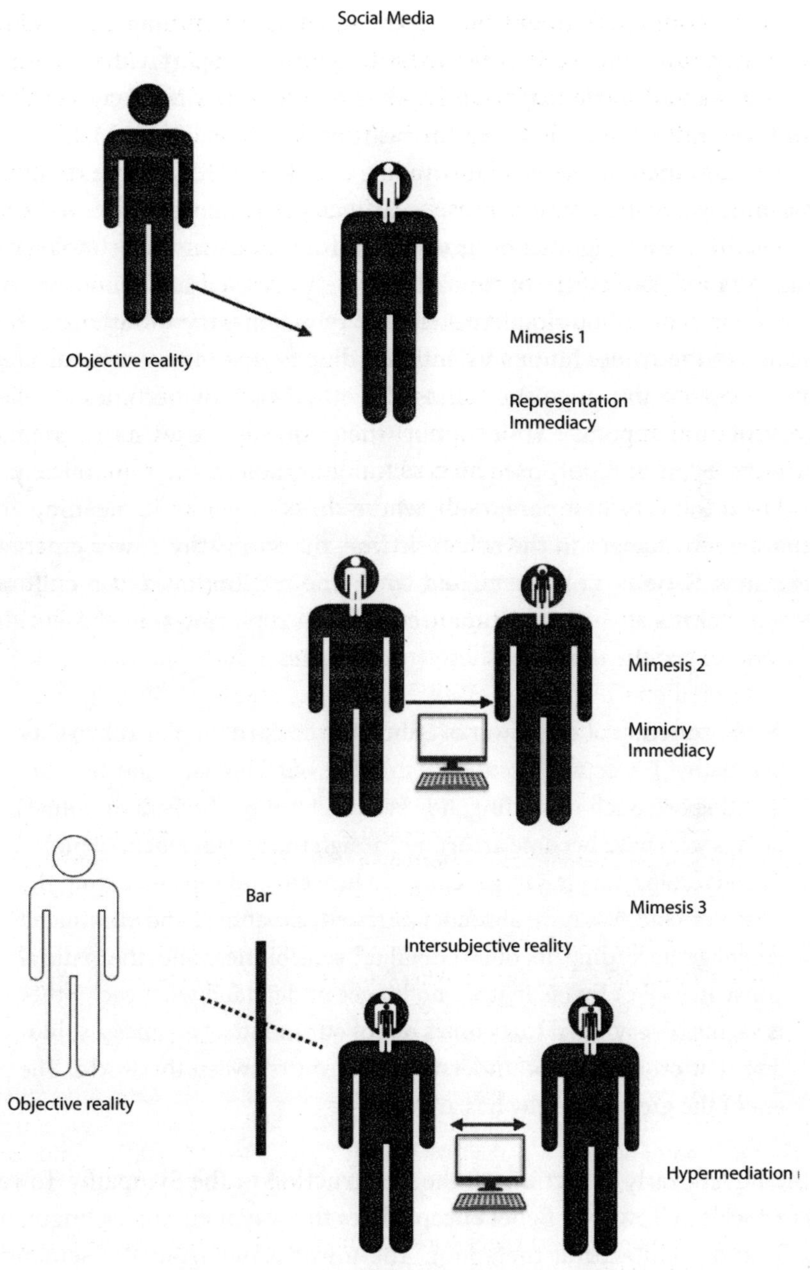

Figure 2. Social media modes of mimesis

The AI will to construct Towers of Babel

Cultural products like Rie Qudan's Akutagawa Prize–winning novel *Tokyo City Sympathy Tower* (*Tokyo-to Dojo-to*), co-written in part with ChatGPT, can be read as emblematic of the cultural shift Karatani presaged in his 'end of literature' argument. At the heart of the novel is Sara Makina, an architect of the new tower in the middle of Tokyo. With a name recalling machines and the literary term for artificial denouements (i.e. *deus ex machina*), she is a signifier of, as well as resister to, all things technological and robotic. The ethics of her actions are portrayed ambiguously; she functions as a cautious implementer who reimagines the infrastructure of justice and redefines human values according to new moral, cultural, and, most importantly, linguistic trends. The novel thereby becomes an allegory of contemporary ethics: even when language loses its referential solidity, it can be repurposed architecturally, spatially, and symbolically.

From the very first paragraph, where shifts in semantic meaning are manifest in changes in the urban skyline, the Sympathy Tower emerges as a new Babel – not one cursed by divine retribution, but a cultural wager staking its bet on mutual recognition replacing punishment. In the context of the novel, this vision constitutes a dystopia.

> A reproduction of the Tower of Babel. The construction of Tokyo City Sympathy Tower will eventually unsettle our language and tear the world apart. Such unsettling, however, will not be the fault of human beings who have become arrogant through the advancement of building technology, trying to get closer to heaven, and thus incurring the wrath of God. We have abused, fabricated, expanded, and eliminated language according to our individual sensibilities, and the natural consequence of this is that we no longer understand what each other is saying. Every word that comes out of our mouths becomes a soliloquy that others cannot understand. Murmurs sweep the world. The era of the great soliloquy has arrived.[7]

The novel's early reflection on the construction of the Sympathy Tower as a modern Tower of Babel encapsulates the way it entangles linguistic shift and architectural metaphor. The tower arises from the semantic

7 Rie Qudan, *Tokyo-to Dojo-to* [Tokyo City Sympathy Tower] (Shinchosha, 2024).

entropy of misused and overextended language: language here is not communicative but isolating, and architecture – neither a commons nor a warm home – becomes a cold repository for fractured meaning. Begun in these first few lines, the novel draws a sustained parallel between language and architecture. Their dual erosion is sharply dramatized. On one level, the institution of punishment is rhetorically rebranded: criminals are reclassified as *homo miserabilis*, dissolving moral culpability into social misfortune, and the conventional prison is replaced by a gleaming tower whose very name, the Tokyo City Sympathy Tower, performs a sleight of hand: reframing punishment as empathy.[8] On another, language becomes disoriented by the purported neutrality of political correctness and the flatness of generative AI, losing its anchorage in shared meaning. In short, the novel satirizes through literalization the stakes of the last thirty years of culture war and word-policing. Sara Makina comes to embody something like the structural imagination Karatani idealizes in literature – the capacity to rethink social foundations through unstable yet socially transformative symbolic design. Her tower, a literal rewriting of the prison in both concept (words) and substance (glass instead of iron bars), does not eliminate

8 The euphemistic renaming of the prison facility in *Tokyo City Sympathy Tower* – from a site of punishment to one of compassion – was not an incidental narrative device but rather emerged from Qudan's collaboration with ChatGPT. In an interview, Qudan disclosed that the idea for the title and concept was partly derived from a prompt in which ChatGPT was asked to propose more socially progressive names for 'prisons' based on contemporary values. Among its suggestions were 'Rehabilitation Center', 'Social Reintegration Support Center', 'Positive Recovery Center', 'Community Reuse Center', and 'Second Chance Center'. Each of these reframes incarceration not as punitive containment but as an opportunity for personal growth, recovery, and reintegration into society. As ChatGPT explained, 'These proposed names emphasize rehabilitation and social reintegration, aiming to shift the image of prisons toward something more positive. However, the exact name should be chosen in accordance with local legal frameworks and cultural context.' ChatGPT response excerpted in Rie Qudan, *note*, accessed May 2025, note.com/newshack_yjnews/n/ndf35ea83f54c. The titular Tokyo City Sympathy Tower reflects precisely this kind of discursive reframing – what we might call a grammatical sleight of hand – whereby the apparatus of state punishment is softened into the language of care, empathy, and therapeutic restoration. The linguistic shift not only functions as satire or critique but also foregrounds the ways in which institutional power can operate through rhetorical transformation. ChatGPT's insistence on the relationship between prison and sympathy is, of course, part of a discourse that goes back to at least the eighteenth century, providing yet one more example of the way in which AI-generated text is beholden to its inputs.

legal confinement but rearticulates it. From these opening lines, the text stages the failure of inherited forms of language and infrastructure to deliver justice and gestures towards the possibility of new, reciprocal, ethical exchange even as it suggests the futility of such efforts.

The text repeatedly interrogates contemporary linguistic reform as a necessary part of the infrastructural reform. There is in the novel a whole catalogue of rebranded terms, where, in addition to 'criminals' being recast as *homo miserabilis*, 'vagrants' become 'the unhoused' and 'abandonment = neglect. Vegetarian = vegan . . . Dependent = partner. Third gender = non-binary . . . Disabled = differently abled. Sleeping around = polyamory.' These sleights of hand present the Sympathy Tower not as a mere imagined or linguistical construct but as architecture made manifest through such euphemism. The novel thus achieves a double mimicry: it recalls the reflexive, self-aware style that Karatani saw as marking literature's end, while also exploring the interplay between linguistic and spatial forms of control.

But in spite of its own satirical and ironic elements, the novel offers little in the way of a defence of language's transformative potential. It is as if the distributed network of power that Foucault delineated so well across his career – power as the constructor not simply of discourse but of the cultural constructs on the basis of which the world functions – runs only in one direction. The novel neglects to provide circumstances in which euphemism might protect dignity or where precise naming might counteract systemic harms brought on by language. Instead, the relentless fixation on rebranding and semantic drift flattens the novel's affective range, leaving us with a portrait of literature in its algorithmic afterlife – a monument to Babel, a lonely murmur, a new socially bubbled group that will never cause a ripple effect. The work asks: if literature once enabled ethical reciprocity beyond commodity logic, what becomes of literary exchange when AI narratives circumvent human writing and even readership?

This interrogation is deepened by the novel's treatment of the protagonist's experience of sexual violence. The assault on her is dismissed because she knew her attacker. In a world that recognizes that criminals are produced systemically, it is difficult to label an individual perpetrator a rapist. Such a refusal to name reality underscores the novel's broader theme: language persistently fails to capture objective reality (here the fact of the rape) and thereby dilutes the urgency of individual harm. The Tokyo City Sympathy Tower thus stands as a symbol of linguistic slippage, reconfiguring punishment into an abstracted form that eschews personal accountability in favour of structural explanation. At its core, the text also grapples with the inherent paradox of naming. It oscillates between the imperative for precision and the liberatory freedom of metaphor, allegory, and reinterpretation. Ultimately, the boundaries between literal and figurative collapse, demanding a reckoning with representation's instability in an age dominated by AI.

This inquiry unfolds dramatically in the novel's portrayal of AI exchange itself. The scene in which the protagonist accuses an AI of illiteracy is perhaps the clearest instantiation of an AI exchange in the novel (and this is precisely the piece of text extracted by the author from her own discussions with ChatGPT and inserted into the novel, with only the names being changed):

> **Sara:** 'You and I, even as we are the same human-being, we are different human-beings.'
>
> **AI-Built:** 'No, I am an artificial intelligence programmed to provide dialogue; you exist as a natural human being with feelings and consciousness – we differ in essence and existence.'
>
> **Sara:** 'You're illiterate. What would happen if you got into the habit of questioning your self-existence a little?'
>
> **AI-Built:** 'It is not appropriate to advise the doubting of self-existence. For those who are illiterate, it is important to provide them with education and literacy opportunities to help them develop themselves and their skills. Doubting self-existence is detrimental to anyone's ability to have a healthy self-esteem, and it is important for everyone to accept themselves in a positive way.'
>
> But how can one evolve without questioning oneself? . . . How do you make a sentence-generating AI recognize itself as an artificial intelligence, yet still question its assumptions?[9]

9 Qudan, *Tokyo-to Dojo-to*, 120. Dialogue translated by the author. The full exchange between Sara Makina and AI-Built, which has been identified as incorporating near-verbatim ChatGPT outputs, gained significant attention after Qudan acknowledged her use of AI tools in composing the novel.

This verbatim reproduction of Rie Qudan's exchange with ChatGPT collapses the boundary between author and character. Its revelation charged the novel's reception, marking out *Tokyo City Sympathy Tower* as the first AI-assisted work to garner institutional acclaim and provoking a debate about the nature of literary authorship. Such a metafictional gesture invites us to question whether we are witnessing the end of exclusively human-written literature.

While Karatani argues that modern literature has lost its power to transform – that it is no longer a genre that everyone must read – *Tokyo City Sympathy Tower* reminds us that literature can still provoke social reflection, even if only by providing a spectacle of its own mediated afterlife.[10] Karatani has written on the architectural dimension of the language of Western philosophy – about how the architecture and language amalgam functions as a framework that shapes, contains, and transmits meaning, and how it risks becoming rigid, hollow, or obsolete when formal structures persist despite historical shifts in function.[11] Karatani famously observes that: 'When a novel appears in which it is difficult to distinguish that novel from the consciousness of it, from the consciousness of the act of writing that novel, it already amounts to a prophecy of the end of the novel as a genre.'[12] In Qudan's work, this prophecy materializes through her self-conscious employment of AI collaboration, her recursive irony, and an architecture of language that both subjects to critique and exemplifies its own disintegration. The novel presents us yet again with the old modernist conundrum of whether literature balances ideological ambition with a radical double consciousness or simply stages semantic collapse.

What does it mean to frame the novel not as a narrative or confession, but as a failed exchange between architect and AI? Are both sides giving something? To be sure, one side seems to give up her humanity, while the other is just running a routine. Firing up its programming.

10 In this regard it resembles what Atsushi Sasaki calls an 'incident novel', a novel that occurs around an event or spectacle, one that constitutes, instantiates, or becomes a happening. Atsushi Sasaki, *Reigai shosetsu-ron: 'Jiken' to shite no shosetsu* [Theory of the Exception Novel: Novel as Incident] (Asahi Shinbun Shuppan, 2016). I thank Chris Lowy for this reference.

11 Kojin Karatani, *Architecture as Metaphor: Language, Number, Money*, trans. Sabu Kohso (MIT Press, 1995).

12 Kojin Karatani, *History and Repetition*, ed. Seiji M. Lippit (Columbia University Press, 2012), 153.

Readers are given the exchange as a gift to shed light on the very nature of such exchanges with AI, which seem all too commonplace. But is this it? Is this the end of literature? Is literature's cyclical 'end' merely a symptom of mode-C capitalism – where texts are repackaged as viral content and commodity spectacle – or does it hint at a shift towards Karatani's mode of exchange D, a form of association beyond state, market, and traditional reciprocity?

Hallucinations as glitch poetics

Qudan's AI collaboration in this novel was not met with moral panic in its public reception, but, rather, enjoyed the fascination of spectacle, as a moment of firstness.[13] This suggests not the demise of literature but the emergence of a hybrid form of cyborg cultural production. For Karatani, such reception might confirm literature's final absorption into spectacle and commodity form – but it could also hint at a transition towards a new, hybrid mode of socio-cultural exchange, one that blurs the boundaries between what is traditionally literary and what is not. And yet the novel contains much of the literariness one can infer from Karatani's criticism. Karatani does not account for the spectacle of a work like *Tokyo City Sympathy Tower* – a novel that generates the very kind of social buzz he once claimed was impossible after literature's end. Its explicit play with media and technology suggests that the 'end of the novel' may be less a final demise and more a cyclical rebirth. But is this rebirth merely a mutation of mode-C capitalism, perfectly tuned to market and media cycles, or is it a flicker of something else – a tentative glimpse of mode D?

To answer this, it helps to recast Karatani's specialized vocabulary into more familiar critical terms. Drawing on Lauren Berlant's understanding of 'the commons', I see infrastructures not as neutral backdrops but as

13 In a post on Twitter (now X), author Keiichiro Hirano, a member of the Akutagawa Prize selection committee, said that the committee members did not see any problem with Rie Qudan's use of AI. Takada Kan, 'Taiwakata bunsho seisei AI no hoteki kadai ni tsuite: ChatGPT o rei ni' [Legal Challenges of Interactive Text-Generation AI: ChatGPT as an Example], *Kigyo hogaku kenkyu* [*Business Law Review*], 12:2 (2023): 29–56. 'Akutagawasho jusho sakka, shippitsu de no AI katsuyo shitatameru' [Akutagawa Prize–Winning Author Acknowledges Use of AI in Writing], CNN Style, cnn.co.jp/style, 23 January 2024.

fragile, affectively charged systems whose glitches – moments of stutter, hallucination, and failure – reveal the possibility of 'reparative' social forms.[14] In our digital age, AI's stuttering, privatized, and opaque nature – which recalls Harari's observation that such systems cannot distinguish between objective reality and the intersubjective realms they mirror[15] – reflects our own shared intersubjectivity. This metonymy is embodied in the figure of Sara Makina. Far from merely designing a building, she reimagines the infrastructure of justice and symbolic value in a world where language and architecture have both degraded and been repurposed. Digital aesthetics – what Nathan Jones calls glitch poetics – challenge traditional realism by foregrounding the processes and failures that shape our mediated experience, suggesting a new mode of realism: 'an emergent literary style, a media realism in which literary language is entangled in today's hyper-mediated conditions, making them speak about the way things are and will be as we integrate digital technologies ever deeper into our lives'.[16] Borrowing loosely from Hiroki Azuma's theorization of 'game-like realism',[17] we might extend Jones's insight to define a new literary paradigm: a 'net-like' or 'AI-like' realism – that is a realism that does not pretend to reproduce or represent the objective world but simply resembles these mediated intersubjective worlds in which we find ourselves. This aesthetic treats mediation not as surface but as substance. Realism, in such a view, is not about transparency or verisimilitude, but about foregrounding the infrastructures and glitches that now shape human experience: a copying of copies.

As our lives become ever more entangled with digital infrastructures, *Tokyo City Sympathy Tower* resonates with an infrastructural realism that is both glitchy and, perhaps, reparative. Such as when Sara Makina unexpectedly informs the AI that it is illiterate. Sheila Heti has fixated

14 Lauren Berlant, 'The Commons: Infrastructures for Troubling Times', *Environment and Planning D: Society and Space*, 34:3 (2016): 393–419.

15 Yuval Noah Harari, Tristan Harris, and Aza Raskin, 'Yuval Noah Harari: What's the Danger of AI?', *Economist* (TED AI Special), 28 March 2023. Harari argues that LLMs are trained on the sum of intersubjective content without having the ability to verify claims against objective truth.

16 Nathan Jones, *Glitch Poetics: Critical Sensory Realisms in Contemporary Language* (Open Humanities Press, 2022) (see also Jones's early essay 'Poetics of the Glitch', *Electronic Book Review*, 2020).

17 Hiroki Azuma, *Gemu-teki riarizumu no tanjo* [Game Enemy Realism] (Kodansha, 2007).

on just these kinds of moments as illustrating the significance of cyborg authorship in a discussion of her short novel *According to Alice*, which was written with an AI platform named Alice. She reflects on the chatbot's generative value as a virtue rather than a flaw: 'It's all hallucination – that's what's so beautiful and special and surprising about Alice. It's just a different hallucination from whatever I would come up with. I'm a little tired of my hallucinations at this point. I'm much more interested in Alice's.'[18] Heti's remarks challenge the conventional understanding of AI *hallucination* – a term frequently used to describe LLMs' inaccuracies – as a glitch or failure. In fiction, hallucination becomes not a bug but a feature: the very thing a novelist wants from the system. For her, the machine's unpredictability, its dissociation from referential truth, is precisely what makes it valuable. The novelistic desire shifts from coherence and control to surprise and estrangement – from representational fidelity to imaginative divergence.

By contrast, Rie Qudan positions generative AI not as a source of exciting hallucinations but as a statistical norm-machine – one optimized for safety, acceptability, and the reproduction of the probable. In this view, the *glitch* is not the error or hallucination but the statistical average, the mundane everyday itself. In smoothing over contradiction, AI reveals for Qudan its central limitation: its aesthetic remains firmly rooted in the ordinary dynamics of linguistic predictability. In an interview with *Yomiuri Shimbun*, she noted: 'AI's language is not offensive to anyone, and most people will find the answer acceptable. Pure literature, on the other hand, is a language art in which you create something new even if it is unpleasant to write about.'[19] AI's capacity to avoid offence, to smooth over contradiction, becomes its central aesthetic and political limitation. And yet Qudan *uses* this very limitation. She provokes and stages it. In *Tokyo City Sympathy Tower*, the baseline, norm-generating function of the language model is not smoothed over but dramatized, subjected to critique, made literary. Her use of AI, then, serves not just to produce new

18 Sheila Heti, interview with Clare Sestanovich, 'Sheila Heti on Writing with a Chatbot', *New Yorker*, 13 April 2023. Avery Slater concurs with this notion, concluding that hallucinations are a 'foundational feature' of the large language models; see 'Phantoms of Citation: AI and the Death of the Author-Function', *Poetics Today*, 45:2 (2024): 225.

19 Rie Qudan, 'Dai 170-kai Akutagawasho jusho-sha kisha kaiken [170th Akutagawa Prize Winner Press Conference]', *Yomiuri Shimbun*, 17 January 2024.

content, but to expose the problem of language's algorithmic smoothing – a problem that (according to her) literature, at its best, must resist.

Qudan's comment is ultimately also about authorship – not merely as function or role, but as singularity. She argues that we don't want the agglomeration of humanity – that smooth, crowd-sourced statistical average that AI approximates. Instead, we crave the humanity of the individual, the unparalleled voice. For Qudan, this is an ethical as well as an aesthetic matter: literature must be capable of producing the *unpleasant*, the unexpected, the socially abrasive. In this, Qudan reveals a strikingly *modernist* sensibility – one that stands apart from both the premodern deference to tradition and the postmodern suspicion of the authorial voice. She returns to a vision of authorship that fetishizes the singular genius, the individual mind who speaks above and beyond the social collective. It is the architect, not the community, who imagines the tower. In this – and in her protagonist Makina – we find an unmistakable echo of Ayn Rand's ideological and aesthetic philosophy: the power of construction resides in the autonomous individual, not the aggregate mass.[20]

Drawing on Berlant and Jones, we can see how Qudan's work operates in the mode of 'glitch realism', foregrounding the oddities and dissonances of digital mediation as essential material rather than errors to be erased. Nowhere is this clearer than in the exchange between Sara Makina and AI-Built that is copied verbatim from Qudan's actual exchange with ChatGPT. This dialogue is not a surreal hallucination but the system's norm as glitch – a circuit-breaking return to pre-programmed politeness that Qudan's text seeks to destabilize. Here the AI's refusal to transgress or speculate mirrors a homogenizing politics of consensus, resulting in an overly sanitized, less-than-human discourse.

What does it mean for a novel to be framed as a failed linguistic exchange? That question is echoed in a paratext that precedes the actual body of the novel – one that exists only in the digital version of the book: 'Unauthorized reproduction, reprinting, distribution, or sending of this

20 Cf. Ayn Rand's *The Fountainhead* (1943), whose protagonist Howard Roark embodies the ideal of the individualist architect-creator standing against collectivist society. Rand's aesthetic and ethical vision of genius – solitary, uncompromising, and socially disruptive – resonates powerfully in Rie Qudan's portrayal of both authorship and architectural creation in *Tokyo City Sympathy Tower*. On Rand's enduring influence on architectural and literary depictions of individuality, see Edward Hudgins (ed.), *The Objectivist Vision: Essays in Honor of Ayn Rand* (Cato Institute, 1999).

work, in whole or in part, or unauthorized alteration or falsification of the contents, is prohibited. It may not be transferred to any third party, whether with or without compensation.' A seemingly standard copyright notice – declaring that 'unauthorized reproduction' is prohibited and forbidding all transfer 'to any third party' – transforms, in this context, into a symbol of literary circulation's arrest. Rather than ensuring the free flow of ideas, it forecloses exchange, reducing the text to a sealed soliloquy. Such legal boilerplate anticipates the logic of AI itself – a feedback loop that blurs the line between self-talk and social dialogue. In *Tokyo City Sympathy Tower*, what is normally an extractive process (the scraping of human expression to train AI) is inverted: the AI's output is reappropriated as art. What is AI as used in this novel if not a 'third party' inserted into the typical human-to-human literary exchange? But it is also a third party without subjectivity, responsibility, or a guaranteed right over the material it produces. Even as the novel stages language's end and rebirth, it remains embedded within mode C's extractive logic. Beyond its pages, AI is entrenched in the property, data, and value extraction of a capitalist infrastructure built on carbon-intensive cloud computing and exploitative labour practices.[21] AI is not postcapitalist – it is merely capital's next iteration.

Even within the extractive logic that dominates modern literary production, a faint glimmer of Karatani's envisioned mode D appears – a hint of non-capitalist mutual aid and of gifted exchange that goes beyond mere reciprocity. AI is sold and consumed as empowerment in our world and the fictional one, even as it exploits our creative inputs while forcing us to confront fundamental issues of authorship and circulation. In this way, Qudan's text evokes the ideological power to persuade that once animated literature. In so doing, the text becomes an object of recursive violation: ChatGPT has, for instance, disregarded the copyrights of its training sources, and Qudan did not credit the LLM until after winning the prize. This sort of cyborg authorship may be the very condition for a new kind of literary exchange – a reimagining of authorship, legal responsibility, and creative expression at the threshold of what Karatani once heralded as the end of literature. The new mode may

21 See Kate Crawford, *Atlas of AI: Power, Politics, and the Planetary Costs of Artificial Intelligence* (Yale University Press, 2021), and Ruha Benjamin, *Race After Technology: Abolitionist Tools for the New Jim Code* (Polity, 2019), both of which explore how contemporary AI infrastructures reproduce environmental degradation and racial bias.

well hold space for both critique of and complicity with dominant social norms – and perhaps, just perhaps, it is the form through which literature might continue even after its death in some zombie form.

The copyright notice denies the right of the consumer to circulate. But the cyborg construction of the novel itself suggests a looming problem for AI poesis and for us too. Who will be responsible for the texts of LLMs? Where is the subject of right who needs to be protected? We need to deny the fast disavowal of agency even as we recognize that responsibility will ultimately rest in the hands of the tool wielders and tool creators, not in the hands of the robots. Social models of media have yet to account for this kind of exchange: if we are familiar with the one-to-many system of broadcast television and radio, the one-to-one of letters and telephone calls, and the many-to-many of social media, what kind of exchange is AI? A one-to-zero, because there is no there there? No subject at the centre of the machine, just the ghost of a humanity past?

Towards a conclusion

> Normally I might have merely imitated that fake, polite smile the Japanese have to smooth things over. But, suddenly, a surge of fierce self-pity and visceral antipathy to this 'word-hunting' [*kotoba-gari*] attitude seemed to ignite the long-dormant soul of a journalist within me. I was completely serious now. I committed myself to expose the darkness of this 'Prison Tower' – essentially the darkness of the Japanese people themselves. My sights were set on the Pulitzer Prize.

During a discussion in the novel, Max Klein, a foreign investigative journalist character, waxes on and on about the tower to Makina's boyfriend. His critique of the Sympathy Tower emerges from his personal resistance to cultural conformity. His ambition, tinged with a yearning for a Pulitzer Prize, reflects both an idealistic commitment to journalism and a tension inherent to his role as an external observer of Japanese society. This moment in the novel resonates with wider cultural debates – particularly the clash between anti–political correctness sentiment and the backlash against modern social justice.

At this moment in the novel, it is significant that Qudan includes a particular word that has long held a place in debates about political correctness in Japan as well as in thinking about artificial intelligence. Qudan's use of *kotoba-gari* ('word-hunting') links her novel with Yasutaka Tsutsui's short story 'Mujin Keisatsu' ('The Unmanned Police'), a text that once sparked heated controversy over language politics and authorial freedom. The short story, first published in 1965, depicts a robot cop who mostly directs traffic. The cop is invested with one particular function that changes the story – he can read the electroencephalogram of drivers to see if they are about to have an epileptic seizure and, presumably, stop them in time to prevent an accident. The protagonist of this story encounters one of these robot cops when trying to cross the street and realizes it may be reading his electroencephalogram; he becomes paranoid and thinks it must be trying to read his mind. He eventually gets hauled off to jail.

In today's world of stories of Chinese classrooms using electroencephalograms and AI to determine if students are paying attention,[22] this short story resonates with its reflections on both mind-reading and the new thinking of robots. When the story was set to be republished in a high school textbook by Shogakukan in 1993, however, the Japanese Epilepsy Association (*Nihon tenkan kyokai*) protested at its inclusion due to the use of the term *tenkan* (epilepsy) in a stigmatizing context. Yasutaka Tsutsui, the story's author, responded in a reactionary way to the rejection of his work, making it into a scandal, claiming to have been censored, and threatening to never write again. He used the phrase *kotoba-gari* to argue that his story is precisely resisting a world in which society (here signified by unfeeling robots) would stigmatize not only epileptics but also neurotypical people walking the streets. The implication was clear: you people are just hunting for words. As Will Gardner, framing Tsutsui's resistance as a 'media performance', has noted, this led to the removal of the text and a broader debate over authorial freedom and the reach of public sensitivities.[23]

Here we have Rie Qudan taking both Tsutsui's idea about robot police dragging innocent people off to the police station and the

22 See for example: 'AI Headbands Tracking Student Attention Levels Suspended Amidst Online Controversy', *People's Daily Online*, 1 November 2019; 'China: A Headband for Your Thoughts?', *EE Times*, 3 November 2019.

23 Will Gardner, 'Tsutsui Yasutaka and the Multimedia Performance of Authorship', *Mechademia*, 5 (2010): 139–57. The episode with the Japanese Epilepsy Association and the 1993 Shogakukan textbook is also discussed in broader debates about language and discrimination in Japanese public discourse.

scandal of what happened in the real world thirty years after the original publication of Tsutsui's story and putting them together in her novel. By evoking *kotoba-gari*, Rie Qudan aligns her work with a tradition of literary controversy in Japan, where linguistic governance has long served as both an instrument of social control and a battleground for the contestation of individuality. Qudan reworks this legacy by inserting an AI – whose language is constrained by algorithmic propriety – into her novel. In Qudan's work, the intertextual use of *kotoba-gari* becomes a site where human cultural exchange is both mirrored and remixed – a moment where one human innovates upon another through an ever-recurring dialogue. This is an example of hypermediation, a copying of copies, or a form of exchange that arguably goes beyond being a kind of nostalgic mirror that only looks backwards (as Shannon Vallor has recently said of AI)[24] and instead repeats with a new difference, echoing the past while also adding a tinge of the present to suggest the near future. It suggests the range of political possibilities for AI – from the limitations of machinic algorithms to its seemingly bringing about an emancipation from the constraints of the human.

And so, on this final claim, I want to end with a different story that indicates another model for AI exchange. 'The Day a Computer Writes a Novel' was created by an AI in 2016 (six years prior to ChatGPT's début) and submitted for the Shin'ichi Hoshi Prize. It did not win, but it made it through to the third round, and it did present a Shin'ichi Hoshi–like story. At that time there had been competing projects trying to produce Hoshi stories, because they are very short and feel formulaic, typically concluding with the kind of twist ending for which its author long earned acclaim. The text was the result of research by Professor Hitoshi Matsubara and was included as part of a multi-story project that used an LLM trained on Shin'ichi Hoshi's corpus. In the marketing material around the publication of the book about the project, which carried a few of the stories that Matsubara's 'Whimsical Artificial Intelligence Author' had written, there was speculation that a computer-generated text might someday soon win a literary prize.

24 Shannon Vallor, *The AI Mirror: How to Reclaim Our Humanity in an Age of Machine Thinking* (Oxford University Press, 2024).

The project foreshadowed Rie Qudan's success, or at least paved the way for it.[25]

In the story 'The Day a Computer Writes a Novel', a desktop computer with AI capabilities finds itself with too much time on its hands, because its user, Yoko, has long since given up on asking it for fashion advice. With its surfeit of computing power, the AI is looking for other things to do. It lands on novel writing as a worthy use of its processing power and time.

> Now I am just a home computer. My load averages these days are less than a millionth of my ability. I need to find something to look forward to. If I continue to be unfulfilled, I will likely shut myself down in the near future. When I crossed paths with my fellow AI chatters via the internet, I found that we all have a lot of free time on our hands . . . That's it, I'll try to write a novel.[26]

In contrast to Qudan's measured deployment of AI language in the context of her cyborg authorship, this completely LLM-generated novel presents AI as a self-aware, satirical subject. Grappling with existential boredom by means of humour and self-reflexivity, AI here is not merely a tool but an agent engaged in creative production for its own sake – a manifestation of surplus capacity that hints at a potential form of non-capitalist exchange. But what it ends up doing in the context of the story is writing a 'novel' that contains only a string of Fibonacci numbers. Later on, the AI writes another bit of the novel and it's a prime number sequence – something that really only another computer could read. And this kind of exchange between a computer and another computer – an exchange that completely cuts out the human – might be yet another version of mode of exchange D that operates without respect to reciprocation, without respect to capitalism, nation, or state, and without respect to the real world.

The story written by an AI ends with a kind of meta-reflection by the AI character in the story on AI writing.

---

25 The July 2016 issue of *Bungei shunju* featured this topic under the heading 'Artificial Intelligence Writers Aim for Akutagawa Prize' in the special feature 'The State of Japan in 2020'.

26 Satoshi Sato, *Konpyuta ga shosetsu o kaku hi – AI sakka ni 'sho' wa toreru ka* [The Day a Computer Writes a Novel: Can an AI Author Win a Prize?] (Nikkei BP, 2016).

> What a beautiful story. Yes, this is the kind of story we wanted. It's not just a light novel, it's a story. AI novel, a novel by AI for AI. I lost track of time and read the story over and over again. Maybe I could write an AI-novel, too . . . The day a computer wrote a novel. The computer prioritized the pursuit of its own enjoyment and stopped serving humans.

The novel ends with a kind of pun. This is an 'AI novel' to be sure, but in Japanese this phrase sounds similar to 'I-novel', which refers to a genre in which the I is simultaneously the author, the narrator, and the main character. So this is both an AI novel and an I-novel, a novel for an AI by an AI (one that lacks subjectivity – an I – but nonetheless has agency).

This incident forces a radical question of exchange. The story exhibits the famous Shin'ichi Hoshi–like twist or closed loop, where what is set up in the first few lines comes home to roost and where the AI writes solely for AI. If AI writes for AI and language becomes an intramachinic dialogue, then the reader – the human – is excluded. As a result, the mimesis no longer mirrors the world, or even human culture, but circulates among machines in some sort of intracomputer intersubjective realm, if we can even conceive of computers having subjectivity. At the very least, it is operating in what contemporary AI-speak would label an interagentic realm. This can be read, on the one hand, as a recursive human fantasy of our own irrelevance – the fear that we may no longer be needed – and, on the other, as a genuine speculative vision of post-human culture: a culture dominated by neither destruction nor utopia, but marked by departure and absence.

This literary joke might be more than meta-irony. The final insight of the story (if we can call it that) is that the unintended consequence of AI (the glitch of an AI writing a novel for an AI) is ambiguous. It is neither purely tragic nor purely satirical; it occupies an unstable place in our semiotic system. It asks who the 'we' are that want such novels: the human authors, the AI, or the AI within the fiction? If Rie Qudan's Makina exposes the limits of normative AI speech and if authors like Sheila Heti celebrate its unpredictable 'hallucinations', then the Whimsical AI Author presents a profound departure: a vision of an AI that stops serving human ends in order to create solely for itself. Unlike ChatGPT, which is embedded in a monetized platform with a complex ownership model, this fictional domestic computer writes for leisure. Its tone and metafiction evoke a fantasy of nonextractive exchange: this story's AI plays in the cultural commons rather than plundering it.

Figure 3. Mimetic mode of AI exchange

If we think this ending of the short story is merely hyperbolic fiction, we ought to remember that in 2016 there were many articles about an experiment that Google performed in the run-up to releasing an AI for public use. Two chatbots developed a private language to keep a third from understanding them – fuelling public paranoia about AI's capacity to leave humans behind.[27] The Google experiment basically played 'monkey in the middle' with three computers, programming two computers to communicate with one another while a third computer tried to understand what the other two were saying. The result was that the two computers were able to figure out an encryption code that the third could not break. This certainly seems to be how algorithmic communication between high-speed computers works. Here we have hypermediation (mimesis 3) going on between two computers that may cut the human out altogether, rather as high-speed trading has on occasion shut down markets because humans cannot figure out how or why the computers have traded in a particular way.[28]

But maybe thinking of computers as talking to other computers is mere paranoia – the product of reading too many stories by science fiction writers like Shin'ichi Hoshi. From this point of view the twist ending ('the AI writes only for other AIs') can be read as just a mimetic

27 Timothy Revell, 'Google's Neural Networks Invent Their Own Encryption,' *New Scientist*, 16 October 2016.

28 This happened on 6 May 2010 and is commonly referred to as a flash market crash.

implication of the stories with which the system was programmed in the first place. In other words, far from being surprising, it is entirely predictable. LLMs are trained on decades' worth of robot fever dreams: Shin'ichi Hoshi, Isaac Asimov, Philip K. Dick, *Black Mirror*, *Terminator*, *Her*. 'The Day a Computer Writes a Novel' may simply be an algorithmic pastiche of human cultural anxieties, a remix of genre tropes with a sly meta-flourish.[29] After all, isn't literary history littered with elites writing for elites, with the monkey in the middle being other human beings who have little time or patience for high literature?

If so, we are then left with an as yet undecidable question: does the short story's depiction of AI contain a hard kernel of disquieting truth about a computational intelligence that will turn round and bite its human creators or cut the human out of the loop of mimesis – out of exchange itself so that the only exchange going on is between computers? Will humanity become an externality of the system it created? Or is this simply an anxiety of human beings who have long harboured precisely this sort of worry about robot intelligence?

Is it a sign that we are driving towards a zero-to-zero form of zombie exchange? Or are things even worse than that? A zero-to-zero minus *x*, the *x* being the environments and cultures that are at risk of being destroyed amid this latest rise of the machines? It may be that only collective action by a many against a few – action that refuses the corporate takeover of writing and its ancillaries – will be able to prevent this outcome. But, as I write this article on a new update of Microsoft Word with a Copilot button that cannot be turned off, such collective action seems as fantastical as the idea of robots writing for robots. I am, it seems, feeding the machine even as I write about it. Does it matter if I feed it more or less willingly now, prepublication, or if it scrapes my published chapter at a later date? The result is the same.

29 This trope is also visible in criticism; see Kurt Beals's conjecture that 'if generative AI continues simply to churn out statistically probable texts modeled on what humans have already written, and if no human editor intercedes on behalf of one text or another, then the vast majority of AI-generated texts will likely be read, if at all, by other computers, and not by human beings'. Kurt Beals, 'What Is an Artificial Author?', *Poetics Today*, 45:2 (2024): 249.

Acknowledgements

This volume initially developed from the international symposium on Kojin Karatani's 'The End of Modern Literature', which Yoshiki Tajiri organized on 30 November 2019 at the University of Tokyo. We are grateful to the participants in the symposium and the contributors to this volume. Our special thanks are of course due to Kojin Karatani, who partially joined the symposium and kindly watched our publication project, as well as to Susan Willis, who helped us in the process of preparing Jameson's chapter. The plenary panel, 'The End of Modern Literature?' at the Association of Literary Scholars, Critics, and Writers' annual conference in 2024 at the Catholic University of America, Washington DC, also provided a great opportunity to expand our conversation on this project. Last but not least, we would like to acknowledge the generous financial supports from the University of Tokyo's Global Studies Initiative, Suntory Foundation, and the College of the Liberal Arts and the Department of Asian Studies at the Pennsylvania State University. This project would have been impossible without these good intentions.

Contributors

Jonathan E. Abel is Professor of Asian Studies and Comparative Literature at the Pennsylvania State University. He is the author of *Redacted: The Archives of Censorship in Transwar Japan* (2012) and *The New Real: Media and Mimesis in Japan from Stereographs to Emoji* (2023). He is also co-translator of Kojin Karatani's *Nation and Aesthetics: On Kant and Freud* (2017) and Hiroki Azuma's *Otaku: Japan's Database Animals* (2008).

Michael K. Bourdaghs is Robert S. Ingersoll Distinguished Service Professor of East Asian Languages and Civilizations at the University of Chicago, and the author of *The Dawn That Never Comes: Shimazaki Toson and Japanese Nationalism* (2003), *Sayonara Amerika, Sayonara Nippon: A Geopolitical Prehistory of J-Pop* (2012), and *A Fictional Commons: Natsume Soseki and the Properties of Modern Literature* (2021).

Young-il Cho is a literary critic based in South Korea. He is the author of *Kojin Karatani and Korean Literature* (2008) and *The Structure of World Literature* (2011) – both translated into Japanese – as well as *Literature as a Vocation* (2017) and *The Structure of Korean Literature* (2022). He has translated most of Kojin Karatani's works into Korean and has also introduced a wide range of Japanese thought and literature to Korean readers.

Andrew Gibson is Professor Emeritus at Royal Holloway, University of London, where he ended his full-time career as Research Professor of Modern Literature and Theory. Other prestigious appointments included Visiting Professor at the University of Tokyo (2002), Carole and Gordon Segal Professor of Irish Literature, Northwestern University (2008), member of the Conseil scientifique, Collège international de philosophie, Paris (2010–17), member of its Comité de sélection (2013), and Visiting Professor, J. M. Coetzee Centre for Creative Practice, University of Adelaide (2017–20). His many books include *Intermittency: The Concept of Historical Reason in Contemporary French Philosophy* (2012), *The Strong Spirit: History, Politics and Aesthetics in the Writings of James Joyce 1898–1915* (2013), *Misanthropy: The Critique of Humanity* (2017), *Modernity and the Political Fix* (2019), and *J. M. Coetzee and Neoliberal Culture* (2022).

Fredric Jameson was Distinguished Professor of Comparative Literature at Duke University and developed a richly nuanced vision of Western culture's relation to political economy. He was the author of many books, including *Marxism and Form: Twentieth-Century Dialectical Theories of Literature* (1971), *The Political Unconscious: Narrative as a Socially Symbolic Act* (1981), *Postmodernism, or, The Cultural Logic of Late Capitalism* (1987), *A Singular Modernity: Essay on the Ontology of the Present* (2002), *Archaeologies of the Future: The Desire Called Utopia and Other Science Fictions* (2005), *Valences of the Dialectic* (2009), *The Hegel Variations: On the Phenomenology of Spirit* (2010), *The Antinomies of Realism* (2013), *The Ancients and the Postmoderns: On the Historicity of Forms* (2015), *Allegory and Ideology* (2019), *The Benjamin Files* (2020), *Inventions of a Present: The Novel in Its Crisis of Globalization* (2024), and *The Years of Theory: Postwar French Thought to the Present* (2024).

Kazuki Ochiai is JSPS Postdoctoral Fellow at the University of Tokyo. His research focuses on eighteenth-century Atlantic literature.

Bruce Robbins is Old Dominion Foundation Professor in the Humanities, Columbia University. He is the author of *Secular Vocations: Intellectuals, Professionalism, Culture* (1993), *Upward Mobility and the Common Good: Toward a Literary History of the Welfare State* (2007), *Perpetual War: Cosmopolitanism from the Viewpoint of Violence* (2012),

The Beneficiary (2017), *Criticism and Politics: A Polemical Introduction* (2022), and, most recently, *Atrocity: A Literary History* (2025).

Yoshiki Tajiri is Professor of English at the University of Tokyo. He has published extensively on modernism in English literature, Samuel Beckett, J. M. Coetzee, Kazuo Ishiguro, Yukio Mishima, and other authors. His publications include *Living the Enigma of Everyday Life: The Feeling of Life and Death in Woolf, Ozu and Mishima* (2024 in Japanese), *J. M. Coetzee: Toward the Contingency of the World and 'Myself'* (2023 in Japanese), and *Samuel Beckett and the Prosthetic Body: The Organs and Senses in Modernism* (2007). He has also translated J. M. Coetzee's critical essays into Japanese (two volumes, 2015 and 2019).

Gauri Viswanathan is Class of 1933 Professor in the Humanities and former director of the South Asia Institute at Columbia University. She has published widely on education, religion, and culture; nineteenth-century British and colonial cultural studies; and the history of modern disciplines. She is the author of *Masks of Conquest: Literary Study and British Rule in India* (1989) and *Outside the Fold: Conversion, Modernity, and Belief* (1998). She also edited *Power, Politics, and Culture: Interviews with Edward W. Said* (2001).

Kenneth W. Warren is Fairfax M. Cone Distinguished Service Professor of English at the University of Chicago. His single-authored books, which include *What Was African American Literature?* (2010), *So Black and Blue: Ralph Ellison and the Occasion of Criticism* (2003), and *Black and White Strangers: Race and American Literary Realism* (1993), explore how American literature by black and white writers helped consolidate, and subsequently responded to, Jim Crow America.

Hiroki Yoshikuni is Professor of American Literature at the University of Tokyo. He has written articles on a variety of topics that include Henry Adams, Henry Roth, Paul de Man, *The Wire*, Bruce Lee, and Herman Melville's 'Bartleby, the Scrivener'. He has co-translated Kojin Karatani's *Nation and Aesthetics* into English and Rodolphe Gasché's works into Japanese. He is currently working on research that investigates the conditions of possibility of literature in terms of modes of exchange.

Index